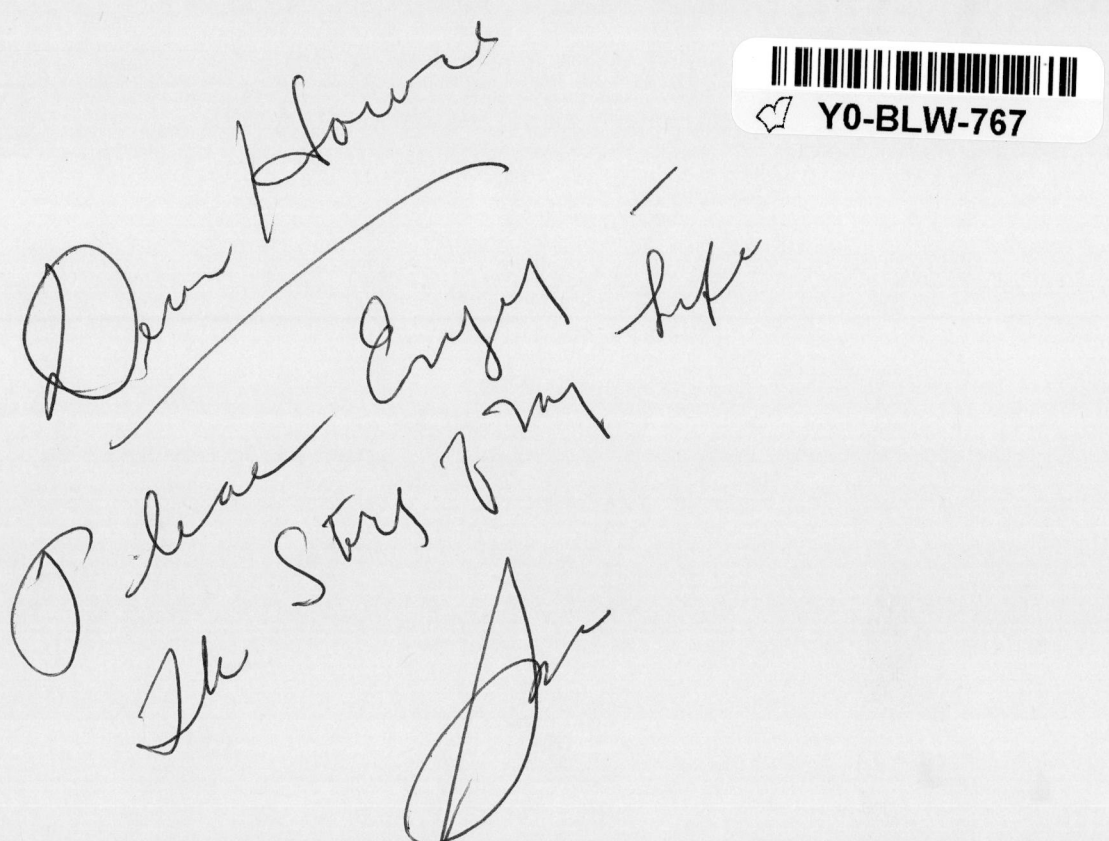

Dear Howard

Please Enjoy
the Story of my life

Joe

Born to Survive

Born to Survive

SAM PFEFFER
with *Joshua M. Sklare*

Copyright © 2011 by Sam Pfeffer. All rights reserved.

Publisher: Montefiore Press
Editing and project management: Textbook Writers Associates, Inc.
Cover design: Julie Gallagher
Text design and production: Gallagher

Printed in the United States of America

ISBN 978-0-98192651-3

A portion of the proceeds from the sale of *Born to Survive* will go to the CHAZAK Foundation.

The *Montefiore Press* is engaged in the writing, production and distribution of private books. Its sole purpose is to bring to light the stories of exceptional individuals who have made significant contributions in their professional, civic and philanthropic endeavors.

Address inquiries to: Joshua M. Sklare, The Montefiore Press, 3333 West Commercial Blvd., Suite 110, Fort Lauderdale, FL 33309, USA

Montefiore Press
Specialists in Private Books
www.montefiorepress.com

*In honor of my entire family,
and especially my wife of sixty years,
Dr. Paula Pfeffer, who have inspired me
to lead such an enjoyable
and meaningful life.*

Contents

Preface ix

CHAPTER 1   Spring Valley, Illinois 1

CHAPTER 2   The Navy and Beyond 47

CHAPTER 3   My Legal Career 69

CHAPTER 4   Business 111

CHAPTER 5   Charities 155

CHAPTER 6   Family and Friends 181

CHAPTER 7   Fullfilling My Remaining Goals 213

A Tribute to My Uncle, Maurice Buckman 259

Photo Album 261

Preface

AS YOU OPEN THIS BOOK you may be wondering, "Hey Sam, why did you decide to write this book? You have had an interesting life, you've plenty of good stories to tell, but why write a book?" It is true that I have been blessed to have led an interesting and at times even an exciting life. But that was not what motivated me, though I hope you will be entertained by some of the stories in the pages ahead.

Rather, I thought it would be important for my family and my future descendants to learn something about my life. You will find in *Born to Survive* the usual stuff of memoirs—where I grew up, where I went to school, and what I did to earn a living are all in here. But there is also a lot more. In this book you will find the answer to a larger question. You will learn something of what is behind the story of my life. That is to say, what is Sam Pfeffer all about and what does he stand for?

I like to think that the most important things in my life have not been things at all, but rather a group of principles and ideals that I have tried to uphold. They stem from my childhood in Spring Valley, Illiniois and most importantly from the values of the religion that I was raised to believe in, Judaism. Whether it is "Love thy neighbor as thyself" or "That which is harmful to you do not do unto others," ours is a religion which places a premium on kindness and sensitivity. I have tried to live my life with an emphasis on helping others and, whether or not I have succeeded, I leave for the reader to decide. What is important to me is that my family and my descendants will give serious thought to these matters, to leading a life that has as its center the virtues of kindness, compassion, and charity.

Now that you know why I have written this book, let me tell you how I went about the process of writing it. I started a couple of years ago by describing my life into a tape recorder. They were all recorded by Toni Causby, who did a great job of listening and then transcribing the stories for me. I am deeply appreciative to her for all her efforts. Though I had transcripts to look at, it soon became evident that I did not have a book. For that I needed to hire a professional. Through my cousin Jerry Buckman, I had the good fortune of meeting Joshua Sklare and placed the project into his very capable literary hands. The end product, which you see before you, is a result of our collaboration and I am tremendously grateful to all that he has contributed. While Josh was the literary force behind this book, Julie Gallagher has done an outstanding job as the book's designer and compositor and I am most grateful for the many hours she spent on this project.

Lastly, I must thank my wonderful wife of sixty years, Dr. Paula Pfeffer. She has stood by me all these years, never questioning my judgement and never hesitating to show her support for any and all of the many ventures that you will read about in the pages ahead. Her many scholarly accomplishments include being nominated for a Pulitzer Prize for her groundbreaking biography of the labor and civil rights leader, A. Philip Randolph. There are no words that can adequately express how I feel about her. Suffice it to say, she has made my life vibrant and my heart happy and it is to her that I dedicate this book.

Sam Pfeffer
Wilmette, Illinois
2011

CHAPTER 1

Spring Valley, Illinois

A Coal Town on the Illinois River

When you meet someone for the first time, one of the questions you are likely to ask is, "Where are you from?" Or, perhaps the question is better stated, "Where did you grow up?" That tells you something about the person's life. If you were to ask me that question, I would tell you that I was born and raised in a small town called Spring Valley, Illinois. Spring Valley is about 100 miles southwest of my current home in suburban Wilmette, Illinois. Although the two places are not far apart geographically, they are worlds apart in many ways. Spring Valley has more in common with small towns throughout the country than it does with anything on Chicago's North Shore. Many Chicagoans have never even heard of Spring Valley nor do they care to know much about it. However, as you read my story, you will learn a good deal about its history and its people and perhaps you will better understand what makes me tick.

*Water tank, Spring Valley, Illinois.
A typical landmark in any small town.*

Spring Valley owes its birth and its growth to the coal industry. Normally, when you think of coal mining, you think of Appalachia, of places like West Virginia, Kentucky, and Tennessee. You conjure up in your mind banjo-playing hill folk, and all of the stereotypes that surround such people and their culture. But Illinois has a long history of mining, not just in its southern region which abuts Kentucky, but well into its center and even in Northern Illinois, of which Spring Valley is considered a part.

Everyone has heard of Cook County and you are likely to know Lake County and perhaps McHenry and Will Counties as well. But Spring Valley is a part of little known Bureau County, named for a French American trader active in the area. Bureau County is one of the 102 counties that comprise Illinois. Its county seat is in Princeton—not the place in New Jersey with the famous university—but a town of 9,000 people which is larger than the 6,000 people who today inhabit Spring Valley.

The county traces its history to the 1830s, but Spring Valley began to develop as a town in 1883 when its coal mines began to boom. To give you some indication of what a boom town means in terms of population growth, the number of people increased twelvefold from 1,000 people in 1883 to over 12,000 by 1910. These were hardworking folks, especially those who toiled in the mines, and the 46 taverns which graced it helped take the edge off many a hard day's labor.

You only need to watch cable news to know that coal mining is dangerous work. It seems as though every year there is a story about a tragic cave-in and the struggle to save the lives of trapped miners. Whenever I hear about such a story, I think back to the mines of Spring Valley. If working the mines can take a man's life in the twenty-first century, you can only imagine how lethal it must have been in the nineteenth and early twentieth century. Such a calamity befell Spring Valley when tragedy struck in the nearby town of Cherry. Cherry is about four miles from Spring Valley and I went to high school with plenty of kids from Cherry. Like Spring Valley, it had a coal mine and about five hundred men and boys, many Italian immigrants, worked its mine. For many, November 13, 1909 was to be their last day on earth. In all, 259 died in what would become the third worst mining disaster in United States history. This time it was a fire, not a typical cave-in which proved fatal to so many. The memory of these 259 miners was never far from the collective memory of our town when I was a boy. I remember my grandfather telling me about the bodies that were constantly being taken out of the mine as the blaze and the fumes grew out of control. The corpses were so many that burying them all proved difficult. My grandfather and uncle helped in the effort, taking bodies to the homes of the deceased. They shed many a tear with the family members of those who had lost their lives.

The men who arrived in Spring Valley and built it into the boom town that was once called "Magic City" were a diverse lot composed mostly of Western and Northern Europeans. Later,

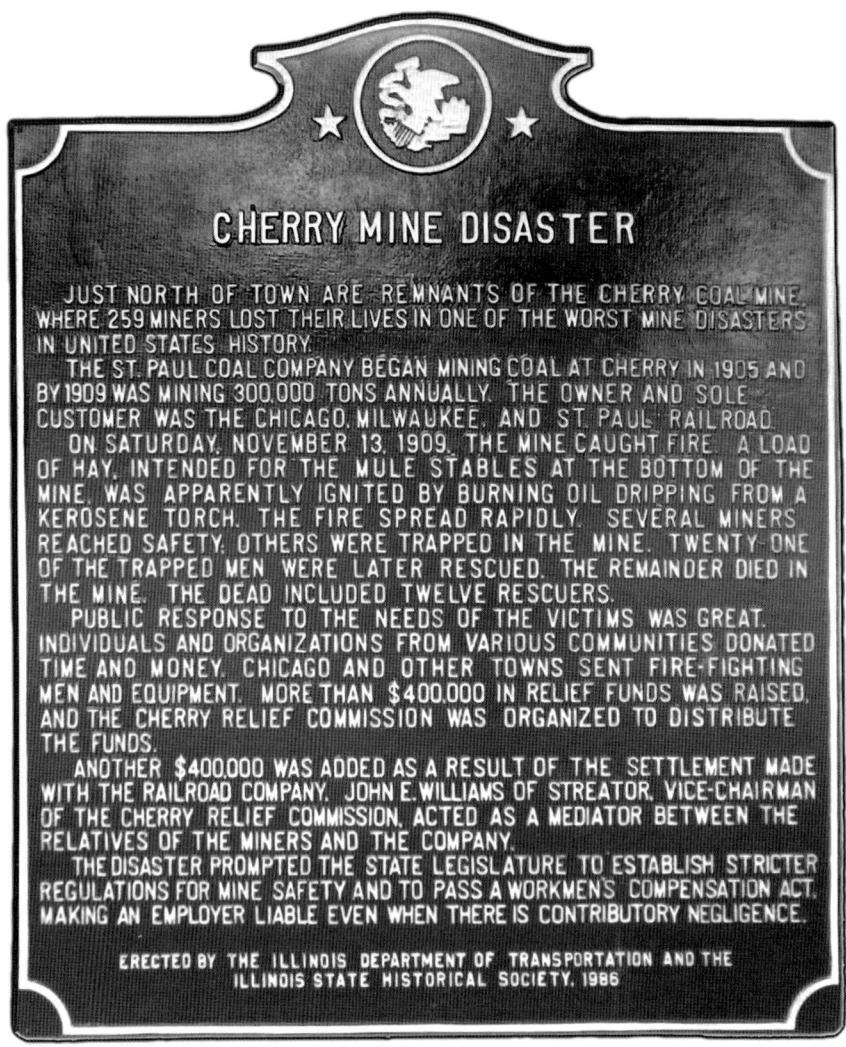

Cherry Mine Disaster Historical Marker

as Southern and Eastern Europeans began to arrive on these shores, they found their way to Spring Valley just as they would to coal mining towns throughout the country. The Italians were particularly strong in Spring Valley and they were originally brought in as strikebreakers, though they would soon become union men themselves. The company bosses were besieged with a great deal of union troubles in the 1890s and they eventually

SPRING VALLEY, ILLINOIS

Postcard from Cherry Mine Disaster showing ruins from Fan House and Escape Shaft

brought in black people from the South in the hopes of gaining cheaper labor and breaking the stranglehold of the union.

Cheap labor they were and coal mining must not have seemed so bad to these African-Americans compared with the life of abject poverty that so many had known as Southern sharecroppers. They established their own community in an area known as the "location," and while there was plenty of tension it spilled over into a full-fledged race riot in 1895, a riot that garnered national attention and became a civil rights cause in Chicago and elsewhere. It became something of a political crisis for Governor John Altgelt, Illinois' first foreign-born governor, who failed to take appropriate action to quell the violence.

Spring Valley's mayor and much of the police force were Italian by that time and they did not move quickly enough to end the rioting. Many blacks were beaten and their property was destroyed as the white miners tried to get them evicted from the town. They failed. Spring Valley had achieved a level of infamy that it could have done without but was a reflection of the circumstances—circumstances that would change. Men fighting for scarce jobs are always a problem; differences in skin color merely exacerbated it. By the time I was a kid, race relations, especially considering what was happening in other parts of the country, were quite good, though mining and the competition for mining jobs were on the wane and would soon be gone altogether as mining was no longer profitable. The boom times were over and it was into such a Spring Valley that I was born. But the town had many things going for it. For one thing, its location on the Illinois River proved an excellent spot for the many grain silos that dotted its landscape and which were used by the many farmers in the area. A small town is a very good place to grow up in, but like every place and every person, it was a place with a past.

The Steinbergs and the Buckmans

My family had begun to arrive by the time of the aforementioned race riots. They were not miners, but, like many Jews they played an important role in the life of a mining town. Most of my young readers probably wonder what Jews were doing in these small towns. Jewish people are today associated with big cities like New York, Chicago, Los Angeles, and Miami. People might be surprised to hear that Jews lived and prospered in nearly every small town in America. Where there were men working in mines, panning for gold, or tilling the soil, they were in need of many things that Jewish peddlers and later Jewish storekeepers were known for providing. My ancestors were part of that story.

Isadore Steinberg was the first to come to Spring Valley, arriving in 1888, about eight years after Jewish migration from Eastern Europe had begun in earnest. He was my great-uncle, the brother of my grandmother, Celia Steinberg Buckman. I was very close to my grandmother and used to hear plenty of family tales including the story behind our family name. They came from Russia and when they arrived at the port of entry known as Ellis Island, they were told that if you had a name that sounded very Jewish, it would not be easy to get a job. It may have been the "*Goldeneh Medihna*" (the country where the streets were paved with gold), but there was a price to be paid for the chance to have some of that gold and many Jews anglicized their names in an attempt to hide their religion and ethnic origin. These anglicized names were also a lot easier to pronounce. The family name had been Saks and they changed it to Steinberg, which they believed to be a good German name. Perhaps it was all for the best that everyone thought Steinberg to be a Jewish name, for it was such an identity which was to be the dominant one for our family.

My great-uncle Isadore Steinberg had established a clothing store named Steinberg's Department Store, catering to the peddlers who came from Chicago with their wares. These items were then sold in his store to the farmers in the area and included anything needed around a farm or a home. Virtually anything from trousers to pots and pans to work materials for sewing garments could be found in this department store.

Many of the peddlers who supplied my great uncle with the goods to sell were religious Jews who needed to have an appropriate place to stay should they not be able to return to Chicago for the Sabbath. They made Spring Valley their way station.

You now know how my grandmother's family wound up in Spring Valley. But how did my grandfather get over to these shores? Would you believe that my grandfather, Charles Buckman, came by himself from Russia at the tender age of 13? At an age when boys today are writing their thank you cards for their Bar Mitzvah gifts, he traveled to a strange land, not knowing any English, and somehow made his way to Chicago. Why was he so anxious to leave Russia? Like many Jewish youngsters, he faced a 25-year conscription in the Czar's army, which was a miserable life and frequently meant a death sentence. Like many Jewish boys, he escaped his fate by fleeing Russia with a group of his friends and was happy to come to this country even if he was penniless. After finding work in 1890 during the World's Fair, he somehow met my grandmother. After they married, they came to Spring Valley in 1893 and had established a grocery and feed store with the help of Isadore Steinberg. Like some storekeepers, they had purchased a building, the downstairs of which functioned as a store while the upstairs served as their living quarters. The upstairs consisted of the kitchen, a parlor and a sitting room. I mentioned the Jewish peddlers staying in Spring Valley over the Sabbath. They frequently stayed upstairs. My grandmother would cook Sabbath meals for them. Of course, my grandparents would never charge them anything; they were not running an inn. One of the most important mitzvot or commandments in Judaism is called *Hachnasos Orchim,* which means tending to the needs of household guests. Our forefather, the patriarch Abraham, was renowned for this and so it is with his descendants. It is a point of emphasis in Jewish life. It would be unthinkable to charge someone for staying over in one's own home. My grandparents followed this example religiously, and, not only did my grandmother feed their guests, but she provided them with a care package as they would no doubt be traveling right after the Sabbath. The peddlers were very grateful, but did not have the economic means to ply my grandparents with a traditional gift as would be the custom today when you are staying in someone's home. The peddlers showed their appreciation by taking items like copper wash tubs and other metal knick-knacks that they had collected along the way and placed them in the backyard.

 In 1898, a terrible fire destroyed my grandparent's building, their home, and their store. All that remained were these metal items left behind by the peddlers. Thus began a new business to be known as Buckman Iron and Metal. It operates still today. The business spans four generations and 112 years and now includes scrapyards in Spring Valley, Ottawa, Mendota and LaSalle. How did this expansion come about? My uncle, and later my cousin, George and his son, Arnold expanded the operation significantly, purchasing these additional scrapyards. My grandfather started collecting metal in a horse and wagon. His great-grandson flies his own plane.

Born to Survive

I titled this book *Born to Survive* and the reasons for my choice will become clear soon enough. I was born on June 16, 1926, at St. Margaret's Hospital in Spring Valley, Illinois, the son of Paul Pfeffer and Gertrude Buckman. I never knew my father, for my parents divorced not very long after I was born. I carry his last name, but that is about it. Once he was out of my life, he was out of my life. He never helped my mother or me in any way, never even sent us a dime. For 84 years, I never knew what happened to him. In fact, it was only this year that I found out, but that is a tale that you will have to wait until the end of the book to hear.

My Spring Valley home after remodeling

Many boys who don't know their fathers or are abandoned by them are left bitter creatures. Many youngsters would hold great hostility for such a thing happening to them. They walk around in a state of perpetual anger. Not me. It would be the start of a pattern. Every time something seemed to go wrong in my life, something which seemed like a bad thing, it frequently turned into a good thing. For I had wonderful *mazel*. I say wonderful *mazel*, because the family life that I had was wonderful. Besides my mother, I was surrounded by many other people who loved me and cared for me.

Things did not start out too great in the health department for me. I was born three months premature and weighed approximately two pounds and had all manner of medical problems. I had the doctors working overtime in those first couple of years of my life. They earned their pay for sure, but the real work was done by my grandmother and aunt. My grandmother kept me in a shoebox and it was not just to save money on a bassinet; I was just real small. She would bathe me with oil three times a day until I was two years old. I have always felt that it was my grandmother who saved my life. When I was two years old, my Aunt Mary, married to my mother's eldest brother, Maurice, took over. By the time I was ready for school, I was a normal, healthy child.

Where was my mother in all of this? She was busy working at my great-uncle's store, helping to support us. We did not have much money and it was understood that everyone would have to pitch in if we were going to be able to sustain ourselves. She continued to work at the store until I was about fourteen years old, when she met a wonderful man, Ben Kligman of Chicago. She would move to Chicago and I stayed in Spring Valley. She remained married to Ben for forty years. Ben had two children, Irving, who was four days older than I, and Leonard, who was nine years younger than the two of us.

If you are expecting to hear about a mean stepfather, you will again be mistaken. Ben was a great guy, and treated me

My beloved grandmother in her later years

with the same love and devotion as his own sons. My mother reciprocated in kind to his boys and so I had a father and two brothers. So now I had four brothers, two mothers and two fathers. Not a bad deal.

Two mothers? Four brothers? Let me explain. There have been many women of valor whom I have met throughout my life, but if sainthood could be bestowed to only one woman, I would have to nominate my Aunt Mary for the honor. It is very difficult to put into words all of the things that she did for me. Until

Standing, left to right: Grandpa Ben whom I called the Governor, my mother, my brother Irv. Sitting: my brother Lenny and myself.

the day she was taken from this world, she showered me with attention and showed me an abundance of love and concern, not only to me but, once I had my own family, she extended this love to my wife and children. Though she gave birth to Jerry and George, I was still her oldest son.

What kind of a woman was Aunt Mary? She exemplified all of the best qualities of the Jewish woman, the type of woman who kept the household together in both body and spirit. Most important of all, though, was the manner in which she carried herself. She showed me the proper path to follow in terms of how to conduct myself and this she did through the example she set. She never raised her voice, never treated anyone harshly. We lived together with my grandparents in the same house until I was about thirteen. My aunt and uncle then moved to their own house, a house in which I was a constant visitor.

My aunt's talents were not restricted to the manner in which she treated people. She was an outstanding cook and baker. Like George Washington, we had a cherry tree, and not only one cherry tree, but two. We also grew rhubarb in the garden. What did she do with all of this good stuff? It became the fruity fillings of many a delicious pie. To me, her best pie was her lemon cream pie. Over the years, I have had many pieces of lemon cream pie, maybe even a few too many. I enjoyed them all but found that none could measure up to Aunt Mary's.

Perhaps Aunt Mary's pies were so sweet because they reflected her inner sweetness. When I married Paula, the two became very close. My three daughters also became very close to her. To them, she was always Grandma Mary. Jerry was four years younger than I and George was four years younger than Jerry. We were raised as brothers and that is the way I feel about them today. I am very proud because not only did both become extremely successful, Jerry as a doctor who served as Chief of Staff of Highland Park Hospital, and George as an owner of scrap metal yards, but they are very fine people, good family men, and devoted Jews. I must say that it is a great credit to them that they never harbored any resentment toward the treatment that their parents showed me. There was never any jealousy there, just a lot of understanding. While we may not have had much money growing up, there was plenty of love to go around.

My Aunt Mary was just one half of a couple who were so close that they seemed inseparable. Uncle Maurice was my mother's brother and he worked extremely hard. He was one of those rare people whose character reflected the best qualities. Let me just say that he was honest, earnest, and sincere; admired by everyone who had the good fortune to make his acquaintance.

On Sunday afternoons, he would sit on the porch of our home and read through the newspaper. There is nothing like a cold glass of lemonade to quench your thirst on a hot country day, and, if you can picture the scene, my aunt would come out with a glass of lemonade that just begged to be guzzled. He would smile at her, never hiding his affection and say, "Mommy, give a kiss."

Once he took a trip to California. Prior to leaving, he handed me a large three-ring notebook. He looked at me in such a way that I knew this was serious business, and, indeed it was. He sat me down and told me that if he doesn't return from the trip, I should open the notebook. What was in the notebook? I never found out as, thank God, he returned safely from his trip. Of course, neither did anyone else, that is until after my uncle passed away. It was only at that time that the contents of the notebook became known. It contained a list of individuals whom he lent money to over the years. He had marked those whom he did not want to repay the loan and those who should repay the entire amount. It was a powerful ethical example that my uncle set.

Some boys idolized boxers and baseball players. Some look up to movie stars and pop singers. I idolized my Uncle Maurice. What was it about him? It was not what you saw on the outside as with athletes or movie stars. Rather, it was his inner nature and the manner in which he treated people. He respected every person and taught me that I had an obligation to assist those who were not as fortunate as myself. He never looked down on a soul, no matter how poor, no matter how troubled his circumstances. I have tried to emulate Uncle Maurice in all that I do, but remember him the most when it comes to charity.

Why charity? Charity is one of the most cherished of Jewish values, perhaps its most cherished one. Later in this chapter I talk about a certain sacred prayer that we recite at the High Holidays. At the end of this prayer, we say, "Prayer, Repentance and Charity avert the severe decree." God expects all Jewish people to perform charity and not just rich people, not just those who have extra money at their disposal, or feel themselves lucky. Poor people are required to give charity. In fact, it is the great rabbinic authority, Moses Maimonides, who says that charity is so much a part of the Jewish makeup that if a Jew does not give charity, we have reason to suspect whether the person is in fact from Jewish lineage. So, I always knew from my childhood days to this moment in the year 2011, that I must give charity. Though I may have grown up in limited circumstances, one of the great lessons you learn is that there are always people with less than us, people that we must help, and there is never any shortage of them. This great mitzvah I saw my uncle perform many, many times and it never failed to inspire me. I have tried to follow his example and the tradition of charity that has been the hallmark of my people. I hope that I have been successful.

I was not the only person who so admired my uncle. One of the differences about living in a small town versus a big city is that you really get to know people in a place like Spring Valley. There was a family, the Cassfords, in town and it was not a small family. They had quite a few mouths to feed and Mr. Cassford did the best he could working hard as a garbage collector. They all struggled mightily to keep body and soul together and my uncle helped them in any way that he could. One of the boys became a police officer in town and he used to write songs and poems in his spare time. He composed a sonnet about a man who was one of the kindest creatures that God had ever placed on this earth. This man sought no fanfare, no publicity for all his many acts of loving kindness; his only desire was to do good. This man was my Uncle Maurice and this beautiful poem hangs over the door to my office, my uncle looming as large to me as ever. It never fails to inspire and I have put it in the back of this book for all who cherish the memory of Uncle Maurice to read and enjoy. He was just one great man.

Uncle Sam, Aunt Doris and Other Relatives

Every American has an "Uncle Sam," that tall, almost gaunt-like character with the flowing white mane, goatee beard, and top hat, with his finger pointed at you, inviting you to serve or otherwise do your patriotic duty. I speak now of my actual Uncle Sam, whose given name was Seymour. He was my mother's youngest brother, the man who was only eight years older than I. He took care of me like an older brother. Like a typical older brother, there were times when he was less than enthusiastic about having to take care of me, but he always did what was expected of him.

Uncle Sam married his wife, Trudy, while he was in the service and ran a successful furniture business back in Spring Valley, Buckman Furniture. When Paula and I got married, he would frequently come to Chicago on business and stay with us. We always gave him our bedroom and we would sleep in the living room. There was never any question about this. It was my way of paying him back for all of the kindness he had shown me as a child.

There were other relatives who had a great impact on my life, like my Aunt Doris, who were around when I was growing up. Aunt Doris was my mother's youngest sister and was a really beautiful woman. Like my mother, she worked at my great-uncle's store. Because of her stunning looks, she hit the big time, getting a job modeling shoes. My grandmother, aunt, uncle, and I would travel to the metropolis of LaSalle, Illinois, five miles from Spring Valley. There, the shoe store owner would put up a screen in the window which would show only the bottom portion of her legs as she would model different types of shoes. These were more modest times and no one ever saw her face as she elegantly sauntered in the various types of footwear. But

Aunt Mary, Uncle Maurice, and Aunt Doris pointing to the picnic barrel

My Aunt Doris with Darryl

Uncle Sam and Grandma Celia Buckman

Walter, Doris, and Darryl Reif with Fannie Reif (seated)

it was among the most exciting happenings that could be found in LaSalle at the time, and, to us, it was as high fashion as what could be found on Seventh Avenue in New York. To us, she was the closest thing we had to a celebrity in the family.

My Aunt Doris first married Charles Bork, who was from a family of wealthy scrap dealers from Peoria, fifty miles south of Spring Valley. I remember when the Bork family would visit, you would think my grandmother was entertaining royalty. After they divorced, Aunt Doris married a gentleman named Walter Reif. Though they never had children of their own, Walter had a son Paul, then 13, from a previous marriage. This son would have his own family with a wife and two sons, one fifteen months old and the other two months old, when tragedy struck. Paul was traveling on a plane with his wife when a crash ensued, killing both of them and leaving two orphans. The fifteen-month old toddler was named Darryl and my aunt and uncle subsequently adopted him. The two month old baby was taken by Walter's first wife who had since remarried. Aunt Doris showered Darryl with great love and affection and he remained very close to our family well after the death of Aunt Doris. I became very close to him, and though we are not related by blood, to me he is like a son. He visits from California two or three times a year, and I love having him with us. These bonds of family are very strong indeed. I have tried to the best of my ability to strengthen these bonds and do what is right when it comes to family.

The Jewish Ghetto of Spring Valley

When you think of a Jewish ghetto, you think of an area where Jews were restricted to living. Venice was the original Jewish ghetto and then there was Frankfurt and plenty of other places, too. Or, perhaps when you think of a Jewish ghetto you think of the teeming tenements of the Lower East Side of New York or Chicago's Maxwell Street neighborhood. When I think of a

Jewish ghetto, however, there is only one place which comes to mind: the Jewish ghetto of Spring Valley.

Why was it called the Jewish ghetto? It had to do with the fact that there were three houses in a row whose residents were Jews. That, in Spring Valley, constituted a Jewish ghetto. In the first house was our rabbi, Rabbi Sachs. The second house was occupied by my grandparents, where I lived as well. The third house was home to the Berliner family. You would think that in a town with so few Jews that everyone would get along. Well, that was only partially true. If you remember the beginning of the movie, "Fiddler on the Roof," you may recall that there are occasional disputes that erupt between Jews. If it was true in the town of Anatevka, so, too, was it true in Spring Valley. There was some bad blood between my grandfather and Mr. Berliner. The only time the two men spoke was to trade insults. These were clearly vestiges from the old country. Warm, hearfelt sentiments would be exchanged between them, like, "Your ears should be filled with dirt and you should grow onions in them." LIke most youngsters, I found it very easy to learn insults and language that was not very nice. When my grandmother heard me repeating these things, she told me never to speak such words or she would be forced to wash my mouth out with soap. And believe me, she meant it.

Mr. Berliner butchered cattle in a building in the backyard of his home. He kept the hides of the animals in a hole in his backyard, which did not necessarily do much to increase property values in the neigborhood. As you can imagine, the smell was not too pleasant and it seems as if every fly in Spring Valley hovered around their backyard. To me it was like a scene out of Egypt during the Ten Plagues.

The Berliners were a large family with seven daughters and one son. Their children ranged sufficiently in age so that their oldest child was a friend of my mother's and the youngest, Eleanor (Eki), is a friend of mine, who today lives in nearby Morton Grove. One of the Berliner girls married a Buckman, a first cousin of my mother. So the Buckmans and the Berliners were not exactly the stuff of the Hatfields and the McCoys, for, with the exception of the two family patriarchs, we all got along rather well.

As sweet as my grandmother was, she could be plenty tough. On the few occasions, or at least I like to think there were not too many of these occasions, when I did upset my grandmother, she was more than capable of meting out serious punishment. The woman, despite her age, was the world's greatest marksman or markswoman, though in her entire life, she never once discharged a firearm. She never used a bow and arrow either, but she was perfectly deadly with a shoe and that was the only weapon she ever needed. Whenever I did anything wrong and would start to run and hide, she would take off her shoe and fling it, which would sometimes travel a pretty good distance. Like a champion tomahawk thrower, the shoe never failed to hit its target, namely me, right square in the behind.

My grandmother had a severe case of arthritis, and though this did not seem to affect her throwing motion, it made walking somewhat difficult. So, after getting hit, I would bring the shoe back to her and apologize. She would smile and we were once again back to being the best of friends.

Though money may have been tight, my grandmother kept us well fed. Breakfast was a dish of oatmeal with toast and milk. Lunch's menu was dependent on the time of the year. Until the birds decided to head south for the winter, we would be treated to salami and eggs, that great low cholesterol treat. During wintertime, we got my grandmother's version of chili.

I remember my grandfather only when he was an older man. He would attend the synagogue on Saturday regularly and I still have fond memories of him taking me along with him. During the holidays and especially during the High Holidays, I would sit by his side and watch him pray. There was an intensity to the way in which he beseeched the Almighty, an intensity that must have had its origins in the old country and in watching his father and grandfather pray.

The intensity reached its crescendo during the prayer we know as "*Unesaneh Tokef*," where everyone in the congregation would proclaim in a loud voice, "Repentance, Prayer and Charity avert the severe decree." These men, wrapped as they were in their prayer shawls, really seemed to mean those words. My grandfather and other men would start to cry. I never understood why he would cry but I too would begin to sob. He was genuinely afraid of his fate and not only for his life, but for all of the people he cared about.

GOING TO SCHOOL

My grandfather's standard mode of transportation was a horse and wagon. He would take the wagon around all week buying scrap metal, traveling not just through Spring Valley but all of the surrounding communities. He would come home for

Entrance to Lincoln School where I attended grammar school

*Hall Township High School, Spring Valley Illinois,
my old high school*

lunch on most days. During the summer, my cousin, Jerry, and I would hide under the seat of the wagon before he came out of the house. When we were about a block from the house, the two of us would get up and sit by his side. He would pretend to be upset with us and act all surprised. Since this was a daily occurrence, though, he obviously knew what was going on and then let us each take one of the reins of the horse, making us feel like big fellas.

Every Saturday night after the Sabbath had concluded, he would pull me in the little red wagon to Kroger's Grocery Store where he would buy the groceries for the week, and treat me to two pieces of chocolate. The big action on Saturday nights was the band concerts. The band would play on a stage that had been built on wheels and would accommodate about twenty-five people. How could we afford such a luxury? Simple, it was free, paid for by the city with the help of local merchants. The merchants helped underwrite the concerts because people would come from all over the area, buying groceries and patronizing the respective merchants.

I would sit and listen to the great music, and my grandfather would sit on the curb next to me. We would be right in front of the band. I guess my grandfather really had a soft touch because he would buy me a double dip ice cream cone, which, though only five or ten cents, was for him a big expenditure in those days.

My grandfather's horse was to come in handy, but not always in ways that I could have imagined. My grandparents emphasized the importance of getting an education and my grandmother must have been very aware of every trick that kids use to get out of going to school for she insisted that if I ever had to miss a day of school, I'd better have a pretty good excuse.

I was in the first grade when we had one of those gigantic snowstorms. There was over a foot of snow on the ground and the fluffy stuff was still coming down strongly. Excitement filled me as I imagined all the fun I was going to have playing outside. In my mind, I could picture the snowman that I was going to build, with a scarf wrapped around him and some old buttons for his eyes. I was thinking about a good snowball fight that I was going to have with a few of my buddies. But before I could enjoy the day, my grandmother put her hand on my shoulder and I was brought back to reality. She told me that if I wanted to be well educated, I could not afford to miss a day of school. Judging by the look in her eyes, there was nothing I could do to convince her otherwise. She instructed my grandfather to unhitch the horse from his wagon and take me to school by horseback. The horse trotted through the snow like a Clydesdale, and, soon enough, we were at the school door. Even though there was not a soul standing by the door, my grandfather opened the door and told me to go into the school. The only other occupant in the school was the janitor who lived in a house next door to the school. He and I spent the entire day together and he was a really nice guy. I guess he was glad to have some company in that otherwise empty building.

*Standing, left to right: my grandmother,
Uncle Maurice, my grandfather.
Kneeling: George, Aunt Mary, and Jerry.
Lying down is the family bulldog.*

At the end of the day, my grandfather came with his horse and took me home. While my own kids would listen to the radio to find out if their schools were closed during snowstorms, I would think of my grandfather taking me to school on horseback. It left quite an impression on me. I realized what my grandmother was trying to get through to me. Every extra day spent at school gave me an advantage over my classmates, an advantage which I was reluctant to relinquish.

Everyone has a favorite teacher, a special kind of a teacher who brings the subject matter alive for the student. In my case, that teacher was Mrs. Catherine Ballerin. Mrs. Ballerin grew up in Spring Valley and began teaching in an era where you did not need to have a college degree. Once the person had successfully taught for a certain number of years, she received a certificate which effectively served in lieu of a degree. Mrs. Ballerin began teaching at the age of seventeen at the old Lincoln school. One of her early students was my mom and by the time I rolled around she was a middle-aged widow.

Mrs. Ballerin was big on teaching the fundamentals. She was a stickler for proper grammar and, as such, was the type of teacher who seems in short supply these days. Under her guidance, I was taught all about the proper use of nouns, verbs, adjectives, and adverbs. She also taught us to avoid certain things, bad stuff like misplaced modifiers, dangling participles, and, of course, the cardinal sin of ending a sentence with a preposition. I learned the fundamentals of our language well enough from this woman that when I took the English placement exam in college, I tested out of the first four semesters.

Mrs. Ballerin would play the piano at school plays and musicals. During the Christmas season, she would play while students would sing Christmas carols. But Mrs. Ballerin's favorite time of year was autumn. At Thanksgiving time, the Chicago Tribune would print the same cartoon every year. It can best be described as Native American Pastoral, replete with wigwams, Indian corn stocks and a full moon. Mrs. Ballerin would insist that we cut out the scene from the newspaper and bring it to class. We would spend one class session discussing the beauty of nature and how lucky we were to be able to view such a beautiful looking scene. Our teacher did not limit her comments to an appreciation of nature. She would point out that every human being was a beautiful creature, created by God in His Heavenly Image. Because of this we were obligated to love everyone regardless of race, creed, or color. I did not always fully understand what Mrs. Ballerin was talking about, but soaked it up real well. Like so many teachers, her real impact on your life came after you left her classroom. While perusing through a book about Spring Valley on the occasion of its 100th anniversary, I came upon a section about Catherine Ballerin. Reprinted there was a letter from one of her students from 1957, then a captain in the United States Army and later a dentist in Spring Valley. I think he expresses there what so many of us felt about this wonderful lady. It makes the point that Mrs. Ballerin was and remains for me a "teacher's teacher."

> Dear Mrs. Ballerin,
> I guess you will be surprised to get a letter from me. I am stationed in Germany, serving in the army.
>
> I was just reading from a book, *The Family Book of Best Loved Poems*, this evening, and so many of the poems I read brought back to my grade school days and especially to you who taught them all to me from the 5th–8th grades. I just had to write you this letter to show you my appreciation and to thank you for what you gave me during those years. You would be surprised how many of those poems I still can recite by heart!—Little Boy Blue, To Autumn, The Daffodils, Solitary Reaper, I Wandered Lonely As A Cloud—parts from Snowbound, and many, many others.
>
> I have school-teacher friends over here and they can't get over how many of these I know. Of course, I'm always

bragging about you to them. I wonder, sometimes, if teachers realize how much of an impression they make on their students and the very important role they play in the character development of every pupil who passed through their classes. I can remember my grade school days as if they were yesterday.

I suppose you receive plenty of letters like this from former students who have awakened to realize what a great person you really are and how much good you have done for them.

Hope you don't think I'm odd in writing this letter- for really, I mean every word of what I have said, from the bottom of my heart.

Very sincerely yours,
Louis Darwish

Amen, Louis. I could not have said it better myself. I only wished that Mrs. Ballerin were still alive to enjoy this book. I hope she would enjoy it and I like to think that she would say to me something like, "Peppy, I am pleased to see that you have some facility with the English language and that my work with you has paid off." Indeed it has, Mrs. Ballerin. Alas, she passed away at the age of 85 in 1971. She left one daughter and hundreds of grateful students. Thank you, Mrs. Ballerin.

The Little Synagogue

During the the three festivals on *Sukkot*, *Shavuot*, and *Pesach* as well as on *Yom Kippur*, right before we recite the *Mussaf* prayers, those of Ashkenazai origin recite the *Yizkor* service. *Yizkor* means to remember and we ask God to remember the souls of our dear relatives who have passed on to the next world, what they call the *Olam HaEmes*. It is traditional for those whose parents are still alive to leave the synagogue during the recital of *Yizkor*. After the

Valley synagogue smallest in U.S.

Photos of the members of the synagogue taken at the end of World War I. My grandfather is seated in the front row, second from right.

prayer is completed, those of us who had been waiting outside were called back in for the remainder of the service.

It was *Yom Kippur,* the holiest day of the Jewish year, and I went outside for *Yizkor.* I was just a child at the time, and, while playing outside, I had inadvertently torn a blade of grass. I just figured the neat thing to do would be to put it into my mouth and chew on it, so I did just that. The Torah scroll was being returned to the Ark and it is customary to kiss the scroll as it was going around the congregation. Some use a prayer book, touching the prayer book to the embroidered cover and then kissing the book. Some use a prayer shawl. Others touch it with their fingers and then kiss those fingers which have touched the Holy Scroll. Well, as the Torah was coming around, I must have forgotten about the blade of grass in my mouth because

SPRING VALLEY, ILLINOIS

Plaque in Spring Valley Synagogue. My Uncle Maurice's name, Mordechai ben Yishayahu is among those names listed.

Standing in front of Spring Valley Synagogue during a recent visit

My cousin Charlie Steinberg showing the two Torah scrolls in the ark. Both were given in honor of my Uncle Maurice, one by the Buckman family and one by the Steinberg family (my grandmother's brother's family).

the Rabbi stopped me cold and then proceeded to give me a hard slap in the face.

It was a bit of a shock, but he told me that people are fasting on the Day of Atonement, and not only am I not fasting, but I am actually eating in the synagogue. Of course, the grass hardly tasted like food, though I suppose I wish I had already swallowed it rather than letting it remain in my mouth like a cigarette. Can you imagine the outcry if a rabbi slapped a kid today? Lawsuits would have ensued, and the rabbi would have been fired, if not arrested. But this was just a different time and a different age. It was understood that you have to give adults leeway in imparting discipline and proper education to youngsters. Everyone just accepted that that was the way it was. And you know what? Even though as a child I was not supposed to be fasting, the incident made quite an impression on me. From then on, I left the grass of Spring Valley for its hungry cows.

Our little shul was not just for the benefit of our Spring Valley *Shtetl*. It was used by all of the Jews in the surrounding areas, from towns and villages like Mendota, DePue, and Grandville. These were Eastern European Jews, and, since they were religious, they would not drive on the High Holidays. They would come to Spring Valley for *Rosh Hashanah* and then return for *Yom Kippur*, the Day of Atonement and the holiest day of the Jewish year.

Where did these guests stay for the High Holidays? Some stayed with my grandparents and others stayed with other Jews in Spring Valley who were within walking distance of the shul. These folks would arrive before the holiday and bring with them all of their own food. They would then set about cooking the food in my grandmother's large stove. What a scene with all of these ladies making all of these great dishes like gefilte fish, brisket and tzimmes. Oh, the smells that would come out of that kitchen! Each lady had her own speciality and she would share it all with the many people that were present.

What was my role in all of this? I had a big job that was absolutely necessary for the successful preparation of the food. I would round up buckets of coal in the weeks before the holidays and have them stored near the cook stove so that there would be sufficient coal for all the cooking to be done. Let me tell you, we are talking about a lot of coal, so you should appreciate the gas and electric stoves of today.

Our guests were quite a collection of different folks. They hailed from all manner of different countries such as Poland, Lithuania, and Russia, and were a hardworking lot. Many were storekeepers like my grandparents had been, having come to the area as peddlers supplying the local populace with clothing and household goods. There was a family named Koopersmith who owned a scrap metal yard in Mendota. Mr. Koopersmith was a great big man, strong with powerful hands, and broad shoulders. He had a shiny gold tooth that was always visible whenever he smiled. The highlight of his year was during the auctioning of the *aliyahs* every year during Rosh Hashanah and Yom Kippur. That was the only time of the year we auctioned the honors and it was a primary way of raising funds though the amounts pledged were anywhere between one dollar and ten dollars. Mr. Koopersmith would step up to the podium where the Torah was read from and, his smile would turn deadly serious as he would plead with his fellow Jews to help the shul by making a big pledge. In the middle of his talk, his eyes would well up and he would begin to cry. People naturally responded, and, as he left the podium, his big gold tooth grin returned naturally enough to his face. It was a performance worthy of an Academy Award.

These holy days were essentially the only vacation that most of our High Holiday visitors would take during the year. After the festive meals, the families would stay up for hours, regaling everyone present with the same stories that they had told the previous years. Invariably, an argument would ensue about some minor detail in one of the stories or some other such trivial matter. Voices would be raised and insults would be exchanged. Frequently, derisive comments were directed to each other's country of origin. One would say, "What would a Litvak like yourself know of such things?" The Litvak would poke fun at the way in which his Galician friend pronounced his Yiddish and then both would gang up on their friends from White Russia: "What would a dumb Russian know?"

They really seemed to be angry at each other. Perhaps close quarters does something to people. Sometimes they went to bed angry claiming they would not return next year no matter how much they yearned to be with their fellow Jews for the holidays. Then, by the end of the holiday, they became best friends again. It was quite a turnaround as they would say good-bye, thanking my grandparents for making it the greatest holiday that they had ever had and extending their blessings to everyone present. Everyone was hugging one another, hoping that God would grant them a sweet year and enable them to return the following year. It was almost a surreal change, but it occurred every year like clockwork.

How did we accommodate all of these guests? Well, we kids would give up our rooms and sleep crosswise, five or six to a bed. None of us thought to complain. We loved all of the excitement that surrounded the holidays. There was a certain camaraderie that comes when a lot of people share a relatively small place. I am sure if you talk to immigrants like Mexicans and Poles today who still may live that way, they would concur. My wife, Paula, grew up in a four room apartment with her two aunts, one uncle and two cousins. She slept on a folding bed in the living room so I always tease her that we live in our current rather commodious home, which neither of us could have ever imagined, due to all of my hard work but that is another story. We enjoyed the comforts to be sure, but somewhere deep down, I think we still have a lot of fondness and nostalgia for those days of yesteryear.

Today, there are many Jews who attend synagogue only on the High Holidays. There are even public schools in largely Jewish areas that are closed on these days. We had a tiny Jewish community but no Jewish child would attend school on these days. Not only would they not be in school on *Rosh Hashanah* and *Yom Kippur,* but they would be absent on the three festivals.

During one of the festivals, one of the Jewish girls in town went to school. The principal noted her presence and asked her why she wasn't observing her religious holiday. She was sent home simply by the fact that none of the other Jewish students were present on these days. It gives you a sense of how we were respected by our non-Jewish neighbors.

Many times over the years I have been asked how it was that we managed to live a Jewish life when we were such a small minority. As this story indicates, in some respects, it was easier to live Jewishly. Not only did we have parents and grandparents enforcing religious norms and traditions, but a whole host of Gentiles as well.

Our little shul and our little *shtetl* would follow the pattern of many other small towns. Jews of my generation would leave for college or the service or for work in the big city and seldom return. Synagogues in small towns were difficult to maintain, and, even in my day it was always a struggle for us to keep a rabbi, and to maintain regular Sabbath and holiday services. Eventually, we could not afford a full time rabbi and by the 1950s could no longer get a regular Sabbath minyan (quorum of ten men). We never had a daily *minyan*, but when anyone from Spring Valley or any of the surrounding communities had a *yahrtzeit*, the anniversary of the death of a loved one which required the saying of the Mourner's Kaddish, a minyan would always be assembled. Once you turned thirteen, it was assumed that you would be responsible for maintaining such a minyan. I still remember my Uncle Maurice going to the shul at 4:00 A.M. to light the cookstove so it would be burning in time for the morning prayers on cold winter mornings. When I say cold winter mornings, I mean just that. I remember one particular January morning when the temperature was a bone-chilling twenty-five degrees below zero. But Uncle Maurice was strong in body and powerful in spirit, and

Photo taken around the time of my Bar Mitzvah

would have never considered doing anything else but lighting that stove and making sure there was a minyan present.

You cannot imagine the appreciation that people felt at being able to have such a minyan. I don't think any one of us who live today in large Jewish communities can fully understand it. I should also make mention of the fact that my cousin, George, took over the family scrap yard business and has remained in Spring Valley. My second cousin, Charlie Steinberg, has also remained in town and still maintains High Holiday services in the old shul. That, of course, is its own remarkable story, particularly in light of the fate of synagogues in other small towns. These buildings have mostly been sold and the chantings of the stirring prayers of the High Holidays can be heard only in the memories of those who once graced these wonderful buildings, as rickety as these structures may have been.

One of the Jewish memories that most of us have is one's Bar or Bat Mitzvah. In the North Shore of Chicago where I live, these are often big affairs; weekend events with big festive meals, Saturday night parties with a band playing or even flying a family to Israel to celebrate the occasion at the Western Wall. If you are the thirteen-year-old in question, the best part has to be the presents. For me, things were a bit different. My family did not send out a fancy invitation together with an RSVP card but rather contacted various out-of-town family members who, together with our Spring Valley Jews, were in attendance on that summer day in 1939. Rabbi Sachs prepared me for the big day and I had a brand new tweed sport jacket to wear, a jacket that would last through high school. Like most Bar Mitzvah boys, I chanted the Haftorah and spoke before the congregation. But the refreshments after Services were the simple fare of *kichel* and herring prepared by my grandmother. The adults washed it down with Four Roses Whiskey, which was known as one of the least expensive brands. It may have been a spartan celebration, but I loved it all the same.

Cousin Jake

The whole notion of family that I was raised with was that everyone stood together; everyone tried to help each other out. My grandmother had a nephew who became a very successful clothier in Salina, Kansas. For those of you who have never heard of Salina, it is a veritable metropolis compared to Spring Valley, several times its size. This relative, Jake Smith, had done well and was known as "Cousin Jake." We would receive regular care packages from him. The packages contained basic staple items, things that we now did not have to buy, giving our family a little breathing room. I never realized that there was anything at all unusual about receiving a care package. Like kids everywhere, you just kind of figure that whatever is happening in your family must be happening in every other family. One day, a special care package arrived from Salina. It was a huge box, considerably larger than most of the ones that we received. My grandmother opened it and I remember still the joy that I felt when I examined the contents of that box. No clothes or foodstuffs in this one. Nothing but a shiny new bicycle for me. I loved that bike and would ride it to school with great pride. When my cousin Jerry started the first grade and I was in the fourth grade, I would put him on the handlebars and we would shuffle off to school. I don't ever remember Jerry hitting the pavement, but I could be wrong.

Opening up care packages was not the only thing I saw. In later years, I remember my Aunt Mary collecting a bunch of clothing and sending it to her relatives. Who were these relatives? They had fled Hitler prior to the Holocaust and were in the process of establishing themselves in America. Recently, I spoke to the woman who helps us out around the house. She is from Poland and tells me that she sends packages of clothing back to her family in the Old Country. So the spirit of Jake, our cousin from Kansas, lives on today.

Down by the River

In small towns, people know each other for very long periods of times. People do not come and go, but stay in the same town for decades. There are limited numbers of doctors, lawyers, and dentists in town. A doctor may treat several generations of families, and they make house calls or at least they used to make house calls. Our doctor was Dr. Henry Jacobs, and despite his name, he was not Jewish but a Christian Arab from Syria. Dr. Jacobs lived only a few blocks from our house and during my latest pilgrimage to Spring Valley, I passed his rather stately looking home.

The story goes that one day I was running a high fever and my mom grew concerned, and, as they say in the old Westerns, went to fetch the doctor. After he examined me, my mother wanted to pay him but he refused to accept anything. She refused his refusal and took the seventy-five cents that she had on her and put it in his pocket. But the story does not end there. Apparently, there was a longer history to all of this. Dr. Jacobs' mother had a grocery store about a block away from my grandmother's. Her rent was ten dollars a month, and in those days, it was a pretty steep amount. She didn't have enough money to cover the rent once and the landlord was getting ready to evict her. My grandmother, though she was a competitor, gave Mrs. Jacobs the ten dollars necessary to cover the rent. As a result, Dr. Jacobs refused to accept money from anyone in the Buckman family. In fact, his mother had implanted within him the notion that whenever a Buckman needed help, it was his responsibility to come through. Such was the gratitude that they felt for our family, all based on this single act of kindness, a kindness that went against self-interest.

Dr. Jacobs used to grow tomatoes. One day, he asked my buddy, Chuck Sebastian, and me if we would like to get some poles to which he used to strap the tomato plants. He needed 25-30 poles and both of us saw this as a great money-making opportunity. We saw ourselves as being tycoons in waiting and jumped at any chance to prove our entrepreneurial mettle. The two of us were equipped with a hatchet and a couple of knives and made our way to the river bank where we cut small saplings which we thought would do the job rather nicely.

We were finishing up our work and were getting ready to leave when we began to hear sirens blaring and cars honking, noises which may have been common enough in the life of a big city but were a rare happening in a small town like Spring Valley. We were coming out of the brush by the river and all of a sudden we were greeted by none other than the man responsible for law and order in our fair town, namely the Chief of Police.

He informed us that we were in real trouble as it was 8:00 in the evening but since it was summertime the sun was still shining so we had no idea that it was so late. It goes without saying that neither one of us had a watch. My grandmother had called the police when neither of us showed up for supper. Apparently, someone had spotted us walking by the river and it was assumed that we had both drowned.

We were taken in the squad car back to our respective families. Chuck's parents and my grandmother and mother proceeded to hug us and then began laying into us, reprimanding us for our irresponsible behavior and the obvious worry that we had caused. For happy-go-lucky kids in the mold of a Tom Sawyer and Huckleberry Finn, we had no idea what we had done wrong. Years later and especially when I had children of my own, I would fully understand what we had done. In the meantime, we were able to complete our mission, delivering the poles to Dr. Jacobs. He must have felt bad about what we had gone through and gave us an extra dollar each. To us, that extra dollar was sure worth the scolding.

Cleaning Out the Chicken Coop

Not every job was as glamorous as chopping saplings on the river bank. Sometimes work is just a lesson in humility. Behind our home, my grandparents raised chickens. Of course, we were interested in both the eggs and the chickens. Anyone who has ever raised chickens in a coop knows that the chickens are not like children. They are not fickle eaters and will devour just about anything put in front of them. Any edible item that might be destined for the garbage would find its way into the chicken coop.

When I reached Bar Mitzvah age, I began to work in the coop. I would put on high boots and help my grandfather remove everything down to the earth for the next year's season in feeding them again. To this day, when I close my eyes the putrid odors of the coop return to my nostrils. I must have been a touch embarrassed by this work because I never told any of my friends and certainly none of my girlfriends of my toiling in the coop. I always worked hard to get the stink out of my pores and my clothes but now I have let the hat out of the bag—or better said, the chicken out of the coop.

STARVED ROCK

Lest my grandchildren think that all I ever did was work, we had plenty of fun, too. There were many exciting places to explore but none was as enjoyable as a visit to Starved Rock. They call it one of the Seven Wonders of Illinois and it is majestic indeed. It is on the southern bank of the Illinois River about twenty miles from Spring Valley and people would come from as far away as

Aerial photo of Starved Rock (Courtesy of Kathy Casstevens)

Chicago to explore its vast 2,600 acres of natural beauty. It has a long history to it and that history involves the Native Americans who once lived there and a siege that one tribe laid on another; hence the name Starved Rock. If you had a healthy imagination as I did, there was plenty to think about as you stared out at the large expanse of rocks and streams that made up the park.

Uncle Maurice had a truck and would clear out the back of it, and we would all sit on a bench in the bed of the truck as we went to the park. We had a family friend who had a cabin on an island right in front of Starved Rock and we would visit him and have a cookout there. Stanley Saj was a customer of my uncle and we felt like millionaires on our own private island. One thing that I will never forget is that this man had a car and it was an unusual one at that. It had pedals and it would float on the water and function like a boat. I could spend all day on that thing.

Making Extra Money

There are always ways to make extra money. As they say, necessity is the mother of invention, and, since it was a necessity to have money, I tried to be inventive. There were opportunities just waiting to be tapped. We received our kosher meat from Chicago and the meat along with bread made the trip on a Trailways bus. The contents were in bags, with the recipients names written on the outside of the bags, and I would meet the bus and take the bags and deliver them to each family. My action was based on tips and depending on the person, I would receive twenty-five to fifty cents for my efforts.

There were other ways to make money. During the Feast of Tabernacles, traditional Jews use a *lulav* and *etrog*. These are known as the Four Species and the *lulav* is taken from a palm tree and in it are branches from a willow and a myrtle. The *etrog* is from a citron tree and resembles a very large lemon. Its only use is for the holiday so the *lulav* and *etrog* business is the ultimate seasonal business. With the *etrog*, it is preferable to have a very nice looking and pleasant smelling type. It was the opposite of dealing with the chicken coop. Since we were all limited financially, we would have only one *lulav* and *etrog* for the whole town. I would get on my bike and take the *lulav* and *etrog* to the Jewish homes so that the blessing could be made on the four species. After the holidays, I would collect my tips from everyone. I made some good money on that one and it was a mitzvah to boot. What could be better than that!

Heading for the Dump

Most kids learn to drive when they are fifteen or sixteen, but I got a jump up on the competition. I started driving in the sixth grade, though without a proper driver's license. I would work helping out in my grandfather's junkyard and whenever a car was brought into the yard and it had some gas in the tank, I was permitted to drive it around within the confines of the yard. Needless to say, it was great fun, and, before long, I was driving legally on the streets of Spring Valley, the first of my friends to drive.

One day, my grandfather gave me an old Ford to drive around. I picked up my buddy, Chuck Sebastian, and, after driving about town, decided to head back to the yard. Spring Valley is a pretty hilly town, at least by Illinois standards and the yard was at the bottom of one of the town's steepest hills. Unfortunately, toward the end of our rather exciting ride, we realized that the brakes were not working correctly. Although we were not driving at a high speed, it became clear that the only way for the car to come to a halt was to drive the car into the town's dump, which was located at the other end of town. The car was built like a small tank and we drove straight into the dump and found the spot to head for in the form of a very large pile of trash. Boom! How did we get out of the car? With great difficulty for sure. We crawled through all types of garbage and proceeded to walk back to the junkyard, trying to get all of the accumulated residue off our clothes. My uncle took one look at us and then got a whiff and remarked, "You boys smell like you just came out of a garbage dump!" which was pretty accurate. All in all, though, it sure beat the chicken coop.

Falling from the Truck

There was a small factory in Spring Valley which made a product that used different types of metals. It used copper, zinc, and aluminum, and my Uncle Maurice would purchase the company's scrap which would be placed in barrels. We would drive over to the company and load the barrels on the truck. Once we filled up the bed of the truck, we would place a large chain across the back to prevent the barrels from falling off the truck and onto the street. I would sit on the top of the barrels as the truck returned to the yard.

Well, that chain was surely important because one early summer day, the driver must have had his mind on something else because he neglected to lock the chain, leaving the back of the truck completely open. Not good! As the truck was moving, the barrels began to fall off of the truck, and guess what went along with them. Yep, if you guessed Sam Pfeffer, you would be right. I went tumbling onto the street in a rather violent fashion, and let me add painful as well.

Carelessness is costly, and, in this case it resulted in two fractured hips. Each was known as a "green stick fracture" because, like the twig of a tree it was not broken off completely, but rather considered an internal fracture. This all occurred at the beginning of the summer, and, as you can well imagine, it did not turn out to be a summer full of fun. I spent several months in the hospital lying on a canvas like that of a ship's sail. Fortunately, I healed just fine, good as new.

The Ward and Its Occupants

One thing about being laid up in a hospital is that you establish a bond with everyone else in your ward. These are people you would never meet if not for the unusual circumstances which bring you together. In my case, there were six other patients in there with me, but one fellow will always stand out. I remember him still today.

He was at the peak of his youth, and the peak of youthful exuberance when Fate intervened. The young man was a star basketball player in one of the nearby towns. He must have been something of a hero in that town, six foot two inches tall, handsome, and they say he was just a really nice guy: a regular Jack Armstrong, the kind of guy whom boys look up to and girls adore. His potential seemed limitless as he was off to the University of Notre Dame on a basketball scholarship. What could be better than that?

Like most high school kids, the night of graduation is a time for celebration: a time for hooting and hollering, for beating

St. Margaret's Hospital where I was born and where I spent an entire summer after my fall from the truck

their chests the way only young men of such an age can. Well, the beer must have been flowing pretty steadily and laughter was surely in the air when he decided to take a ride with two of his buddies. It was a drive that none of those boys wish he had taken. The driver sped around a curve, and losing control, rolled over right into a ditch. As Fate would have it, the driver and the other passenger were unhurt. They simply walked away. Their buddy would never walk again, would hear the cheers of the crowd only within the recesses of his memory, for he was paralyzed and wheelchair bound for the rest of his life.

I could see and hear the many visitors coming to visit him. In addition to his family and friends, there were obviously many well-wishers from his town and his school who clearly loved this young man. It must have shaken everyone up because though I was just a young teenager, there were times when I could feel tears coming to my eyes whenever I would ponder the fate of this guy being relegated to life in a wheelchair. In a strange twist of fate that leaves one baffled, his other two buddies died within the following two years, both killed in separate automobile accidents. What kind of a life did the high schooler end up having? I do not know but have thought of him often over the years, especially when I ever felt compelled to complain about minor aches and pains.

Keeping the Dietary Laws in a Catholic Hospital

St. Margaret's is a Catholic hospital which dates back to 1903, when Father John Power started it. It was staffed from its inception by nuns who were members of an order originally from France with the name of "Sisters of Mary of the Presentation"—a serious bunch indeed and very committed to their work.

While I was laid up in the hospital, I did my best to observe the kosher laws. The only meal where I ate the hospital's food was breakfast. Lunch and dinner were brought to me by members of my family. For breakfast, I would have soft boiled eggs.

Every Saturday, the Mother Superior would make her rounds at the hospital, inspecting every facet of hospital service to ensure that it met her high standards of care. The place was immaculate, so much so that you could easily eat off of the floor. She would walk around with her administrator, and, on this particular Saturday, as they passed by my bed, I began to cackle like a chicken and pulled out two of the soft boiled eggs that I had saved from breakfast. The ever serious Mother Superior, a seeming caricature of the harsh leader of nuns, not only loosened up a bit, but began to laugh. I had never seen her laugh before and it made me crack up. I had to repeat the performance numerous times as she would bring over the other nuns to watch.

Apparently, this story made the rounds because one of the bylines for the Spring Valley paper read, "Pfeffer laid an egg at St. Margaret's Hospital"—obviously a slow news week.

Who Is Sam Pfeffer?

When I graduated from elementary school, in my case the Lincoln School, I had a fairly large contingent in attendance. There was my mother, grandmother, and my aunt. The principal was handing out the diplomas and called out the name Sam Pfeffer. Nobody stood up. Finally, in a staged whisper that was loud enough to wake up anyone who happened to be dozing off, he turned to me and said, "Hey Pep, *you* are Sam Pfeffer." Everyone broke out in laughter.

You have to understand that everyone knew me by my nickname, Pep or Peppy, and since my grandparents were named Buckman, I was known as Peppy Buckman. I had gotten so used to that being my name that I had forgotten my legal name, Sam Pfeffer. It is the name which appears on all proper documents, including grammar school diplomas. Fortunately, I got my diploma.

Math—My Nemesis

If you remember the story about me going to school in the snow, you will have realized the importance that my grandmother placed on gaining an education. I worked hard in school and did well. But if Superman could be taken down by Kryptonite, I nearly was done in by mathematics.

We had the same teacher for math during my last four years at Lincoln School, and, unlike Mrs. Ballerin, she was not a particular favorite of mine. Well, I should add that I was not a particular favorite of hers. Why? Very simple. In 7th grade, I was out in the hall and the discussion turned to our different teachers. I mentioned that I did not like our math teacher too much because she reminded me of a bulldog. Just then my friends started to laugh hysterically and I was confused as I could not see the great humor. To me, she really did resemble a bulldog and not a nice bulldog, but an angry one. Just then I turned around and realized why they were laughing. My math teacher was standing right behind me and heard my less than complimentary description of her.

Naturally, I apologized and though my math teacher seemingly acknowledged my contrition, a phobia of math developed from that point onward. In high school, a Mr. Bradley was my geometry teacher. Mr. Bradley was a close family friend who frequently took me fishing so you would have thought that this should have cured any lingering problems from my "bulldog" comment. But apparently not because I had a less than stellar performance on my first geometry exam. Across the test paper and next to where I had printed my name, Mr. Bradley had written in bold letters, "Pfeffer, you even misspelled your own name." Fortunately, the future still looked bright.

CHAPTER 2

The Navy and Beyond

ENLISTING IN THE NAVY

One of the recurring themes in this book is that you have to have mazel. This chapter of my life is certainly a prime example of that. In my day a high school student with an excellent academic record was allowed to leave high school after the third year and begin college. For me this meant leaving Spring Valley and coming to Chicago where I attended Herzl Junior College. Herzl had a primarily Jewish enrollment and was located on the Old West Side in the Lawndale section of Chicago..

My mother had relocated to Chicago when she married my stepfather and I was living with them and my two stepbrothers. The year was 1943 and World War Two had been raging for nearly four years. The United States had been involved in the war for nearly two years after the attack on Pearl Harbor on December 7, 1941. By the spring of 1944, I was about to turn 18 and made the decision to enlist in the Navy and do my part. Like all Chicago area recruits, I did not have very far to travel for boot camp, held as it still is today at the Great Lakes Naval Station, north of Chicago.

Boot camp is boot camp, rigorous, grueling and boring, but I did well in my sixteen weeks at Great Lakes. The opportunity to become a Navy corpsman presented itself and I jumped at the chance. The corpsman's school was held in the state of Washington near Spokane and for the first time in my life I would travel, even if it was at the behest of Uncle Sam and not Sam Pfeffer. Seeing the magnificent mountains of the Pacific Northwest was a real eye opener, especially for a Midwestern kid used to staring at flat cornfields. The school went fine and, after being graduated, I was rewarded with a 10-day pass which allowed me to visit everyone back home.

Reporting back to the base, I was awaiting my permanent assigment. I fully expected to be assigned to a combat unit in the Pacific. You have to remember the time. Fighting was fast and furious in spots like Iwo Jima, Okinawa, and a whole host of other hot spots. Preparations were in the works for what was expected to be the bloodiest battle in the war, the invasion of the Japanese mainland. It was a battle that would never happen. However none of us could have predicated that. In all of the island battles, particularly in those in which the Marines were the primary fighting force, Navy corpsmen were the medics as the Marine Corps does not have its own medical corps, relying on the Navy to fulfill that role. If you remember the famous photo of the flag being raised on Iwo Jima by several servicemen, one of the men shown was a corpsman. Corpsmen were acquiring battlefield decorations in large numbers not so much for fighting, but for their heroic behavior in tending to the wounded, coming under heavy fire. These decorations included the highest award for valor, the Congressional Medal of Honor, which was often awarded posthumously. That is what I was looking at when I readied myself to receive my orders.

The way it went is that a whole bunch of us would wait in line outside in a hallway and were being called into rooms that were manned by petty officers who would give us our assignments. As one man would vacate, the next one would walk in. Finally, my turn arrived and I steadied myself for what lay ahead. I was told to sit down and looked straight ahead at a fellow who clearly had been around the block in the Navy. He had before him a folder with my name on it, Pfeffer, Sam, and all of the pertinent statistical information and the record that I had thus far accumulated. The first thing that came out of his mouth was delivered with a hint of a smile. "Where in the devil is Spring Valley, Illinois?" I gave him the coordinates, the longitude and latitude as it were, and he asked me if I had ever heard of Peru. Immediately, I realized that he was speaking not about the country in western South America, but, rather, that town on the Illinois River near Starved Rock State Park and only about four miles from Spring Valley. The town was known for two things: being the birthplace of world famous violinist, Maud Powell, and the world headquarters of Westclox. Peru and LaSalle had a high school together and they were considered our big rivals. Naturally, I knew plenty of the kids who attended LaSalle-Peru High School. The chief then asked me if I knew a guy with the nickname of "Pollack." "Of course, I did," I told him. Everyone knew Pollack and if you saw him you could never forget him. He was a great big guy, the kind of guy who may have a nickname of Tiny if it weren't Pollack. Six foot three and enough bulk on him to put a three-hundred-pound scale to its limit. But the guy did not have a mean bone in his body. In fact, though no one would want to mess with him, he was a gentle giant and one of the most lovable guys in town. The chief told me that the big Teddy Bear was his brother.

My connection with Pollack seemed to endear me to his older brother, and, rather than send me overseas, he began to search for a stateside assignment. I did not know exactly how to react to all of this. On the one hand, I did not want any preferential treatment. That would not be fair to the other guys. On the other hand, no one wants to be a dead hero, so I just said to myself, "Whatever is coming my way, is coming my way. I'll take it and pray for the best." Well, the chief spent a few minutes looking

In my naval uniform

through a bunch of papers and told me that the Naval Hospital in Seattle had requested one corpsman so that was where I was headed.

After arriving at the hospital, I was assigned the graveyard shift, which, given where I was working, is probably not the best way to describe the work hours of 11 at night to 7 in the morning. It was fine with me and though I was not expecting to see a lot of combat during this tour of duty, I did see some action, in a manner of speaking, the first night on the job. I was changing bedsheets when I happened to open a door to one of the rooms on the floor while looking for some additional linen. What did I find there but the head nurse tending to one of the patients but not in any traditional medical sense. Though their behavior was clearly against Naval regulations, I decided that in an early version of "Don't ask, Don't tell," that I would close the door, shut off the lights, and pretend that I had not seen what I had just seen.

Two days later the head nurse called me into her office and told me that she was transferring me from hospital duty to barrack detail. This was considered very cushy and I suppose was a reward for my discretion. I was grateful and this proved another reminder that I had mazel.

The Remainder of My Time in the Navy

Much of the time spent in the military is very boring. Sure, when you are watching a John Wayne movie, it all seems very exciting and very glorious but whether you are in a combat unit or a non-combat one, much of the time is busy time or down time. It's just the way it is and you catch on fast to the pace of life. While barracks detail was cushy it was also pretty dull. No matter how much work we did, we could not shake the stale odor of boredom. We would sweep the floors and then sweep them again, and then mop and polish them until you could practically eat off of them. Inspections were no sweat and we tried to seem interested in our work. It was a struggle.

One day, a Navy chief came around looking for something or rather someone. What was the object of his interest? He was looking for a chess opponent, which may seem a little surprising as you do not associate that cerebral game with its roots in places like India and Persia with a hardened Navy chief. But this guy was not typical and I saw an opportunity. I told him that

I had played the game a bit a few years before I enlisted and had not seen a chess board for some time. I did not want him to think that I was some kind of grandmaster, but, apparently, I was the only guy with any experience, so I was told to come around to his barracks. When I got there, he had a board all set up with shiny wooden pieces that had clearly not seen much action. There was only one problem with all of this. Some of the pieces were incorrectly set up which led me to believe that the chief had limited experience and was certainly no chess shark. I repositioned the pieces, careful to avoid embarrassing the chief.

Why the chief was so anxious to play, I do not know. Perhaps he was expecting that the game would sharpen his military mind, but there we sat, one green kid from Spring Valley with one stripe, and him with the emblem of the chiefs, with a fouled anchor and the initals USN contained in it. We started to play what would be the first of several chess games that day. Discretion being the better part of valor, I decided that it would be wise if I did not play my hardest, hoping that he would not notice and I could inconspicuously and gracefully lose. Well that proved difficult. Despite the chief's enthusiasm for the game, he had absolutely no ability and little patience. He would make one careless move after another until I had no choice but to capture his pieces and checkmate him.

I was unsure of whether I would receive a return engagement from the chief, but, sure enough, he appeared the next day and summoned me to his quarters again. After playing, we would have lunch together at the special dining area reserved for the chiefs and though this sort of fraternization was quite rare, he seemed to rather enjoy both the games and my company and we continued this routine for many months. Finally, I received orders to report to the Out Going Unit (OGU in military jargon) for reassignment, presumably for duty with the Marines who were readying themselves for the final assault in the South Pacific. Again, I was ready for what lay ahead and there was much talk about the final assault, the anticpated invasion of Japan.

Thinking that I had better inform the chief that I would soon be leaving the base and he would be in need of a new opponent, the chief did not take the news well. He told me not to pack just yet as he would take the matter up with the officer in charge. Apparently he did and the word came down that I would remain on base, reassigned to baggage detail. The chief must have figured that he could not do without my company, and what could I say? So, baggage detail it was.

Baggage detail sounds more appropriate for a civilan airport than a naval base, but this was military stuff. You may have seen sailors traveling in bus or train stations with their official looking duffel bags slung over their shoulders. You would be amazed at how much can be stuffed into one of those duffel bags. Well, sailors who would come through the hospital would check their bags into the baggage room when they arrived on base. We would then go through the items in the bag and inventory every item, down to the last sock and undershirt. If they had something other than the number issued by Uncle Sam, which they invariably did, they would need to show the proper receipt. If they had no receipt, which was also very common, the article in question would be confiscated. We were talking about items of value here like blankets and peacoats. They would be put into boxes and shipped to the reclaiming department of the Navy to be reclaimed.

If a sailor wanted to take his duffel bag off base, he needed to show a label on the top of it, with the signature of the officer in charge, to prove that the bag had been examined. The fellow who effectively ran the baggage detail was not really a commissioned officer. He was somewhere between a commissioned and non-commissioned officer, holding a rank something like a warrant officer. This fellow would be away much of the time and he needed someone to keep the labels and use them appropriately. He had a lot of confidence in me and would give me a few hundred of these labels with his name already signed.

The question in the military is always how much should you run things by the book? Some who run things by the book, by the manual, or whatever you want to call it, forget that we are dealing with human beings here, and human beings who have been through a heck of a lot. I always felt that you had to have a certain amount of compassion for the guys who were coming through the hospital, some of them with serious wounds and injuries. If not for the grace of God and my good mazel, I could have been one of them.

It was not unusual for a sailor to have several coats in his duffel bag without the proper receipts. These should be indicated on the label. Perhaps the history of how he came across the extra two coats was a bit on the hazy side, but I did not hold it against him. So what would I do? I would confiscate the two extra coats but then throw one of them back in.

My chess playing with the chief continued throughout my time in baggage detail. Finally, I received a set of orders that would have taken me to a new duty station. Again, the chief got wind of the orders and had them changed. By now you may be wondering. This guy was not an admiral, captain or anything of the sort. Do the chiefs run this country's navy? In a manner of speaking, indeed they do. The day-to-day business is largely in the hands of the chiefs. So, I was ordered to report for my new assignment at the base's fire department.

The firehouse consisted of the fire trucks which were kept in the middle of this huge building. It was my new home, as one side of the building functioned as the barracks for the men assigned to duty there and the other side was the quarters for the marines attached to the base. In addition to the large vehicles that were used for fighting fires, we also had a small pickup truck that could be used for fire inspections or to travel to the place of the fire. The reality was that the pickup was used for "security purposes."

The primary function of the truck was to pick up marines and sailors who had one too many. We would get a call from the marines at the gate that someone needed an escort back to his barracks and off we went. These included officers, nurses among them, who needed a ride, and, as a result of this service that we provided, we had accumulated a great deal of goodwill on base.

Chess was not the only hobby that occupied my time while in the Navy. My uncle had sent me my trombone and figured that I would try out for the base band. Many of my friends may be surprised to hear that I was once a trombone player and played the instrument in the years prior to my enlistment in the Navy. It had all come about by accident when, as a twelve-year old, I saw the movie "Swing High, Swing Low" starring Carole Lombard and Fred MacMurray. Fred MacMurray played the trumpet in the film and I simply adored both the movie and the role of Skid Johnson, a handsome ex-soldier who plays the nightclubs of Panama and wins over the beautiful woman. So, I set my sights on learning how to play the trumpet. Well, I told my grandmother of my desires and she suggested that I go see the only man in Spring Valley who gave music lessons, namely Mr. Bertrand who lived only a block and half away.

As luck would have it, Mr. Bertrand, did not have a trumpet, but a trombone and, to induce me to take lessons with him, he offered me a discount off of his regular price, from 50 cents down to 25 cents. I studied with him for a good number of years and got the chance to play in the high school band. Mr. Sweet had been my teacher and the bandleader in high school and we played at the local county fairs where we were paid and received free tickets. I also played some local clubs with some small combos and was geared up to join the base's band.

When I showed up to the band practice, I heard really beautiful sounds coming from those playing. There was a reason for that. The men playing were good musicians; some of them were pros and way out of my league. My trombone playing days were over and I decided to send the instrument back to Spring Valley for sale.

What was motivating me in all of this? If you were a participant in one of the base's extra-curricular activities, you could get a weekend off when you normally would not have been allowed to leave the base. I wanted that weekend and figured there must be a way of getting it. Again, I had a little bit of mazel. In the service, sports were big and many of the bases had teams in various sports like football, basketball, and baseball. Boxing was big and Joe Louis and other famous fighters were inducted into the service and were traveling around doing exhibitions.

I had to eliminate most of the sports available because they were staffed with excellent athletes, some of whom were college stars or even professionals. I was also not a really big guy, maybe 129 pounds soaking wet, so that was an important consideration. So, the most logical sports where my weight would not be a disadvantage were boxing and wrestling because you competed against only those in your weight class. Boxing seemed out of the question because of the experience level of the competition, but I looked into wrestling and met the wrestling coach. A petty officer, he was about my size, maybe 135 pounds tops, and had been a coach at Indiana University when the war broke out.

The coach was a friendly type and he seemed to take an immediate interest in me as he looked me over. I told him that I had no experience but he said that was no problem. He would teach me everything I needed to know about wrestling. His enthusiasm seemed to help fuel my own and so I was on the wrestling team. I worked really hard at it, hanging on his every word and was picking up a lot. It helped that I was roughly the same size as the coach.

If you remember, being on the team provided me with weekend leave every other week. I used the leave for good purposes by going to Washington State University in Pullman, Washington, where I had met a very nice young lady who was a student there. Of course, you did not have to be Clark Gable in those days. Since so many fellows were in the service, it seemed as though the women outnumbered the guys about ten to one. This girl was in a sorority; in fact, she won the award as the prettiest girl on campus. She had invited me to be her escort at the big dance of the year and I told her that I would come. But just then, the base commander went and changed the rules for leave on me. You had to win your match that week to get leave and our coach was one smart guy. He understood that the guys needed leave and he would match guys who had leave coming that week with guys who did not. The dance that I was looking forward to was not my regular leave weekend. But this was not normally a problem as what our coach would do would be to schedule one guy who had leave with a guy who didn't have leave. Of course, the fellow who did not have leave would be the winner. Fate intervened for me, however, as my scheduled opponent became ill and so the coach put in his place a new member of our team who was not a member of our inner circle but was a very tough competitor. He was unaware of the fix and was trying very hard to win the match. I was dominating the guy when he flipped me over and knocked me square out of the circle. This disqualified him and though I was a little bit bruised and sore, I was one happy wrestler. Later I learned that this young man was quite an athlete, a champion gymnast at the college he attended.

The dance at Washington State proved to be a good time, perhaps a little too good, because I missed the bus that left from the school to travel back to Seattle. Therefore, I had to figure out another way to get back to the base. Like many servicemen of that era, I stuck out my thumb by the road hoping to find someone who would be heading the 285 miles westward. Well, the only takers were the state police who must have taken pity on me and drove me to a bus sation where I could pick up my bus that would drop me off in Seattle.

The trip was a long one and I arrived at the base a full six hours late. The marines at the gate knew me and when I told them my story, they began to laugh. But what could they do? They marched me off to the senior non-commissioned officer on duty day who had the authority to punish me as he saw fit for my infraction. Again, my mazel was good as the officer of the day was none other than my wrestling coach. He then asked me why I was six hours late. I figured the smartest thing to do would be to come clean so I told him straight out, "Love caused me to be late" as if love were a force powerful enough to suspend the laws of nature. He smiled back at me and said, "Hey Pfeffer, next time you take a trip like that to Pullman, take me with you." And, you know what? I took him along and he developed an appreciation for the charming ladies of Alpha Chi Omega.

Getting a phone call on base was a highly unusual deal in those days and almost always signified that there was some kind of emergency at home. Any guy would wonder, "Was someone sick? Did someone die?" and all the rest of those God forbidding things that go through your mind when you hear that you have a phone call. So when I heard that my mother was on the line for me, my heart began to pound as I made my way to the base's telephone. I tried to calm myself, taking a deep breath but just then I heard a voice that was unmistakably my mother's on the other end of the telephone without the usual salutation of hello or how are you, "You are going to be killed. Do you hear me? You are gong to be killed!" I told my mother to calm down and tell me what in the devil she was talking about.

Apparently, the cause of her hysteria was the result of a piece of mail that she had received. As a result of my performance on the wrestling team, I had received an accommodation which had gone to my family. Upon opening it, she must have thought that wrestling was something out of the modern movie, "Gladiator," with participants fighting to the death in the arena in front of a cheering crowd. So I set about educating her on the rules of the mat, telling her that our coach was very experienced and that he was extremely careful that no one received a serious injury. I told her about the protective headgear and though I don't necessarily think she became a wrestling fan, I did manage to sufficiently allay her fears. At least, I think I did because I never received another such phone call.

The Pacific Northwest was quite a change of pace for me but I did get the chance to visit family back home. One of the ways that I got to do this was through accompanying wounded guys on the trains. It proved to be my final assignment. There was a navy policy to get long-term patients near their homes while they were recovering, and some of these guys were in pretty bad shape.

The Navy decided that it would try to bring sailors who would be undergoing rather lengthy hospitalizations to naval hospitals that were near their hometowns. Obviously, this was good for morale as it would make for easier visitation. The primary mode of transport was comprised of trains and I was assigned to a group that was going from Washington to Chicago. The patients were escorted by doctors, nurses, and corpsmen. This was strictly a military train and the trip would take about three days. We would get a three-to-four-day layover after we arrived at the Great Lakes Naval Station. This was great for me since it allowed me to visit family aside from my normal leaves and liberties.

The Pacific Northwest climate is known for its dampness and I started to develop major arthritic problems. My condition had worsened to the extent that the doctors felt that I should be discharged early. It was not a disability or medical discharge. It was an honorable discharge, and so I was heading home.

Going Home

I was back in Chicago and was anxious to continue my college education, which I had begun before my enlistment. The GI bill had been signed into law by President Roosevelt in 1944 and this proved to be a wonderful thing for so many of us. Of course, I would have gone to college with or without it but it provided great opportunities for many who had faithfully served. For me, it helped with tuition, but I still worked hard in a variety of jobs to put myself through school. One of my favorite jobs was working in a lady's shoe store. I was graduated from Northwestern, and, after finishing school, decided to head back to Spring Valley before planning my next move.

Why was I so anxious to head back to Spring Valley after being in Washington during my service years and then several years of schooling in Chicago? Well, frankly, I felt I needed some time off and was looking to have some fun. My Uncle Sam (if you remember, he was my mother's brother who was only eight years older than I) had a furniture store there and I went to work for him. This was Uncle Maurice's idea as he did not want to get my hands dirty, which would be inevitable working in the scrap business. While I enjoyed working at the furniture store and most especially my newfound free time when I was not at the store, there was some tension. My uncle had married while in service during the war, and his wife, Trudy, was concerned that given the strong relationship that the two of us had, he was likely to make me a partner, though neither of us had any such thought.

You may have noticed in the last chapter how grateful I was for the wonderful childhood I experienced in Spring Valley. Sure, my family played a huge part in all of this, but the town was just a wonderful place in which to grow up. I was anxious to give something back to a new generation of kids and now that I found myself living in Spring Valley, an opportunity developed.

Across of my grandparents' home, there was a very large lot about a block long. The lot stood empty, its grass growing wildly, and my mind began to wonder at what could be done with it. I approached the neighbor who owned the property and asked him if he had any objection to my cutting the grass and turning the whole place into a baseball diamond that the local kids could use to play baseball. He not only agreed, but liked the idea so much that he lent me a hand in cutting the weeds. I then approached all of the local merchants and told them it was about time that we bring Little League baseball to our fair town.

LIttle League Baseball had been started by some ambitious folks in Williamsport, Pennsylvania, and it was only a local three-team league that first year in 1939. After the war ended and with the great popularity of baseball, the idea began to spread across the country. To me, there seemed to be no better way for a twelve-year-old to spend a spring afternoon, and, using my power of persuasion, was able to convince about ten merchants to become sponsors, thereby defraying the costs of the equipment and uniforms.

We were off and running but it was still pretty much of a bare bones operation. I got together a group of my buddies and we built a screen behind home plate to prevent foul balls from causing any foul injuries. Using the dimensions provided to us by the Little League Association, we laid the base paths, and built a pitcher's mound, and though it did not resemble Comiskey Park or Wrigley Field, it didn't look half bad. Now the challenge was to get the word out. We ran announcements in the local newspaper and began printing and distributing leaflets that encouraged kids to play in the new league. The response was overwhelming and that first year we had one hundred kids sign up. Teams were chosen and that first spring, we had games going five days a week. It became a popular event in town.

The merchants' funding allowed us to advertise their business names on the uniforms, bringing them good publicity, and, hopefully, even some additional business. Despite this, we were still running the thing on a shoestring budget and we would have different people walk through the crowd to solicit much needed funds. People would drop pennies, nickels, and dimes into our collection box. I then took the money to the bank where I had set up an account for the Spring Valley Little League. With this, my first experience in a charitable endeavor, I wanted to keep everything aboveboard so every week I distributed to all of the adults a financial statement which indicated how every dime was spent. Whatever money that was left over was used for awards for the winning team and for a big year-end barbecue that was held at the field.

There was one other thing that I wanted to do for the kids of Spring Valley, and, like Little League, it also involved baseball. I discussed with some parents the possibility of taking the kids to a ballgame over the summer. This time, we were talking about a major league game, and, with all due respect to the Cubs, we decided on the White Sox, since the majority of the town's residents, myself included, were fans of the South Siders. Contacting the team's public relations department, I was able to procure a large block of seats—and we are talking about 200 seats here. I told them how much money we had to spend and they were agreeable even though it was less than the discounted rate.

I had charged each kid who went along fifty cents for the excursion and each parent one dollar. Now that we had the tickets, the question was how to get to the ballpark. I arranged for the rental of several buses. So, for fifty cents, each kid got a seat on the bus, a ticket to the game, a soft drink, bag of peanuts, and a hot dog. The best thing about the game was that it was doubleheader. I say that for my younger readers who may never have heard of such a thing or observed one only when it involved a makeup game. These doubleheaders were prescheduled and the teams usually had them every so often on a Sunday. You ended up with two games for the price of one and the kids really had a fabulous time at the game as the White Sox battled the Yankees.

On the long ride home, we passed through the small Will County town of Plainfield. It was a sleepy town to be sure, but one with which I was very familiar. I had passed it many times when traveling between Spring Valley and Chicago and would frequently stop at the local snack shop where I would always order the same thing: a milkshake and a toasted cheese sandwich. The proprietor knew me by name, and, as I instructed the bus drivers to stop there, I got off and walked into the snack shop and was greeted with, "Same thing, Pep?" I told him to venture a look out the window and he saw the buses. His jaw began to drop when I gave him the order: "Two hundred hamburgers and two hundred drinks." Despite the size of the order, would you believe that he was able to fill it? How did he do it? He lived next door and got his wife, his daughter, and some neighbors to help out. It may have taken a while but the kids didn't seem to mind. For them, it was a day to remember. Whenever I would return to the snack shop in Plainfield in the future, the owner would always ask me the same thing, "Hey, Pep, are you alone or did you bring your buses?"

My Road to Law School

My social life had taken off as I was dating a girl from Ottawa, Illinois—and not just any girl. This girl came from a very prominent family. They owned the scrap yard in Ottawa, a local bank, and an apartment building in Chicago, among other things. By the standards of my aunt and uncle, they were veritable tycoons. My aunt was friendly with the girl's mother and was highly encouraging of the relationship. Besides the strong family connection, the practical feeling was that I would be set for life if I married into this family.

The girl was younger than I, having just finished high school and was interested in getting married rather than going to college. My family was starting to drop hints that it was time to pop the big question, and, when I failed to do so, those hints became a little stronger. It bordered on an ultimatum which was essentially, "Marry the girl or go back to school." It was nothing personal, for the girl was very nice, but I was just not ready to get married. So, the relaxing times in Spring Valley were soon to come to an end. It was time to go back to school.

Dr. Sam Pfeffer—it has a nice ring to it don't you think? It could have been so had my timing been different. I had taken all of the courses required for acceptance into medical school and things were a bit easier in terms of the admissions process in those days. It was the week before school started and as I went to visit all of the medical schools in the Chicago area, I received the same story: they liked my academic record but if I wanted to go to medical school, I would have to wait for the following year. Time to come up with Plan B.

As I was trying to come up with a different plan, I happened upon a friend of mine in town. Standing on Main Street in Spring Valley, Bill Wimbiscus asked me how I was doing and what my plans were. I told him about my situation and he then told me that he was getting ready to begin his second year at DePaul University Law School. He asked me if I had ever considered becoming a lawyer and I told him until that exact second, it had never occupied a thought in my brain. But I was desperate at the time and if Bill had told me that he was enrolled at Morticians' College, you would probably be reading a book written by the founder of the Pfeffer Funeral Home instead.

Well, there was just one problem here. Law school was starting up again the following Monday and this was Thursday afternoon. Not much time there. I should have told you earlier that Bill Wimbiscus was really Bill Wimbiscus, Jr. and Bill Wimbiscus, Sr. was a prominent judge and lawyer in town. (This was back in the days when one could serve as a judge and still maintain a law practice.) We walked over to his dad's office and found him hard at work there. Judge Wimbiscus had known my family for many years and was eager to help. What really came in handy was that he also happened to be a lifelong friend of the dean of the law school in question. He called up Dean Taft, and, after telling him some nice things about me, informed the Dean that I had a lifelong ambition of becoming a lawyer and was anxious to enroll in his law school.

The word came that I should be in his office on Monday morning to talk the matter over. This was the first day of classes and the Dean must have realized that my lifelong ambition had a touch of impulsiveness to it and suggested that for the first week I "audit" the courses. If, by the end of the week, I decided that law school was for me, then I could begin in full as a matriculating student the following week. That seemed fair, and sure enough within a week of my chance meeting with Bill, I was looking at a career in law. I came back to Spring Valley that weekend to tell my family of my plans. My uncle approved of my plans, and with Jerry eventually to become a doctor, what more could a Jewish family want?

Law school is a grind for some people. I really took to it, and, in additon to doing well in my coursework, became president of Nu Beta Epsilon which was the Jewish law fraternity. The main focus of the organization was to bring in a variety of legal practioners who would speak to us about their experiences and issues in the law. Judge Abraham Marovitz came to speak to us one day and it was a speech that would have a great influence on my thinking not just about the law, but about society as well.

If there is such a thing as a self-made businessman, you would have to consider Marovitz a self-made lawyer. His parents were European immigrants and his Maxwell Street childhood was as hardscrabble as they came; he took on any job that he could find, hawking newspapers before gaining employment as an errand boy for a Chicago law firm. His boss became so impressed with the young man that he suggested to Marovitz that he give law school a try. The only problem was that Marovitz had not gone to college, but that was not a problem in those days. He must have had mazel because off he went to law school, and the rest, as they say, is history. After practicing law, he became a state senator and then a superior court judge before serving on the federal bench.

That day I sat spellbound as Judge Marovitz spoke to us about a topic that was very close to his heart: juvenile delinquency. As one who liked to involve his audience in his talk, he posed a question to us: "What was our definition of a juvenile delinquent?" As people began to share their definitions, it was clear that there was a very broad range in which people thought about this matter. He then began to expound his own view of the matter. He said that if a person lives in an area where everyone sells drugs and he also sells drugs, he cannot be thought of as a juvenile delinquent. He is simply following a behavioral norm. If however, he sends out his sister to be prostituted in order to support his drug habit, and that would presumably violate the norms of the neighborhood, then that would classify him as a delinquent. More than anything, he had the power to change your way of thinking about things. From a sense of morality in absolute terms, he made us think about it all in relative terms.

Coming from Spring Valley as I had, much of this was news to me. The big city and the big city ghettos—no not the Jewish ghetto of Spring Valley but the black ghettos of Chicago—had different problems. As I listened to Judge Marovitz speak about these people on the fringes, people who were headed for trouble, I knew that part of my life's work would be helping them. What really impressed me about Marovitz was that he was not so caught up in his own success. He had never lost sight of what was really important in this world and I hope that I never have either.

Good mazel continued to follow me in law school. I learned that if you were a military veteran and had completed your second year of law school, you could sit for the Bar exam. I know that this sounds unthinkable today but it reflects the special circumstances that followed the Second World War. You have to remember that guys lost so much time in service, some as many as four years, that they were anxious to make up for lost time. Many had married and needed to start supporting their families. They were anxious to begin their practice and so was I.

There was only one problem in sitting for the Bar a year early. I was a veteran but I needed the permission of the Dean, that very same dean whose office I had sat in less than two years earlier. He had done me a favor by letting me into law school less than a week after speaking to Judge Wimbiscus on the phone. Now, I needed a second favor, and he allowed me to take the Bar exam. Before I left his office, however, he had a few parting words for me. "You know, Sam, it is very important to keep our percentages high on Bar passage. Don't let us down." And I didn't, as I passed it on the first try.

I was pleased, the Dean was pleased, but there was one person who was not pleased. She was a very important woman in my life, namely, my grandmother. On a visit to Spring Valley, I informed the lady who made my grandfather take me to school by horseback in the midst of a blizzard that I would not be returning for my third year of law school. She was not happy. Why? The last graduation she had attended of mine was when I finished grammar school. I left high school a year early to begin college in Chicago. I finished Northwestern in the summer so I did not participate in its commencement exercises. So if I did not participate, neither did she. She had missed two graduations and was not about to miss a third.

My grandmother had not only nurtured me but literally saved my life when I was a tiny infant. How could I deny her some good old fashioned *nachas*? So off I went for my third year of law school. At least I did not have to worry about passing the bar, and the way I figured it, it was worth the year just to see the look on my grandmother's face when I received my diploma. She sat in the front row, beaming with pride when the dean got to the Ps and called my name. I should mention to you that I did not expect this to be my last graduation. I still harbored plans of going to medical school after practicing law for a few years. As you will see, that soon changed. Of course, you, the reader, may well be wondering at the end of this chapter, "Sam, you did not seem to plan things out very well." You would be just about right. Some people like to plan their future out to the last detail. I allowed fate to take me on an interesting ride.

CHAPTER 3

My Legal Career

BY PASSING THE BAR A YEAR EARLY, I was able to start taking on cases while still in law school. This gave me a distinct advantage and though it would sound crazy to a third-year law student today, my fellow students had exposure to people who were looking for a lawyer but could not take on the cases themselves. They began referring cases my way. It worked out great and I did pretty well that year. Some of the cases they sent my way were more than a little bit unusual. Perhaps none was stranger than the woman who kept twenty-five cats as pets. As you may gather, the woman was a bit on the eccentric side. As you may not be surprised to hear, the City of Chicago took exception to the number of feline friends that she kept in her home. The City had received enough calls from concerned and aggravated neighbors that it filed a complaint alleging that this arrangement posed a health hazard. Motions on the case were brought before a judge, who, on a typical morning, would hear about three hundred motions. (Such procedure no longer exists and has not for many years. That is all he did.) He was one of my favorite judges, very knowledgeable in the law and with a great sense of humor to boot. He would bend over the bench with his glasses perched at the end of his nose, looking like the wise old man that he was whenever he posed a question to one of the lawyers. The City's attorney presented the facts of the case and again emphasized the serious health risks that the twenty-five cats represented.

The lawyer clearly overdramatized the whole business. He made it seem as though there were an imminent danger to the good citizens of the Windy City. The judge, employing his wry sense of humor, said, "Oh, you mean this is a kitty case."

The case was continued about six times and each time our judge would say, "O.k. we are going to hear that kitty case." I guess the judge must have enjoyed the comic relief from what must have been a rather boring case docket. What was the final disposition of the matter? We agreed that my client would give away all but three of her cats. The lady may have been a touch eccentric, but she was a poor eccentric, and, in lieu of my fee, I received four cats. I allowed the classmate who had referred the case to me to keep the fee. I am not sure that Clarence Darrow got his start this way.

Regal Purchasing Company

I was a practical guy and though you could admire men like Arthur Goldberg or Louis Brandeis, great scholars and practioners of the law that they were, I had always been preoccupied with making a living, a preoccupation that surely was influenced by growing up in the Depression. Of course, I had worked my way starting from my undergraduate years through law school on a variety of different jobs such as selling shoes. As I was in law school, my buddy, Herman Sturman, was attending medical school. We may have been busy with school, but that did not preclude us from going into business together. It proved to be a most interesting experience.

The name of our fledgling enterprise was the Regal Purchasing Company. What kind of company was Regal Purchasing Company, you ask. Our motto was "Live like a king with the money you save" courtesy of Yours Truly. Through my family, I had access to the Furniture Mart and the Merchandise Mart (where manufacturers had their showrooms) which meant that I

MY LEGAL CAREER

> **LAWNDA:** -8560
>
> **Regal Purchasing Co.**
> (NOT INC.)
>
> Jewelry · Furniture · Appliances
> Sporting Goods · Clothing · Novelties
> SAVINGS 20-50%
> Live Like A King on the Money You Save
>
> MR. SAMM   1526 SOUTH KOLIN

My Regal business card used by Herman and me

could buy things at the same price that retailers could. I also had access to a wholesale company named Glabman Furniture. In addition I had a friend who owned a clothing store and another friend who owned an outfit that sold bedding and drapery. Through these connections, we had a whole lot of stuff to sell.

We had cards made up with the Regal Purchasing Company logo embossed on them and our famous motto, "Live like a king with the money you save," brightly displayed. We even got a friend and fellow classmate of mine from DePaul who was from Elmhurst in the western suburbs, William Bauer, to work for us. (Bill achieved great notoriety in his legal career. An extremely fine gentleman with great integrity, Bill worked his way up to State's Attorney and then was appointed United States Attorney for the Northern District for Illinois before being nominated for a seat on the United States District Court and later the United Sates Court of Appeals, eventually serving there as Chief Judge.)

We passed out our cards, but since we did not have our own work phone number, the phone numbers on the cards were our two mothers' home phone numbers. In the beginning, everything went according to plan. We received orders on everything imaginable and you have to remember that at this time, there were no discount stores. Whenever we sold something, Herman and I would split the profit. Since we had no delivery trucks, Bill's touring car was used to deliver the items.

Sometimes success can lead you to make a strategic error. If we had just kept on doing what we were doing, we would have been fine and we would have continued to make decent money. But, like many budding entrepreneurs, we had big plans. We wanted to be big shots and needed to expand our customer base. At the time Copenhagen, the snuff and smokeless tobacco brand, was manufactured on the West Side and we were able to get an appointment to see its Personnel Director. The idea was that we would put one of our cards in each employee's pay envelope. We stressed that it would be a benefit for the employee and not cost the company anything. After listening to our pitch, the man had one objection. We did not have a union label on our card. We explained it away by telling him that we had a buddy who printed the cards for us, an explanation that he accepted.

I told you we made an error. The response to this new marketing strategy was overwhelming. In fact, we were flooded with calls, or, rather, I should say that our mothers were flooded with calls. And that was the problem. Our mothers were kind enough to carry us for nine months, or, in my case, a little bit less, and go through significant pain in delivering us, not to mention caring for us. They were happy to answer calls here and there, and even to take orders. But they were not prepared for the onslaught of calls that followed and we had soon used up all of the maternal goodwill. In frustration both ladies had their phone numbers changed. And who could really blame them? There went the Regal Purchasing Company, disconnected along with the phone number. Had we been sophisticated enough to hire a telephone answering service, who knows what could have been? But it was to the practice of law that I was headed. The outside ventures would have to wait.

Before I get to a serious discussion of my legal practice, I want to go back to my good friend, Herman Sturman. Herman married a girl named Gladys Freiman. Gladys' parents, Rose and Sam, owned a hotel across the street from the Chicago Stadium on Madison Street. Though the area is now gentrified and highly

My closest friend, Dr. Herman Sturman, with his lovely wife, Gladys

desirable for condos and restaurants, but then there was an area known as Skid Row. They lived two blocks from the hotel and while the area has now undergone serious gentrification, it was, at the time, a pretty rough place.

Every Friday night, Rose would have her entire family over for dinner. She would invite her sons and daughters-in-law, including the parents of her daughters-in law, and friends of the couples of which I was one. After dinner, the men would sit in the living room and play pinochle. The younger folks sat around the dining room table and played a card game called garbage. The women had their own favorite game; in their case, it was kaluki.

Of course, the highlight of the evening was dinner. Mrs. Freiman was what in Yiddish is called a real *baleboste*, a fine cook and homemaker. Dinner was traditional Eastern European fare, which meant chicken soup, gefilte fish, chopped liver, entrees of meat and chicken, vegetables, potatoes, and, if you were still hungry, her desert speciality was a scrumptious chocolate cake. We washed this feast down with Old Colony strawberry soda.

It seemed as though Rose, who was probably typical of these types of ladies, never sat down at the table for the meal. She always seemed busy coming back and forth from the kitchen bringing things out and clearing plates. One night she had baked one of her chocolate cakes which had been nearly consumed. All that remained was one rather skinny looking piece. Apparently no one had the nerve to take that last sliver. She looked down at the lonely piece and exclaimed, "You didn't like my chocolate cake?"

Rose was a supremely stoic gal. She didn't even shed a tear when she tragically revealed that she had contracted inoperable cancer. I was in the room at the time and the rest of us were sobbing like babies as we contemplated the world without this wonderful lady. She looked at us all and said, "What are you crying for? Kings die, queens die, even presidents die. What did you think, that I was never going to die?"

The Freimans were a close-knit family. Once a week, Rose and her older sister Esther, would take Gladys and her cousins to a movie downtown and then go out to eat at a cafeteria. Esther's hearing was limited and she was known to doze through a portion of the picture. Rose, the European lady that she was, had a limited English vocabulary and had her own version of what the actors' lines were. Afterward, at the cafeteria, Rose and Esther would discuss the movie and argue about it. Siskel and Ebert they weren't. To the casual observer, it seemed as though they were talking about two different movies as one would refer to one of the characters as the villain while the other considered him the hero. Gladys and her cousins never attempted to intercede in these cinematic debates. It was all just too funny and probably more entertaining than the movie to want to interrupt, the type of performance that befitted these two grand dames.

One of Glady's favorite stories about her mother was when, as a new bride, she called her mother. Apparently, the conversation went something like this.

> *"Hello Ma. How are you?"*
> *"I'm o.k."*
> *"What are you doing?"*
> *"I'm watching T.V."*
> *"What are you watching?"*
> *"I'm watching Red Buttons."*
> *"I thought you didn't like Red Buttons."*
> *"I don't, but Pa likes him."*
> *"How is Pa?"*
> *"He's o.k. He went to a lodge meeting tonight."*

One Sunday morning after Paula and I were married, we met Herman and Gladys for breakfast. On Sunday morning, there was a Jewish hour on the radio. Gladys' parents never missed a program. Always a practical joker, I decided to call them at this time and disguised my voice. Her mother answered and I identified myself as calling from a Chicago radio station and told her the name of the station and inquired what she was listening to. She wanted to know the reason for my question. I told her that I was giving away $25.00 to the first person who could answer my next question. I told her that only she could answer the question and not seek any help from anyone else in the home. She agreed. What was the question? It was my way to be a bit of a wise guy so I asked her one of the wise guys' favorite questions, "Who is buried in Grant's tomb?" She put her hand over the receiver and said, "Vait a minute." She then yelled over to her husband. "Sam, who is buried in Grant's tomb?" Apparently, Sam did not need a long time to think the matter over. He replied, "How should I know. I vasn't at the funeral."

Herman and Gladys, like a good number of Chicagoans of the era, had moved to Los Angeles not that long after they were married when Herman had finished medical school. Gladys had three children within a period of twenty-four months and each time her mother would fly out from Chicago to help out. After the third child was born and she was boarding the plane to return home, Rose turned to her daughter and said, "You know Gladys, I vas thinking that next year, your father and I vould like to go to Hot Springs." What a lady! They sure ain't making them like that anymore.

After law school, I worked in an insurance office which was adjacent to a law office which was leased by a lawyer named Joseph Honoroff. I had a desk in the insurance office, and in lieu of rent, I would answer the trial calls for Mr. Honoroff and his partner. In addition, I handled some of the subrogation work which involves one insurance company suing another over alleged liability, and would send these cases to a senior attorney, who, in turn, would have me handle the case. If we were successful, I would receive 50% of the fee. Checks were being made out to him. But what happened was that he would receive the fee and not inform me, and keep the whole fee for himself. It irritated me so that I decided to leave, making plans to rent my own office. I went to Joe and told him that I was leaving. Joe said that he would get rid of the other guy and that I could rent an office in the suite and that he would give me enough work to cover the rent. So I remained with Joe until a few years later when Joe had a heart attack. During his recovery, I handled all matters for Joe. After Joe's death a few years later, I took over the space.

Joe was an interesting fellow and I got to know his family quite well, including his mother-in-law. His mother-in-law seemed to have the qualities of the strong Jewish woman. An ardent Zionist, she had gone to the Holy Land during the 1948 War of Independence and volunteered, passing out shells to the men and women fighting on the front lines. She had two nephews who had survived the war in Hungary and she was anxious to bring them to America. One way to do it was to arrange marriages with American girls. In this case, however, the nephews were already married. The mother-in-law arranged fake marriages to two nurses. One nephew went back to his wife in Europe. His wife was a beautiful woman, though during the war, she became the girlfriend of a high ranking Nazi official and this nephew survived working as a gardener on the estate. Eventually, after divorcing the American nurse, this nephew came over to America with his Hungarian wife. This pair ended up causing the whole family much aggravation and embarrassment as they set up an extortion ring in Las Vegas, with his wife enticing unsuspecting conventioneers and with the husband photographing and extorting money, a scenario as you would imagine on some television crime drama. It all came crashing to an end by an angry dentist who reported the crime to the FBI. After investigating the ring, the FBI arrested both of them, and eventually they were convicted. When the FBI came to arrest the nephew, they found him at Joe's apartment. Joe drove with the nephew on the way to the FBI office. The FBI agents in the front seat listened intently and the nephew spoke to Joe in Yiddish, presumably about the location of the extortion money. After they arrived at the location, one of the agents said in Yiddish, "Thanks for the information."

Joe's mother-in-law was indicted in the federal courts for setting up the fake marriages. She was sent to federal prison for a short time and not only did she survive the ordeal but she had her cellmate write the family letters. Apparently, the cellmate was a more literary type named Iva Toguri D'Aquino, otherwise known as Tokyo Rose. Joe's mother-in-law could not quite figure

Gene and Vera Becker

The Gabrics with Ralph Jr.

out how such a lovely woman could be put in prison for the crime of merely speaking on the radio.

Joe's father-in-law operated as a custom's peddler and would work the poorer neighborhoods in which the people essentially bought various items in what amounted to the installment plan. His wife assisted him in the business and she employed a driver for her husband and would go with him on her route telling him to take a right turn, then changing her mind and turn left, go this way, go that way, all of which resulted in them getting a fair amount of tickets, all of which they would contest. Guess whose task it was to go to court? You guessed it: Yours Truly. Once we appeared before a judge and Joe's mother-in-law insisted that she was in the right, implying the ticket may have been written due to anti-Semitism on the part of the officer. The judge had

Our practice
Standing left to right: Me, Ralph Gabric, Eugene (Gene) Becker.
Kneeling: Joseph Cerveny.

the name of the officer before him and proceeded to tell Mrs. Honoroff that the name of the officer in question was none other than "Irving Goldberg."

Now I had so much work on my own that I brought in another lawyer to help me. Eugene Becker was a classmate of mine and worked for one of the insurance companies before he came to work for me. Within a few months, our relationship changed and we became partners. A few years later we needed another attorney. Gene had a friend at Liberty Mutual where he had previously worked. This was Ralph Gabric, who joined the firm as a third partner. We eventually brought in a fourth person, Joseph Cerveny, when I purchased Old Orchard Chevrolet and the office split. Ralph's practice was largely Workmen's Compensation, which he handled out of our office in Wheaton. Ralph took over the office and gave up any interest in exchange for full ownership of the Wheaton office. At that time, Cerveny became a partner. It was something of an ideal partnership. We each had our speciality. I was focused on estate and business law. Gene focused on personal injury work and did it very well and Ralph had carved out a niche for himelf handling Workmen's Compensation cases.

Besides complementing each other professionally, we just had an excellent relationship with one another. There were no bad feelings or jealousy, just a lot of appreciation and admiration. It did not end there. Despite our different backgrounds, we became not only friends but more like family. Again, I felt like I had great mazel with those guys.

My partner, Ralph Gabric was an exceptional man. Full of charisma, he became chairman of the DuPage County Bar Association and later the Illinois Bar Association. LIke Bill Bauer, you could not have found a more highly respected man in the law. He and his wife, Joan, lived in the Western suburbs and had a particularly talented son named Ralph, Jr. While in high school, Ralph, Jr. wanted to enroll in some college courses at Northwestern University for the summer, which, of course, was near our home. Ralph, Jr. was known as Rossi and we suggested to his parents that he stay

At my office

with us for the summer and they were amenable. Rossi was an accomplished pianist and when I would return from the office that summer, he could be heard, playing our piano. The beautiful music would envelope our entire home. Our entire family greatly enjoyed having him for the summer. He was something of a Renaissance man, for, in addition to his musical interests, he studied chemistry as an undergraduate. However when it came time to choose a vocation, the apple did not fall far from the tree. He went to my own alma matter, DePaul Law School, and is today a top notch litigator in Chicago, handling mostly patent cases.

It is true that our practice was commercially successful. But there is more to a career than strictly that. As you may have picked up, I believed there was so much more to life than making money. Sure, you have to make a living, and, hopefully, a good living at that. But more than anything, I would tell people that you have to have a heart. My partner, Ralph, had a great big one and he believed in service, in giving back. He made pro bono work mandatory when he was president of the DuPage County Bar Association and inaugurated a program to assist indigent individuals who were in need of legal help. We call this kind of thing legal aid today, but Ralph felt that doing well and doing good went hand in hand. Although we lost Ralph in 2002 and miss him a great deal, his son continues to spearhead the program that meant so much to his dad. What a legacy!

Anyone who has picked up this book will note that while I am a very proud Jew, I am also known for my ecumenism, equipped with a strong desire to reach out to people of different faiths. And that was even felt at the firm. Ethnicity or lack thereof frequently fits into the compositions of most law firms, even small ones like ours. Some are Waspy, and some have a Jewish or Irish Catholic orientation. One of the fundamental tenets of Pfeffer, Becker, and Gabric was that we covered the three major religions in America at the time, Protestant, Catholic and Jew. Will Herberg, the famous sociologist whose book took those three faiths as its title, would have been proud of our firm's makeup. My statement on the matter was that I am a member of the Jewish faith, Becker belongs to whatever church is nearest his home, and Gabric, a Catholic school graduate, was deeply rooted in his faith.

I was our point man on estates, and, one day, Gene Becker asked me if I could meet with his minister to discuss his estate plan. I said I would be happy to do so and after coming up with a plan, I had the appropriate documents drawn up. Gene's minister insisted that I bill him like I would any other client but I flat out refused to take any money from him. But as Passover neared, he sent me a huge basket of fruit for the holiday, a very nice gesture.

Though Gabric's priest had taken a vow of poverty, we nonetheless discussed an estate plan for him. I had the papers drawn up and again he insisted on paying the bill. Again, I refused and eventually he relented. In appreciation, he sent the office a case of Christian Brothers Brandy.

If you are thinking that it is two down and one to go, you would be just about right. One day I received a call from the rabbi of my congregation who wanted to come in and talk about his estate plan. He came in with his wife and though the estate was not large, it was quite complicated. Again, I had the appropriate papers drawn up. Though I had done significantly more work for him than for either of the other two clergymen, how could I accept money from my own rabbi? I flatly refused, so guess what he sent me in appreciation? His gift to me was that he sent me another rabbi.

One can be the most brilliant lawyer and the most honest and ethical practitioner in the world but it will mean nothing without clients, and paying ones at that. Though the three of us had our own unique styles and talents, we had one strong commonality: we were all very focused on the client. Of course, we knew that we did not have the resources to compete with the large or even the medium sized firms. But one of the downsides of the larger firms is that they tend to be most interested in large clients, the ones that they figure are going to rack up a lot of billable hours. Smaller clients often get short shrift.

Art and Glenna

My relationships with clients occasionally took on some unique aspects that exceeded the traditional manner of these matters. Frankly, I was often fascinated by some of the characters whom I met in the practice. Perhaps no clients were more intriguing than Art and Glenna. They lived in the Sauganash area of Chicago and if you remember Ma and Pa Kettle minus the fifteen children, then that would be them.

How did I get to them? They were referred to me by their insurance agent who thought I may be able to help them with a particular problem with the one group of people you don't want to have a problem with: namely, the Internal Revenue Service. Though they seemed thoroughly unsophisticated, they were not bumpkins in the usual sense. The owned a small business which manufactured "fitments." If you have never heard of fitments, don't worry, because neither had I. But they serve a very important purpose, because when inserted into a bottle, they allow only one drop to come out a time, helpful in matters of perfume and other liquids that you don't drink. It was a small operation they ran, with three women working the machines which produced thousands of these things every day and one man who assisted Art with the packaging and shipping.

Art and Glenna lived simply. Glenna even had one of the old-fashioned washing machines, complete with a wringer. They took a small salary, but, in reality, the business was what people today would call a "cash cow." Their big client was Mary Kay Cosmetics, and the business seemed to run itself, taking in plenty of money year after year. What was the problem? The business paid no cash dividends out and therefore it appeared to be hoarding cash in order to avoid taxation. At that time, the IRS was cracking down on companies that were accumulating cash for no legitimate reason. It was a violation of the Internal Revenue Code called excessive accumulation. If found guilty of such an offense, a fine would be imposed and the entity would be forced to pay out monies as a dividend.

The person who became aware of the impending problem was Art and Glenna's accountant and he had informed them that he was incapable of tackling it. He suggested a prominent law firm to handle the matter. They went to this prestigious firm and proceeded to deal with an associate who seemed thoroughly uninterested in their predicament. They then went to their insurance agent who was a friend of theirs and there came the referral.

If the fancy downtown lawyer had bothered to look, he would have noticed that these were two very successful people. They could afford first-class legal representation as easily as any corporate client. But the problem that they had was a tricky one and would require some creative thinking to come up with a potential solution. As with any client, I tried to learn all I could about their business, and spoke to them at length to see if there were some way to justify the accumulation. While visiting their storefront operation, I asked Art if the machines that produced the fitments were under any patent. He said he personally owned the patents on those machines. Just then, the proverbial light went on in my head. I immediately saw an opening.

In questioning the two, they told me it was their intent all along to pay Art for the patents and have the company own the machinery. We immediately took steps to justify the accumulations, having that reflected in the corporate minutes. I brought in appraisers, and they put a price tag on the machines. All of this was put into writing.

We were not out of the woods yet. A year later the IRS formally advised the company that it had excessive accumulation. Extensive negotiations were conducted over the next few years to resolve the matter. These things are never fun and you can imagine that people can get fairly anxious as they await the final disposition of the matter in question. In our case, everything worked out. The IRS agreed that the accumulation was justified. I was proved correct in my approach and I put the rest of the plan in motion. Art sold the patents to the corporation for the value set by the appraisers. It all amounted to substantial savings for Art and Glenna, and, as you can well imagine, they were most grateful to me. They not only became clients but close friends. I even managed to convince Glenna to give up her old wringer washing machine and buy a newfangled washer and dryer. Though they had considerable resources, they did not give much thought to spending money on themselves. For so many people, making money is a means to enjoying the good life. Not so for Art and Glenna. The one luxury that Art enjoyed was the afternoon that we would spend together every year in December having lunch and cocktails. It was a rare moment away from Glenna and the business and served as my yearly holiday gift to him.

Given the extent of their net worth, I often discussed the importance of setting up a proper estate plan. But, like Ma and Pa Kettle would have, they simply refused to do anything of the kind. They had no children or close relatives and therefore insisted that I become the sole beneficiary of their estate. While I was flattered by the offer, I made it clear to them that this would not be ethical.

One day Art and Glenna decided to take a trip. They instructed me to draw up a short and quick will. I advised them that this would be a mistake, that given their situation a sophisticated estate plan would necessitate a trust as well as a will. Art again insisted on me drawing up a document in which they left everything to me. Again, I declined. I did hurriedly draw up a document which included a will and a trust, giving away what amounted to a number of million dollars to any charitable organization approved by the IRS for such purposes.

I wished them a safe and happy trip and told them that as soon as they returned we would have to prepare a proper estate plan. Guess what? When they got back, they would not allow me to draw up any documents. What could I do? I was very fond of them and realized that these were just not normal clients.

The event that worried me from the start of my becoming their attorney finally transpired. Art had a heart attack and passed away. Glenna immediately called and asked me to come to their home. I drove to their house to help Glenna make funeral preparations. So long as I had known the couple, they had never gone to any church. I had never even known what religion they followed and asked Glenna what religion Art had been brought up in. She said that she thought that Art had been a baptized a Catholic and so with the assistance of their Catholic neighbor, we arranged for a funeral mass to be conducted by a priest. After Art's death, the priest solicited Glenna for a substantial donation to help defray the costs of converting a nunnery into a school building. The cornerstone laid there would be in honor of Glenna and in memory of Art. She told the priest that she was not interested in the proposition, but gave him permission to speak to me about the matter. I met with the priest several times and thought that this project would be a fitting memorial to Art and a wonderful honor for Glenna. It took some talking to convince Glenna that they had more than enough funds to underwrite this sort of thing. She reluctantly agreed and we cut the check to the priest. The cornerstone was laid and all of that was very nice, but we never heard from that priest again.

Glenna was no longer able to run the business so I had arranged for its sale to the employee who had worked for them for all these years. I tried my best to look after Glenna as she was aging and eventually began suffering from dementia. She did have lucid moments and I was of the opinion that she should remain in her house rather than go to a nursing home. I met with her doctor and a social worker. They agreed with me and we tried to do everything we could to take care of her. We hired around-the-clock caregivers. We also paid her neighbor to take her to social events.

Her dementia began to get worse and her doctor felt that she was no longer capable of making decisions for herself. He was right. Her neighbor had taken her to a fundraiser for a well-known North Shore Catholic girl's school. Supposedly, Glenna had pledged a quarter of a million dollars, subject, of course, to my approval. I then received a phone call from a lawyer friend who also served on the school's board of directors. William Kelly Jr,. was a highly respected attorney and felt that since he knew me well, it was appropriate that he meet with me. I told him flat out that she was incompetent and suggested that he go speak with her. If he felt that she was competent than he would get the $250,000. If, however, he saw that she was not competent, then the school was out of luck. I also informed him that upon her demise I had sole discretion as the trustee to make distribution of any not-for-profit organization that met the IRS criteria. I would make sure that the school would receive the full $250,000. He stated that my word was all he needed, shook my hand, and left it at that.

Glenna eventually died and when she did, the Archdiocese of Chicago filed a claim on all assets of the estate. They argued that since her primary charitable concerns were for the Catholic school that all of the money should go to the Archdiocese. This I felt was unjustified on their part. When the estate was formalized, I had planned for the school to receive the $250,000 as promised. I had a series of meetings with the Archdiocese's attorneys, and on one occasion, Bill Kelly joined the meeting and explained exactly what had happened. Bill stated he would testify to that in court. Eventually, Bill called me and told me that the Archdiocese would accept the $250,000, but wanted $25,000 to cover the lawyer's fees. While I was not enamored of its request, I felt that the matter should be settled and decided to do just that. What happened to the rest of the money? I made sure it was wisely dispersed to more than sixty worthy causes over a number of years, taking care that I gave no preference or exerted no prejudice other than the worthiness of the charity itself. The greatest legacy that could be bestowed upon Art and Glenna was to ensure that their years of hard work would result in doing the maximum amount of good. That was a serious responsibility.

Elizabeth F.

You might think that clients like Art and Glenna would be a once-in-a-career type of interaction. Never again would you represent a remotely similar character or characters. But they were not to be the only ones. One day, I received a call one day from a broker friend at the A.G Becker office in Roseland, on the far south side of Chicago. Becker was a well established brokerage firm based in Chicago and would eventually be sold to Merrill

Lynch in the 1980s. The broker who I knew had a client named Elizabeth F. whom he felt was in dire need of an estate plan. Since I had something of a reputation in the area and had drawn up the estate plan for the head of the Roseland office who was Elizabeth's personal stockbroker, he felt that I would be an ideal person to help her.

Elizabeth F. lived in South Shore and was a retired schoolteacher, but don't let her rather modest career earnings fool you. As I was soon to find out, she was a wealthy lady due to having inherited money, not from her husband, as she had never married, but rather she was an heiress to small family fortunes on both maternal and paternal sides, being the last survivor of both of these lines. Prior to our meeting, I had asked her to bring all of the appropriate documentation that would allow me to set up an estate plan. The documentation that I speak of would list her assets, and therefore indicate her net worth. When she came in to my office for the meeting, I asked her for the documents listing her assets. She responded by telling me that she had not brought them. Why not, I asked? She told me that she did not know me well enough to entrust me with such confidential information. I told her that without such information I simply could not help her. I further informed her that I would not charge her for the meeting as nothing was accomplished. At the door, I told her that when she felt comfortable enough with me to return with the relevant documents, then I would be happy to help her. From the expression on her face, it was not clear whether I would ever lay my eyes on Elizabeth F. again.

Well, I finally heard from Elizabeth F., but it was not about the estate plan. She had called to ask my advice on another matter. There was at the time a Personal Property Tax assessed in Cook County which attempted to tax things like furniture and other such household possessions. It was all quite ridiculous and in 1970 the state legislature did away with it. Before its rescinding, you would get a bill for $100 or $150, but it could be easily contested by taking it to court. We would ask for proof of what the assessment based on. Rather than go to litigation, it would be dismissed. The state just hoped that most people would pay rather than bother to fight it. But we provided a service to our regular clients which did just that. The whole thing was a big pain in the neck for us. It did not pay for us to take individual property tax bills to court but we would take them in groups of 50 or 100 and contest them. In all cases, we would win and the client would owe nothing on the Personal Property Tax. It was not a bad deal for us either as we would then charge our clients a minimal amount, something like $25 or $35, far less than the amount the state had billed. Well, Elizabeth was very upset about the tax as I think she got charged around $150. I told her to send it to my office and when it was dismissed I called her to let her know. She was overjoyed and wanted to know how much she owed us. I told her that if she really wanted to she could send us a check for $25 but otherwise to just forget about it. This seemed to change everything as she made an appointment to come in. She told me that she now had complete trust in me.

Just like with Art and Glenna, it was tough to convince Elizabeth of the importance of an estate plan that would minimize her estate's tax liability and its legal bills. Hence, the idea was to set up trusts rather than just the standard will that goes through probate. Of course, there were certain cash bequests. She had a cousin whom she wanted to leave a substantial sum to and several friends as well. I talked her into making some large donations while she was still alive, including what would become a theater at Columbia College in Chicago. There was still the matter of her estate and I encouraged her to set up a charitable trust but she always delayed.

Like many older people, one day Elizabeth broke her hip. After being discharged from the hospital rather than go to a rehab center near her South Shore home, she ended up at a nursing home in Wilmette because her cousin lived in nearby Evanston. Since I was so close by, and at her request, I became a frequent visitor during this time and we became quite close. Once, I brought my girls over to visit and was badgering Elizabeth about the charitable trust, hoping that I could get the work done and reviewed while she was still in Wilmette. She looked at my cute daughters and said, "Sam, I want you and your family to have the remaining millions." As with Art and Glenna, I told her that I was flattered by her offer but that would violate professional ethics.

Did I have a magical spell over this elderly lady? No. But we spent a tremendous amount of time together and I became a trusted advisor as well as her lawyer. I also listened to her talk about her problems, her concerns and saw this as more than just my professional responsibility. When you have clients like Art and Glenna and Elizabeth F., your role expands, partly because you are the one person they feel they can rely on. They know that you have their best interests at heart. But I still could not get her to set up the trusts the way I wanted to in order to avoid probate. One day while we were trying to get things finalized, she asked me, "Tell me Sam, will you make more money on the trust or by going through probate?" I told her that a will that goes through probate is best financially for me, for I would spend the most amount of time working on it. But again, I warned her that it would not be in her best interests to do this. She told me that was what she wanted, so what could I do? We drew up a will with a charitable trust and made arrangements for it to be signed.

For the signing, which took place in the nursing home in Wilmette, we had her accountant and the two vice presidents of the First National Bank serve as witnesses as well as a videotape crew capturing it all so no one could ever contest the validity of the will. In front of the cameras, I asked Elizabeth if she understood that a will would not be in her best interests, and, as her attorney, I advised her against it. She admonished me on tape, "Sam, how many times do I have to tell you what I want? If you cannot do it, then I will find a lawyer who can." So we did it against my objections.

Sadly, Elizabeth eventually died. What happened to the several million dollars that was the focus of all the attention? Well, I had set up a charitable trust with myself as joint trustee with the then First National Bank of Chicago (as cofiduciaries). I divided the money among many charities, all recognized by the IRS and as diverse a bunch of entities as one could imagine. You could blame it on my ecumenical sensibilities, but I did not want it to seem as though I was favoring one group over another, so when it came to religion, again Will Herberg would have been proud. Monies went to the Sisters of Mercy, to various Protestant institutions, and to a variety of Jewish ones like the Hebrew Theological College in Skokie, as well as other educational institutions. After several years and sixty different institutions later, we had given away all of the money. What was left of Elizabeth's fortune, like Art and Glenna's, had been well spent and would work to aid humanity.

Helene W.

One day, my secretary told me that there was someone who wanted to see me and that she was in the waiting area. The woman had been referred to me by her stockbroker. I told my secretary to let her in. Before me stood Helene W., whom I was to learn was in her 40s, but looked twenty years older. Her appearance and clothing were quite disheveled, and even her wig was slightly askew. She resembled something of what one considered a street person and was carrying several shopping bags with her. I soon found out what was contained in those bags. Nothing very valuable; just a few million dollars worth of stock certificates. She had signed blank assignments, and, therefore, these certificates were negotiable instruments. I realized that this was a serious situation, and though it was late in the afternoon, I had my secretary come into my office and we had all of the stock certificates itemized and put in our office safe, I then handed her a proper receipt for them. I explained to her that I did not want her to carry the certificates with her as they were negotiable. With these blank assignments it was like carrying a few million dollars in cash. She agreed.

I was to later learn of the circumstances behind Helene's wealth. Her parents had died and she was the sole heiress of their rather significant estate. She was one of those tragic people who are all alone in the world, with no one to look out for her, much less share a life with. There was some entended family, an aunt and some cousins, but she was estranged from them. As with Art and Glenna and Elizabeth F., I realized that it was important to come up with a solid estate plan and asked her what she wanted to do with her significant assets. She provided me with four charities that she was partial to and would be the recipients of her entire estate. Though it was not necessary, I was in constant communication with Helene as she would phone me once or twice a week to discuss the stock market. It was clear that she was lonely and had no one else to talk to.

One day I received a phone call from the Chicago Police Department which informed me that Helene had passed away and requested that I meet them at her apartment. How had they known to call me? Written across all of the mirrors in her apartment were the words, "If anything happens to me, please call my friend Sam Pfeffer" together with my phone number. As with Art and Glenna, I made all of the funeral arrangements and she was buried next to her parents. It was a particularly sad occasion as it was just the rabbi who conducted the service together with only me in attendance at the cemetery. There was no one to mourn her, but I soon received a call from a lawyer who said he represented Helene's aunt. He said the aunt just happened to be his mother-in-law and she would like to speak to me. Well, she called me the next day and accused me of stealing all of Helene's money. I told her that the will had been filed at the Probate Court of Cook County and that if she wanted to see the document, her son-in-law could obtain a copy from the Court. Her son-in-law subsequently called me and informed me that he told the aunt that everything seemed to be in proper order and that the will would have to be contested, which would be a very expensive proposition for her since the four charities would be represented by major law firms. Not withstanding all this information, she wanted to go ahead and sue the estate alleging the will did not reflect Helene's wishes, though the son-in-law would not represent her in this action. After this call, I heard nothing more, the money was distributed and the estate was closed.

The Psychic

Like so many professionals, I relied on referrals to build my practice. Once I started to represent one person in a certain field of endeavor, and was doing a good job, his or her colleagues would soon follow. One group that I drew a number of clients from was the Press Photographers Association of Chicago, especially those who were working for the "Chicago Sun-Times." (For the reader of today, it would be very difficult to realize how significant a role the newspaper played in the lives of people.) Interestingly, these guys all seemed to get their hair cut by the same barber, whose name was Joe D. There was another man who I am sure many of you are familiar with, Irv Kupcinet, who used the same barber. Known as Kup, he was a local legend, a great football player, broadcaster, and media celebrity who also wrote a well-known piece in the newspaper known as "Kup's Column."

It was mid-November of 1963 and apparently Joe D. had told his customers connected with the "Sun-Times" that he had a strange feeling that the president would be assassinated on his upcoming visit to Texas. To be sure, there had been plenty of threats made against Kennedy at the time, but after the events in Dealey Plaza transpired, Kup ran a column. He told the tale of how his barber friend, Joe D., had confided in him, that the president's visit would end in tragedy. Joe D. must have come to the conclusion that he had all of the makings of a psychic and must have figured that there has to be more money in that line of work than in cutting hair. Before long he had put down his scissors and hung up his psychic shingle.

Being a psychic may not be all it's cracked up to be, and before long Joe found himself in trouble. Two ladies who were interested in his services had come along one day and had brought along some stock certificates to their meeting. Agreeing to whatever service he rendered, he placed the certificates on his desk and then proceeded to go into a deep psychic mode of one sort or another, telling each of the women that he had an exceptionally good feeling about these stocks. He did not tell them what they should do with the stocks, whether to sell them, buy more shares, or take any action in particular, only that he had a good feeling about them.

Unfortunately for Joe, Wall Street did not share his good feelings about this stock and it soon became worthless. The ladies did not take their financial loss in stride. They went straight to the United States Attorney's office in Chicago and filed a complaint. They claimed that Joe was acting as a stockbroker by giving advice and the problem as they saw it was that the only license he possessed to render such advice was earned at barber college. If correct, this was a clear violation of securities law and they were getting "clipped by the barber."

Joe D. received a letter from the United States Attorney's office requesting his presence to discuss the allegations made against him. Joe was in a real bind and was searching for a lifeline. He contacted one of his former haircutting customers and the man, who was a client of mine and a press photographer at the Sun-Times told him he'd better get a lawyer and get one fast; he recommended me. Joe came to my office with the official looking letter and we discussed the matter. I questioned him extensively about what he had told these ladies and he assured me that he had given no advice. He had expressed only how he had felt about the stock certificates. And if he had told them only how he had felt about the stock, then I felt that he did nothing wrong. Prior to going to the meeting at the office, Joe reiterated to me that he only rendered advice which was every American's God given right: the right to feel.

We went to the United States Attorney's office and met with several attorneys for an informal meeting, though Joe was under oath. Joe was questioned for about an hour and I was also allowed to question Joe. As I had instructed him, he constantly repeated the mantra that he never gave any advice, only that he expressed how he felt. In summation, I reinforced that what was at stake here was a "man's right to feel" implying that it was as sacrosanct as "life, liberty and the pursuit of happiness," worthy of inclusion in the Declaration of Independence or perhaps an additon to the Bill or Rights. Everyone in the room laughed and the meeting was concluded.

Joe was naturally relieved by the outcome and most grateful to me. I did not know that Joe had friends at the National Enquirer, but apparently he did. Though that paper has recently broken an important story on Senator John Edwards and may even wind up winning a Pulitzer, it hardly had a great reputation in the journalistic community. Famous for its wild headlines that you would see as you were in the checkout line at the supermarket, it was, for all intents and purposes, a gossip rag. Well, Joe's friend came to take pictures as we left the U.S Attorney's office and returned to my office for further pictures and statements from me. They had me pose perusing a very thick-looking law tome with Joe standing beside me. The entire matter was dropped by the U.S. Attorney's office but the headline at the National Enquirer was precious: "Lawyer defends man's right to feel."

The Norwegians

Although I was not an international lawyer, my practice nonetheless seemed to have an international flavor to it. How did I get involve with the Norwegians? I had a young client who was looking to invest in a business, who somehow made contact with two gentlemen some from Norway. They had typically

Scandinavian-sounding names: Ingvar Tolefson and Per Ohrstrom. The Norwegians were looking for capital and all three agreed to retain me as the attorney for a new entity. Before we get to the Norwegians, I should say a word about my client. He was the nephew of a famous figure in Chicago annals named Dan G. who was a captain in the State's Attorney Police during the early part of the century. Dan was a machine guy who used to collect protection money from the Everleigh sisters and similar businesses when they operated a high-class brothel on South Dearborn Avenue that was patronized by many of the City's elite. Well, Dan was a political force in the City, though I never knew him until late in his life when his law enforcement and political career had long ended. His nephew was a total straight arrow and had no involvement in anything as colorful as his uncle had.

The Norwegians exported into the United States many products including whale meat. Their principal export was kelp, large seaweed which was plentiful in Norwegian coastal waters and was used as a mineral and vitamin supplement in animal feed. There was a variety of companies that manufactured the supplement and our Norwegian friends represented one of those companies. They also wished to have a pill made from kelp, which was used by pregnant women in the Scandinavian countries. In effect, they had a pill named Algamin 60, having it manufactured in the United States for distribution here.

I advised them not to be hasty and make sure everything was carefully thought out and planned. I felt that they did not have sufficient capital for the tablets so I set up meetings with various advisors in advertising, public relations, and business consulting. They decided to limit their sales efforts to Minnesota and North and South Dakota, which had a significant Scandinavian population, then move on from there.

The Norwegians were determined to make it here. They acted as ship's chandlers for Norwegian ships that would be coming to U.S. ports and found some success importing kelp, which was used for animal feed supplement. But more than anything, these viking types were great fun. It was clear that they had the hearty spirit of their Norse ancestors.

Ingvar was a fascinating type. Well over six feet tall and two hundred and fifty pounds, he had a girlfriend who was just as stout. A former Norwegian army officer, he was a hero back home because during the war (though I was never able to verify the story), he was instrumental in saving the King from the clutches of the Nazis by bringing him to neutral Sweden.

We had a problem importing kelp, which was used for animal feed. Some competitors were bringing in kelp which did not meet government standards. Although there was nothing wrong with our kelp, all kelp was seized and impounded and we had to petition the government to get ours released. I decided that the solution was to go to Norway and induce the government there to place quality control standards on the kelp. This way all of the kelp that was exported from Norway would have the Norwegian government's stamp indicating that it met all of the requirements of our FDA. I was hoping to do for kelp what was already being done for sardines. Since I was planning on visiting the country, I studied Norwegian for a year at the University of Chicago in the hopes that when I went, I would be able to speak their language a bit. Of course, I realized that all substantive discussions would be in English. That was not my reason for studying Norwegian. I was anxious to escape the stereotype of the typical American who is not interested in the language and culture of foreign countries, and my hosts were indeed impressed that I was willing to go such lengths.

Ingvar, Per, and Captain Dan's nephew all traveled to Norway. Arriving in Oslo, we stayed at the-then elegant Bristol Hotel. There were famous Norwegians all around the dining room and I met most of them including Tygue Halvden Lie who had retired after serving in a variety of governmental posts. He was best known for the two terms he served as the first Secretary General of the United Nations. Another interesting individual was Jens Evensen, a prominent lawyer and government official who was

The salt dispenser given to me in Norway by the wife of the Secretary of Commerce

serving as Minister of Trade and Shipping. You have no doubt heard the word "quisling" used to describe one who betrays his country and collaborates with an enemy government. Vidkum Quisling had led the Norwegian Government during the German Occupation and Jens Evensen was one of the people responsible for prosecuting Quisling and other traitors after the war. In an ironic twist, Evensen's own top aide, Arne Treholt, would become a quisling, convicted years later of spying for the Soviet Union.

There was a genuine generosity of spirit that imbued these Norwegians. One night they held a dinner in my honor and I was seated next to the wife of the Secretary of Commerce, the final arbiter of all trade in and out of Norway. The man was something; he spoke a dozen different languages and he admired the fact that I had spent the year learning Norwegian. In the middle of the office was a huge circular table. On it was a bowl filled with ice to keep Ringas Beer and Aquavit (local liquor) for his guests. For our last night in Norway, we were all invited along with Norwegian government officials for dinner at the home of the Secretary. I was honored by being seated to the right of the hostess. I commented to the hostess on the ornamental beauty of the salt dispenser that was in the shape of a Viking ship with a small spoon. Much to my suprise, I received a beautifully wrapped gift box from the hostess. What was inside? The salt dispenser that I had so admired.

In additon to the time spent in Oslo, one of the greatest aspects of the six-week trip was visiting Kristiansand North (known as the land of the midnight sun) and Oppdal. In Kristiansand, I met a traveling troupe of actors who were sponsored by the Norwegian government to entertain people who lived in isolated areas. The last night that the troupe was in Kristinasand, its members invited me to a party. I enjoyed myself a little too much perhaps, because the following morning when I arrived at breakfast the smell of fried herring was more than I could handle and I spent the rest of the day in my room recovering.

During my stay in Oslo something most unusual occurred. Unusual for Oslo, that is. There had been a rape and murder which occurred early in the morning and while there were no witnesses to the crime, a milkman who had been on his bicycle making deliveries caught a glimpse of an individual running away from the scene, a fact which he reported to the authorities. With the aid of this description, the police were able to capture the alleged perpetrator and the subsequent trial attracted great fanfare. Jens Evensen, the famous former prosecutor who had now become my friend, was attending the trial and brought me along as his guest. The man was found guilty of rape and murder.

As a sign of our friendship, Jens Evensen gave me the last piece of stemware that the Nazis did not take during the occupation. He wanted me to have it as a memento—a very touching and meaningful gesture.

One of the other notables I met in Oslo was the fellow who invented fish scales jewelry as well as inventing major glass marble reflectors. He was a wealthy fellow, and, with his wife, lived in a lovely estate. Our group was invited to a party held at their home. What I remember about the evening is that for every couple in attendance, there was a driver who was assigned to take them home so they would not have to worry about having a cocktail and then driving home. As they were ready to go home for the evening, a driver would take a pedal bike and put it into the trunk of the car and then take them home, biking back to our host's home afterwards. To me, it was a most unusual but simply excellent idea to think of the safety of all of their guests.

Paula and I sitting with Joe and Carol Koenig at our home

What else impressed me about our hosts was that every room in their home was filled with books. It was clear that reading was of great importance to them.

Joe K. Sr.

Of all of the interesting folks that I have met through my law practice, none perhaps was more interesting than Joe K. He turned out to be much more than a client, and would turn into a friend and a partner in philanthropy, whose life has been downright fascinating. So fascinating in fact, that even a good fiction writer could not have come up with a better story.

Joe was born in Yugoslavia in 1934, in a town where half of the inhabitants were like his family, ethnic Germans. In the aftermath of the war, Joe's family, like so many Germans in Eastern and Central Europe, suffered a great deal. His brother was inducted into the German Army and disappeared at the end of the war, his fate unknown. Much of his family was interned by Tito's regime. His grandmother, aunt, and cousin died of starvation in one of the camps. At the age of twelve, Joe was sent to a forced labor camp, remaining there for 1½ years. Together with his father, stepmother, and thirty three other prisoners, they made a daring escape across the border into Romania. From there, they walked into Hungary before finally reaching Vienna a month after they had begun their journey to freedom. But his new life in America would have to wait as Joe contracted tuberculosis and was forced to spend $1^1/_2$ years in a sanitarium. He eventually recovered, and as a displaced person, was sponsored by a relative in the Midwest, making his way to the United States as an eighteen-year-old.

Though he had been graduated from grammar school while in Vienna, like so many whose lives had been torn apart as the result of the war, circumstances did not allow Joe to obtain much in the way of formal education. But he was blessed with a tremendous mechanical aptitude and a photographic mind for machinery. He could go to a tool show, come home, and begin to engineer the same piece of equipment that he had just seen.

Through a series of events, Joe got involved in the extrusion of plastic material for garden etching. Though he had a unique skill set, turning one's talents into a moneymaking venture is never easy; just ask Thomas Edison. By the time someone had referred me to Joe, he had already been through two bankruptcies, one business and one personal. But, like a character out of a Horatio Alger tale, he was determined to make it. Joe wanted me to represent him in a new plastics company that he was starting up. Not having much money, we agreed that I would take a small piece of the company in lieu of a fee, and, as the operation grew, and he began to do well, he would pay my fees. Joe was good to his word.

Believe it or not, most of the work that we did together transpired well after the clock struck midnight. Joe would be up all night running his plant and for some reason I have never been able to sleep very much. I would joke with Joe that this arrangement was beneficial to him, just as with long distance phoning during that era, night rates were cheaper than day rates. The company did, in fact, become successful and naturally enough, Joe was very pleased. The American dream seemed to be playing itself out for this immigrant son. Though things appeared rosy, I felt it was my obligation as his legal advisor to warn him of any impending problems, hopefully before they became irreversible. Though you might not imagine it, you can go into bankruptcy from having a lot of business just as you can from the usual reason of not having enough business. You might ask how that can occur. Well, the situation is that you can have a lot of receivables, you can have plenty of inventory, but you are cash poor. Joe had gotten a small business loan through Harris Bank, and though pleased with his success, the bank was concerned about his ambitious plans for expansion. It had a very large and successful client that was looking to acquire a manufacturing company in Joe's field, and a senior vice president who had been Joe's contact person in the bank, set up a meeting in hopes of facilitating a deal. It sounded like a perfect fit for Joe's financial needs. The outfit wanted to buy the company from Joe and have him run it. They asked him for a price and Joe told the potential buyers that he wanted $2,000,000 for the company. They were agreeable to the price but told us that they would give him the first million at closing and the second one would be based upon the performance of the company, to be paid over time which sounded logical to me. Joe disagreed, and, after we retreated to my office, told me that the only reason that I was pushing the sale was so that I could get bought out of my 10% ownership stake, which amounted to $200,000. I told him that while that sounded tempting, I wanted him to take the deal because I was concerned about his expansion's effect on the company's finances. To prove just how serious I was, I signed over my stock certificate and gave it to Joe. I told him that you now own the company 100 percent. Nonetheless, like so many proud entrepreneurs, Joe could not bring himself to sell and within six months, he was in bankruptcy again.

If you thought this was the end of Joe, you would be sorely mistaken. He had not even begun to make his mark. The man was simply without fear, and his self-confidence never waned, a fantastic lesson to all of us. He started over again, and, by 1970, had bought some machines and formed a company that would become known as Trim-Tex. How did this venture fare? Well, the firm recently celebrated its 40th anniversary and is the leader in the plastics extrusion business for the building industry. Not only was it successful financially, but it is a major innovator in the field. Trim-Tex products helped eliminate the need for trim in metal beats drywall, lowering costs. Upon retirement, Joe's son, took over the entire operation of the company. Joe really loved the busines and his only regret, despite his tremendous success, is that he is no longer involved in the company he built.

Pronto

We had the Norwegians. Then a German refugee from Yugoslavia named Joe K. Now it was time for a Frenchman or rather several Frenchmen to enter the scene. Rene Dayan, a Chicagoan originally from France, was a client of mine. Together with his brother, he had been an early franchisee of MacDonald's after his brother did interior decorating on Ray Kroc's home. HIs brother, Raymond, being from France, obtained the exclusive rights for France and would build 14 MacDonald's there. The first one that he built was on land owned by a successful businessman by the name of Andre Sfez. In addition to his real estate holdings, Andre was a restauranteur and a successful one at that. He was looking to expand in the United States. Raymond suggested that his brother, Rene, would prove an ideal partner for such a venture.

The product of an immigrant Jewish family from North Africa, Sfez's family had come to Paris after the war, and they worked hard selling food on pushcarts, a common immigrant practice all over the world. Andre was an astute businessman and pooled his family's money together and began to buy buldings on the Champ Élysées (One of Paris' most prestigious avenues). The post war real estate market was good to them and by 1960, he opened his first eatery, a nice pizza place called Pizza-Pino. While expanding this chain, he began to open more upscale places. When I first met him, he explained why he wanted to have a variety of different types of restaurants for customers to choose from. If you were in a hurry and wanted to grab a quick bite with your girlfriend before going to the movies, then you would go to Pizza-PIno. If you wanted a more romantic dinner, he had a second place for you, and if you wanted to spend the entire evening eating dinner, then he had a third place that fit the bill. In addition to the real estate and restaurants, Andre also owned frozen food facilities including an ice cream plant.

Rene had arranged a meeting with Andre to take place in Andre's lawyer's office in Manhattan to formalize a partnership between the two parties. Andre spoke little English but that did not prove any barrier in doing business. He traveled with a private secretary, who, in addition to speaking fluent English, was a very astute businessperson. Andre covered our expenses, putting us up at a commodious suite in one of New York's finest hotels. My suite had so many closets that I lost a rain coat in one of the closests. We spent a couple of days hammering out an agreement and worked through the night on one of the most important elements of any partnership—the one which deals with the provisions if either party wants to dissolve the partnership. The buy-out section was about ten pages long. We thought we had covered any possible contingency, and over breakfast the next morning, we met with our clients and read out loud the language that we drafted. As it was translated from English to French for Andre, he got up from his chair and in a very loud voice, used an English word that we were all familiar with, "No!"

What was Andre's objection? He explained through his secretary that he wanted the essence of this section to read, "If either party wanted to get out of the partnership, the two parties would meet, and, sitting across from each other at a table, would each write a number that he would take to buy or sell his interest. The one with the higher number had the right to purchase the business for the price stated and the other partner had no recourse but to accept." That was simple enough. After all was completed, Andre suggested to Rene that I function as the new corporation's lawyer. A prime east-side Manhattan location was found for Pronto Italian Eatery and the place opened to great fanfare in 1976. It was an immediate hit. I would come to New York once a month, and would of course go to Pronto for our meetings. The place attracted plenty of celebrities and pretty girls. Before he was infamous, O.J. Simpson was famous. A football superstar with the Buffalo Bills, he would come fly down to New York City after games and became a regular at Pronto. Even though our meetings were called for 7:00 p.m., Andre and Rene would scarcely show up until at least 9:00 p.m. One night, Ernie Banks, known around Chicago as Mr. Cub, came in and though I was not acquainted with the future Hall of Famer, someone took him to the back of the restaurant to meet me. While waiting for Rene and Andre, we became fast friends over a few drinks.

What was Prontos like? The room was very light. The style was French bistro and they cut fresh spaghetti in the open, part of a trend which would become very popular. The food was not really all that great but the whole place just had a lot of cachet to it. But what made the story of Prontos ever so special was the story of Andre himself. He was a dreamer to be sure, but more than anything, he was a dreamer who went out and made his dreams come true. He would occasionally talk about his days starting out and once told me that when he was selling hamburgers in his pushcart he made up his mind that one day he would not only make one million dollars but would spend one million dollars. That he did and then some. But I was very impressed that despite his wealth, he was very connected to his roots and his family as well. He included his relatives, with whom he had started out, in an equity position in every business venture. He would have many other restaurants in his future but once his partnership with Rene dissolved, I was not involved with him. Still, he was really something.

An Early Christmas Present

Another one of my most interesting clients was a man named Ed M. who was in the sale and repair of safes and other security apparatus. We were quite friendly, and, one day, we were joined by his real estate broker as we went to see a building that Ed was interested in buying. After we viewed the building we decided to grab a bite at a German restaurant named "Matt Igler's." We ordered a round of drinks, and, true to my taste, I asked the waiter to bring me a glass of Chivas Regal, my then favorite brand of scotch. For those of you familiar with Chivas, you know that the bottle has a distinct shape to it. The bottle is more oval shaped and not as long as most brands of scotch or any other booze for that matter. Although the bartender was in a separate room, the configuration of the mirrors allowed me enough of a view to see that he wasn't pouring from the Chivas bottle. When the waiter returned, I asked him if the liquid in my glass was indeed Chivas Regal. He assured me that it was.

I tasted the scotch and though I don't claim to be a connoisseur, there was no doubt in my mind that this was not Chivas. Again, he assured me that it was Chivas. I told him that I would bet him the cost of the meal. If I was wrong and it indeed was Chivas, I told him that I would give him a tip equal to the amount of the dinner. The manager, a well dressed middle aged fellow, noticed the goings-on and came over to make sure everything was o.k. I told him that it was not, informing him of the bet that I had with the waiter. The manager took my glass back with him and retreated to the bar. I could see a major argument was ensuing. The manager returned with another glass of scotch and he promised me that this scotch was indeed not Chivas but, rather, the best brand of scotch that he had. He apologized and told me that they ran out of Chivas and that whatever else our party drank would be on the house. Truthfully, had I not seen the bottle that the bartender had poured from, I probably would not have been able to tell the difference. But I guess I was enjoying the James Bond-like moment though in my case it was scotch and not a vodka martini. My client was simply amazed by the whole thing. The lesson to be sure is that if you tend bar and you are out of something, then come clean. Honesty is the best policy. But my client kept thinking that not only did he have a lawyer who knew something about the law, but more importantly perhaps, he knew something about scotch and liked to regale people with the Chivas story.

Ed had divorced his wife, and was marrying a younger woman, in this case she had been his children's babysitter. His oldest son was eighteen at the time and they had three younger children as well. Ed invited me to the wedding and Paula and I sat right in front of his children who were in the back row, trying to give them support in what must have been a very difficult moment. We certainly felt for them.

After the ceremony, we drove to the hall for the reception. We must have arrived a bit early as the food was just coming out. People were slowly filing in and we noticed a mother and three children sitting at an adjacent table. While most of the ladies at the wedding were wearing fancy outfits with plenty of jewelry, this mother was wearing what was clearly a very inexpensive dress. Her older son, who looked to be about thirteen, was wearing a dress shirt and a tie. The little girl was wearing a very cute dress, though one could tell it was also quite inexpensive. The younger son, maybe eight or nine, was dressed in a sports jacket, shirt and tie. The kids were extremely well behaved, asking their mother's permission to go to the food table. Their comportment was so unusual for kids of that age that you just had to wonder what parenting secret was behind this display.

During the course of the reception, I went over to their table and engaged the thirteen-year old in conversation. What was his connection to the couple, I asked him. He informed me that his father, who had passed away in the previous year, was a first cousin to Ed. The young man then told me what a wonderful man his dad was and how much he missed him. But he was more full of pride for the man than pity for himself. The dad had been a mechanic and the boy's dream was to become a mechanic like his father. He was a sharp kid and must have realized that I had made a mental note that he was without a jacket at a formal occasion. He explained to me that he had a jacket but had outgrown it, and his brother, who was a few feet away, was wearing his blue blazer. It was obvious that his mom could not afford a new sportcoat, but he assured me that he would eventually get one. I asked about school and his outside interests. His schedule was a busy one as he would rise early in the morning and deliver papers from his bike. Something was clearly the matter as he was telling me about the paper route and I asked him what it was. He told me that the bike was very old and was giving him trouble. It was clear that his mother was in no position to buy him a new one. What was really bothering him was not that he was not going to have fun riding the bike, but that it was jeopardizing his paper route. It was not only important for him, but for the sustenance of the family; half of his earnings went to his mother. This was some family, and during the rest of the reception, I spoke to the two other kids and the mother. I was just so impressed with them as they seemed to be from another place and time, more like out of the Depression-era Spring Valley of my youth than Chicago of the 1970s.

It was clear to me that something needed to be done to help these people. I contacted Ed and he provided me with their address. I went to the bicycle store and bought a shiny new bike for the oldest son in September, with the thought that it would be delivered around Christmas time. I kept the bike in my basement, but in November, I decided since the young man was having trouble with his bike, I should not wait until the holidays but bring it over to him right away. The family lived in the very southern end of Cook County, about twenty-five miles away from my home. As you can well imagine, it was a small home, a two-bedroom one bathroom setup with a kitchen. It was clear that this was a very religious family for the only picure I saw in the home was of Jesus with a bleeding heart. When Paula and I walked in with the bike, they were all completely beside themselves. They were in tears at the whole thing and could not stop thanking us. I also paid for Ed to deliver food to the family at Thanksgiving and not mention to them that I had paid for it. They were extremely happy but wanted to do something to reciprocate. These were very proud peoplc and it was hard for them, despite their economic circumstances, to accept any help. They would have been much more comfortable giving to others. There was also another angle to this, a distinctly ecumenical one. These nice Irish Catholic people had never become acquainted with Jews before but they met us, something you would think of coming from folks who lived way out in the country rather than within the borders of Cook County. What did these folks do to thank us? They bought a Chanukah card and wrote Paula and me the most heartfelt letter of thanks that we have ever received. Whenever I would have contact with Ed, I would always ask about them and how they were doing. I don't know how things turned out, but hope they had good mazel, because no family deserved it more. On the positive side, it sure shows how struggles can bring people close together, and, in a sense, help build their collective and individual character. I really admired them and was glad that a small gesture meant so much. It really does not take very much to make a difference in someone else's life. For the price of a Schwinn, or even a lot less, you can accomplish a great deal.

CHAPTER 4

Business

REAL ESTATE

Ours was a unique law practice. For not only were we involved in the practice of law, we often made some rather unique forays into the business world. These were among the most interesting twists and turns of my life. They helped convince me that I was really blessed with *mazel*.

Real estate was one of the many areas in which we became involved. Our first venture was the purchase of a condominium resort in Keystone, Colorado that we used for vacation purposes and eventually sold. We also became investors in a number of hotels and motels, deals that were brought to us by people we knew. We even purchased an apple orchard. This was no small orchard as we once owned 3,000 golden delicious apple trees in Hotchkiss, Colorado after a client of Gene Becker's had brought this investment to our attention. After investing in a number of these deals, we eventually sold our interests.

We were always looking around for good buys and eventually found a building on the southeast corner of Jackson and Kedzie, on the West Side of Chicago. On the first floor of the building was the O'Brien Funeral Home, which had been a long standing business in the neighborhood. There were also some stores there and even a small restaurant. The key tenant was the funeral home, which included an office and a full mortuary. Over time, the area had become predominantly black, so we figured the right course of action would be to hire a black mortician to operate the funeral home since Illinois law required a licensed mortician to operate the business. To justify a return on our investment, we entered into a lease with the operator that was based on a percentage of profits generated by the funeral home.

When we were in business for a couple of years, we were paid a visit one day by the assistant to the operator who informed us that his boss was not recording all of the funerals. We learned that the City of Chicago requires all funerals to be registered with the Bureau of Vital Statistics in order to arrange for a permit. What the operator would do was to have another funeral home obtain the permit as if it were handling the funeral, in order to shield the income from us. He would then pay off his rival. We terminated the lease with the operator and entered into a new lease with his assistant. Business was pretty steady as these things go, but with the race riots in the late 1960s, there was considerable worry that, like many local businesses, the funeral home would be vandalized or even burned to the ground. I got a call from our man who was running the show and he reported that a group of wayward youths had gathered with torches and were intending to burn the place. Our guy apparently was thinking on his feet and had placed one of the deceased bodies out in front of the building. Frightened, the group scattered, never to return.

Being a landlord can be a major headache. Just ask anyone who has had the privilege. We learned from the lady who operated the restaurant that we had female tenants who were using their apartments to ply their trade in what is commonly known as the world's oldest profession. This was completely unacceptable to us and we had them served with eviction notices. The restaurant owner phoned us and revealed that the rear porches were being dismantled by a group of men. I was caught off guard but I sent a photographer to take photos of this rampant destruction.

We were to learn that some of the dismantlers were, in fact, city building inspectors who were friends of the female occupants in question. As a result of this, we were cited for having unsafe porches. I was understandably concerned when we received a notice from the State's Attorney office that a hearing was being convened with the possibility of pursuing criminal charges against us. The hearing date was set and when I arrived, I recognized a few of the faces in the waiting room. They were some of our now infamous building inspector dismantlers.

In his remarks, the State's Attorney stated that this was a very serious violation. The men testified as to the conditions. I was then asked if I had something to say. Well, you hate to break up a good witch hunt, but what could I do? I opened my briefcase and took the pictures out, placing them on the desk of the State's Attorney. He asked the witnesses if they were the same people as those pictured in the photo, and, what could they say? None of them had a twin brother. The ladies of the evening vacated the building and the city inspectors were fired.

We decided that we had had enough excitement for one lifetime and made plans to sell the building. At first we offered the property to a nearby Catholic school, but it refused the property even though the school was getting the property as a charitable gift. Failing that, we figured the best thing to do would be to sell the building to a neighborhood resident and found the building's janitor an eager buyer. We sold it to him at a very good price and even financed the deal for him. Two months after the deal closed, the CTA Repair Station, which was located across the street, had an explosion which severely damaged the west side of our building. The janitor received a hefty settlement, and, after doing the repairs to the building and paying us the entire amount he owed us, he ended up with well over one hundred grand in his pocket. What can you say? The man simply had very good luck.

That was not the only substantial building that we owned. We had an apartment building located at 2208 West North Avenue, in the Wicker Park neighborhood. The area and the building had been predominantly Polish at one time, but, as everything else in Chicago, the neighborhood changed and over the span of just a few years became overwhelmingly Hispanic. Thinking we were savvy to this development, we hired a Mexican woman as the manager. Unfortunately, the building was primarily Puerto Rican, and we found out soon enough that the relations between the two groups were not good.

The ethnic change in the building's composition meant a whole host of new problems. Tenants would remove the light bulbs that illuminated the exit signs and they were notorious for leaving the garbage outside rather than putting it in the cans we had provided. The idea in those days was to encourage tenant participation, so when a new tenant moved in we would give that person a certain sum of money to buy paint and paint the apartment himself. The tenants usually chose the cheapest brands so that they could keep the difference in price for themselves. The cheapest brands also had the largest lead content. One family had a daughter with Down Syndrome whom they kept locked up in the apartment when they went to work. Unfortunately, she ate some of the paint and ended up with lead poisoning. It was a very sad ordeal and it took a lot of time and energy to resolve the situation.

Our problems did not end there. There was a church across the street from the building and the minister would incite his parishioners by telling them that we were slum landlords who were making money off the backs of poor, hardworking people. He would portray us as the bad guys. This minister even went so far as to make up posters that depicted us driving large luxurious automobiles with money bags in the back seat—money bags that were filled with the loot of his congregants. Well, you can see where this was going.

In truth, we were putting forth a great deal of effort and expense to ensure that the building was free of any violations, but the bad publicity was killing us. The manager contacted me and told me that there was going to be a meeting held at the church one evening. Topic of the meeting: to devise a plan of action against the building's owners. I told my partners that I planned on appearing at the meeting. I suggested that we get a quitclaim deed and hand over the deed to the minister, making the church the new owner of the building. I reasoned that over the long term we had made money on the building and by donating it to the church, we could take the tax deduction. They thought I had lost my mind, that I would be shot or maybe even stoned when I walked into that hostile meeting. Call me crazy but I insisted on going.

I may be a bit crazy but stupid I am not. Neither was the minister. I walked in and the throng of people gathered there fell completely silent. Nearly every parishioner's jaw dropped in unison and the place went eerily quiet. I went up to the minister and told him that my partners and I had been doing some deep soul searching. We had indeed become rich off of the building just as had been claimed and now we wanted the church to become rich too, so we were giving them the building. We had seen the light. We decided to repent. We had been saved from the evils of capitalism.

From the silence came loud cheers as I suddenly was transformed from villain to hero. With the deed in my hand, I tried to hand it to the minister. He started yelling, "No, no, no, no!" at which point I would counter him with "Yes, yes, yes, yes!" and back and forth it went for a while. Finally, after continuous cheering from his parishioners, he asked them for quiet as he thanked me for my kindness and told me that my gesture alone was worth everything. He could not in good conscience accept it but would instead accept my everlasting friendship as we embraced and the people went crazy with approval. It was all great theater. Remember when I said the minister was no dummy. Well, that was the truth as he knew what was involved in owning that building and wanted no part of it. After our hugs and embraces that evening, the reverend never gave us any further trouble. We made a contribution to the church every year and presumably this angry man of the cloth found another alleged villain to demonize in his sermons.

A few years afterward, we came to the conclusion that, just like with our building on Jackson, we had enough headaches. But rather than sell the building, we decided the most prudent course of action would be to tear it down. What was left was a vacant lot and while considerable effort went into selling it, it attracted no buyers. Of course, we still had a problem with this lot. People would dump their trash on it. We cleaned it up and arranged for a neighbor who repaired cars to park his cars on the lot. It was free to him, the only stipulation being that he personally police the lot.

We did manage to make a lifelong friend in the ward, though it was after we tore down the building. He was a young man at the time who had been a gang leader in the ward and was now running for alderman. Luis Gutierrez was an articulate and bright young man when I first met him. When I was running Old Orchard Chevrolet, the mother of one my employees (who would often bring customers to us) asked me to attend a fundraiser for her friend, Luis. It was held on a Sunday night at a small Latino-operated tavern. I was there and it was quite a raucous evening with music, singing, and plenty of boozing. In the middle of the floor was a huge sombrero into which people would throw their dinero. Most of the money thrown included an assortment of dimes and quarters, with some dollar bills scattered in for good measure. My intention was to leave ten dollars in the hat which would have made me a real hero. But when I opened my wallet, all I found were two one-hundred dollar bills. What could I do? Luis was standing next to me so I took out one of the hundred dollar bills and gave it to him, which was surely the largest contribution to his campaign until then. Through the rise of his career, and he would go on to become a congressman and one of the most powerful Hispanic politicians in the United States, he never forgot my donation to his campaign. One hundred dollars sure went a long way.

What happened to our property? Just as so many neighborhoods in Chicago had seen racial and ethnic changes in their makeup in the 50s and 60s, there would be a move toward gentrifying many of these neighborhoods in the subsequent decades. Good luck resurfaced and I sold the lot that at one time we could not sell for $5,000, for close to $100,000. Lest the reader think that the problems that we had were strictly a reflection of race or ethnicity, that assumption is wrong. We owned another building in Maywood, which is located about 10 miles west of Downtown Chicago. Its residents are primarily working-class African-Americans. The apartment building we owned there was beautiful and the residents took an active role in maintaining it. We had nary a problem.

I have always been blessed with the ability to make friends. I became acquainted with Charles Jordan, whose family had been lifelong residents of Maywood. One day, I was *schmoozing* with Chuck and he told me that there was a local barber shop which functioned a little like a social club. Chuck said that the place was open 12 hours a day and its 4 chairs were constantly busy. The owner wanted to sell and we could get it for a good price. I told him that I would talk it over with my partners. I guess they weren't too excited about the prospect of owning a barber shop, and, while I admit it lacks some appeal, I was game. I decided to go in on a 50-50 partnership with Chuck. I would supply the cash and he would run the operation. It proved to be a winner and he was a fair partner. Haircuts and shaves added up and it did well for me before I sold my interest to Chuck.

M & S Grill

If owning a barber shop sounds a little different, wait till you hear this tale. It all started with a phone call from a lawyer friend who specialized in bankruptcy law. Along with a group of his colleagues, he wanted to buy a restaurant that was bankrupt and was going through the bankruptcy court at the time. There was a concern that if he and his guys became involved, the price would go up. Since I was relatively unknown in the bankruptcy field, he asked me to buy it for them. I did it as a favor and they were appreciative.

This same lawyer called me a few years later to tell me that one of his clients owns a building on Cicero between Division and Chicago. It was a three-story apartment building with a restaurant on the first floor. There had been a short-order grill in the building for over thirty-five years and the owners were retiring. My colleague had another client whose brother ran a similar type of establishment. I was introduced to Mike by my colleague and he told me that he always dreamed of having his own place. The problem was that the man had no money. If I was interested in buying it, Mike could run it. I met the building's owner, an elderly Italian gentleman, and signed a lease.

Mike and I decided to form a partnership known as "M & S Grill" with Mike being the general partner and me being the limited partner. The place was profitable from the get-go. Our arrangement called for Mike to take a salary and then we took twenty percent of the profits and put them into the bank, splitting the remainder. After six months, I had recouped my entire investment and the place was going great guns. I would have parties there on Saturday night, serving my friends all of the usual fare that these places are known for.

Everything was moving along until about two and one half years into the arrangement when the income from the operation began to show a steep decline. The only explanation was that Mike was skimming some of the cash instead of sharing the profits as we had agreed upon. After debating the issue with him, I told Mike that he would become the sole owner, providing me with three hundred dollars a week for the next twenty-four months. After that, I was out of the picture. He insisted that I remain a partner but I told him no go. I had papers drawn up to reflect our new arrangement. For the next six months, I would go to the restaurant to collect my money every week. One week, I received a frantic call from the building's owner. The man wanted to know what happened to Mike. It was now Wednesday and Mike had been a no-show since Saturday. I called Mike's house and spoke to his wife. She had not seen him since Saturday. He was AWOL and where he had wandered off to was anybody's guess.

I immediately hopped into a cab and will never forget what I found when I got to the restaurant. Everything was gone except for a case of ketchup and a malted milkshake maker. Though I was no longer the owner, I felt responsible for the turn of events. I went to see the building owner and told him that I would pay the rent until he was able to find a new tenant. Within a few days, he found someone who proceeded to run the place for the next thirty years.

What happened to Mike? It turns out that he had run away with one of the waitresses who worked in the grill. I thought I had heard the last of him. But one cold winter day a year or so later, my secretary buzzed my office and told me that there was someone to see me. Who was it, I asked. You guessed it: a guy named Mike requested an audience with me and I told her to let him in. Well, you should have seen the poor bedraggled spectacle who came through my door. His head was bowed and he looked totally despondent. He practically kissed my feet as if I was a Mafia don with the power of life and death, apologizing for all his past wrongdoings, and promising me that he was a changed man. He had seen the light, and, to make it up to me, he wanted to give me the title to his car. There was just one hitch; the car was in Arizona and he needed two hundred dollars to repair it and bring it back to Chicago.

I did not need much time to think the matter over. I instructed Mike to straighten up and with all five foot three of him now as erect as a Marine Corps recruit, I told him to take a look out of the window of my eleventh-floor office. I opened the window with considerable force and staring straight into his eyes told him, "Mike, you are going to leave my office in the next thirty seconds. The only question is how. You can take the elevator or go through the window—your choice." Mike ran out the door like a world-class sprinter and that was the last I heard of him. What was Mike's problem? Of course, he was a little weak on integrity but he screwed up his life only after things were going well, not when they were going poorly. The latter seems more understandable than the former, but it teaches you that there are some people who are simply unable to handle success. Mike was one of those people.

World Hockey Association

My partners and I did get involved with some exciting businesses, or in this case, one particularly exciting business. There is probably nothing which excites people more than the world of sports. In our office, Gene Becker was the sports guy, someone who, in addition to being an excellent lawyer, had a deep love for sports, especially hockey.

As I am writing these words, the Chicago Blackhawks have just won the Stanley Cup. The town is abuzz with pride. The last time this event occurred was in 1961, when Bobby Hull was a young star with the team. A bit of a hockey craze ensued in the sixties and early seventies and one of the byproducts of the craze was that rinks started to be built and youth hockey leagues were organized.

One group built a beautiful rink in Oakbrook Terrace and my partner Gene Becker was familiar to two people in that investment group. As this group had some unique capital needs and the economy had hit a rough patch, Gene had our firm brought in to see if we could be of some help in securing financing, and that was how we were introduced to the world of sports.

Skip ahead to 1971 when Gary Davidson and Dennis Murphy, founders of the American Basketball Association, were looking to do for hockey what they had done for basketball. They founded an alternative league to the NHL which became known as the World Hockey Association (WHA). They began the search for prospective owners by scouring the country. They came to Chicago where they had heard about the group that owned the arena in Oakbrook Terrace, thinking they might be interested in putting an investor group together in what was perceived as an up-and-coming hockey town.

Well, as the things turned out, our firm ended up with a proprietary interest in the Cougars. Gene Becker was brought in as the team's president, and, for a year, functioned as such. The WHA had signed big name players from the NHL and its key signing was Bobby Hull, nicknamed the Golden Jet, who signed with the Winnipeg Jets for a million dollars. While that was great for the WHA, it severely dampened hockey enthusiasm in Chicago, a fact I recently learned from Gene. Talk about a mixed blessing. The Cougars could not book the Chicago Stadium because of the Hawks and was forced to play in the International Amphitheatre, which was a less than stellar venue. In the club's second year when they were in the playoffs but could not play in the Amphitheatre because the arena had booked a production of *Peter Pan*. Can you imagine *Peter Pan* displacing a professional hockey team in the middle of the playoffs? Well, it happened, and due to these and other difficulties, the team folded after three seasons.

Hyperloop

We were very proud of Gene, and though the sporting adventure did not work out in the end, that was totally beyond his control.

If you will permit me a sports analogy from a different sport, you can't hit a home run unless you swing the bat. And we were not afraid to swing when we found a prospective deal to our liking. Sometimes you strike out. Sometimes you even hit into a double play. Hopefully, you get a base hit; a single, most likely. But there are those times when you knock it clean out of the park.

It's always risky to fund a start up company. But we sensed opportunity with a company which we later named Hyperloop. Before we get to it, I must first speak about a company called Sciaky, which was based in Chicago and has an interesting history.

As the United States was contemplating the possibility of entering the Second World War, it realized that it had many deficiencies in industrial manufacturing which now would be critical to the war effort. One deficiency was in the area of manufacturing welding equipment. The Sciaky family owned a large company which did just that. The only problem was the Sciakys were in France, but the American government was able to bring them to the United States during the early stages of the war. With them came their technology and the government built a large plant in Chicago. It manufactured a substantial supply of welding equipment which was used in the many defense plants throughout the country. The company prospered.

As they say, it is all about whom you know and Gene Becker had a friend and neighbor named Merlyn Schlenker who worked in the sales department of Sciaky. Merlyn, in turn, had a friend and colleague named Marcel Sommeria, who had invented a servo electric drive, a mechanism that sent electric impulses to the tool machine that would control the cutting movement. All machine tools were previously controlled using a hydraulic drive so the servo electric drive was a major breakthrough in the machine tool industry and had the potential to significantly impact manufacturing.

Since Gene knew both Marcel and Merlyn well, having developed some of the early plans for the company during racquetball games, he brought the opportunity to our attention. We convened a meeting with Merlyn, Marcel, Gene, Ralph, and me to discuss the formal details of the formation of a company to market Marcel's invention. We agreed to invest $10,000 and divided the equity among Merlyn, Marcel and the three of us. At this meeting, Ralph and I listened to the proposal from Gene and though I was game, Ralph had some reservations. He was willing to go along with the proposal but said if we ever made any real money on this deal, he would kiss Gene's behind on the corner of State and Madison Streets.

It was time to divide up responsibilities and titles. Merlyn, an excellent salesman, was chosen as president of the new venture with Marcel functioning as vice president of engineering. Gene and Ralph became vice-presidents, with me assuming the duties of treasurer. We rented an old post office in Bridgeview on the South Side near Harlem Avenue and 75th Street as our headquarters and began to manufacture our product. Almost from the beginning, it was clear that we were quickly outgrowing our facilities. The building's owners were both residents of the town, with one of them being the mayor, and they were contractors to boot. They proposed building a brand new facility to our specifications and were willing to rent it to us at a reasonable cost.

Things start happening fast when you are in a major growth mode. One of the greatest challenges any new enterprise faces is having adequate financial resources upon which to draw. We were greatly undercapitalized at this point and were faced with the option of mortgaging our homes or seeking an investing partner. We decided on the latter and were able to secure funds from the LaSalle Street Capital Corporation, an SBIC (Small Business Investment Company). Some of the cash would be put toward equity and the rest would be a loan with attractive terms. We would have significant working capital at our disposal. LaSalle Street insisted that the board of directors be reduced to four members, with it taking one seat. Its member would not be an officer of the company, but would oversee the entire operation. The name of its representative was Dan Donahue, who, in his role as president of LaSalle Street Capital Corporation, had ample experience managing startups.

Dan Donahue was one of the most knowledgeable men in business whom I've ever had the good fortune of knowing. He had a great facility for finance and organization. The leadership that he brought to the enterprise was one of the keys in making Hyperloop a success. In addition to his high intellect, he was a typically gregarious Irishman, six foot three inches of good old-fashioned fun. Occasionally, it got the better of him as when we traveled to England to attend the European Tool Show which was being held in Birmingham and to meet with the Lucas Company there. Upon going through customs, a rather serious looking official asked Dan what we were planning on doing in England. Dan may have enjoyed the cocktails on the plane ride a bit too much because he said, "We're here to sell guns to the I.R.A." Why he said this is beyond me, but before you could say Irish Whiskey, we were taken into private rooms, searched, and questioned. Our British friends clearly did not share Dan's sense of humor; as a matter of fact they seemed to lack any sense of humor. They took him at his word and refused to release us until the Lucas company was able to confirm our story.

Lucas was a very large company, and, unlike many American companies, it was extremely old, dating back to the mid 1800s and its founder, Joseph Lucas, inventor of the gas lamp used in mining. It seemed an ideal partner and we entered into a contract for Lucas to become our sole representative for all of Europe. I arranged to meet with members of its legal department at its headquarters about thirty miles from London. We did so much work together that in three years I visited England a total of twenty-one times. I would frequently leave on Thursday and come back on the weekend. Once, during an important negotiation, I spent six weeks in Europe.

I still remember our first meetings with the Lucas people. We began on Monday and were provided with two secretaries to take minutes. Working with the Lucas attorney, our goal was to finish

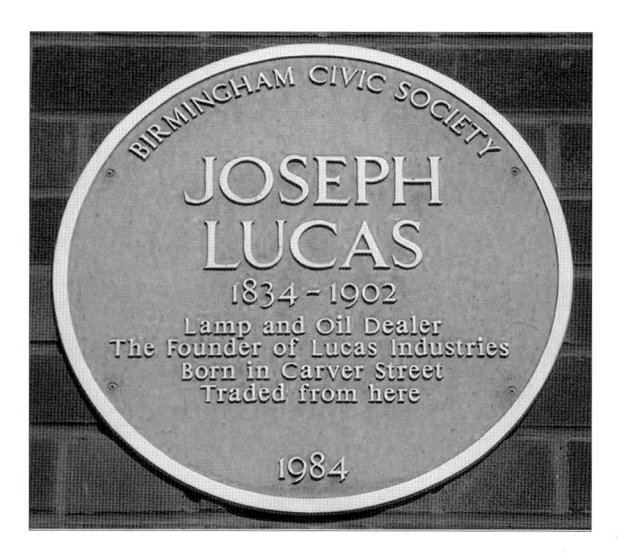

Joseph Lucas plaque

all of the details of a formal contract of representation between Lucas and Hyperloop by Friday afternoon. I thought we were in good shape to make that schedule and that I was slated to get a copy of the document when I ran into a snag. Though the documents were written in English, there are differences between American English and British English, differences that could have a material bearing on the terms of the deal. It was not for nothing that George Bernard Shaw said that "America and Britain are two countries separated by the same language." I called the attorney for Lucas, and, with a secretary present, we changed the language so that there could be no room for misinterpretation.

If you remember from our display of tomfoolery at the London airport, Dan Donahue and I had traveled to Birmingham, England for a large machine tool show. Perhaps the airport experience was a sign of things to come. Every hotel in that great industrial city of the West Midlands was booked and all we could find was a small motel that had only one room with two double beds. We took it. In the room, there was a large sliding glass door that led out to the patio. I arose early the next morning, as I do every morning, to say the morning prayers while donning *tefillin* (phylacteries). These religious items are two black boxes with leather straps. One is placed above the forehead, with the strap going around the head and over the shoulders. The other box rests on the upper bicep and faces the heart, and is then wrapped around the arm, hand, and several fingers. Well, Dan, despite his knowledge in many areas, was unaware of this religious practice and when he saw these strange looking boxes on my head and arms assumed that I fallen through the sliding door and was applying the boxes like a tourniquet to try to stem the bleeding. Dan phoned the desk immediately and told the clerk to send an ambulance. Fortunately, I had just finished my prayers and got the phylacteries off in time to explain the situation to the paramedics. Like the officials at the airport, these rather serious Brits were not amused by the incident.

Our Lucas people were always wonderful hosts, making our many trips to England very special. They made a point of taking us to the finest restaurants and nightclubs in England. In addition, we also had the opportunity to go to special events like the Wimbledon Tennis Tournament and to visit Stratford-on-Avon. They put us up at different hotels and one Saturday night when I was staying at the Paddington Hotel, what with its plumbing fixtures made of full bone china it was as British as it got, several colleagues took me to dinner and I walked back to into the hotel lobby at about 11:00 p.m. As I waited for the elevator, I heard the roar of laughter coming from the main ballroom. The main ballroom was up one flight of stairs and I walked up to see what was going on. I peered in and saw that everyone was having a jolly good time and then with a smile on my face, I readied to walk down the long staircase to take the elevator back up to my room. Just then, a gentleman heading into the ballroom warmly said to me, "Why don't you join the party?" When I politely declined, he said, "You're an American. Now I insist that you join the party." I walked in somewhat reluctantly and was introduced to the people who had organized the dinner dance which were the ladies' auxiliary of a freemason lodge.

They were tremendously friendly and I was plied with drinks and had a grand old time into the wee hours of the morning.

Entertainment is part of doing business. And we did plenty of business. On one of my trips to Germany, we met at the headquarters of a German company to which Merlyn and I were hoping to sell our product. After the customary exchange of business cards, one of the German businessmen asked me, "Herr Pfeffer, you have a German sounding name. Do you speak German?" I turned to the man and said, "I am third-generation American and I do not speak German." I neglected to tell him that I took four semesters of it in college. Though I did not speak the language well, I did retain some of what I had learned.

Prior to our meeting, Merlyn and I discussed the price at which we wished to sell our product and the lowest price that we could accept. We met at 7:00 a.m. at the factory office of the company and the Germans knew that we were scheduled to fly to Amsterdam at 11:30 the very same morning. After much back and forth in German, they gave us a price. From listening to the previous discussions between them, I knew that this was not their final price. I closed my briefcase and said, "Gentleman, this leaves us no room for profit. Why don't you consider a more reasonable price and we could negotiate a contract." Merlyn was ready to shoot me because their offer was still more that our minimum price and he was really hot for a deal—so hot, in fact, that he was ready to blurt something out when I proceeded to give him a swift kick under the conference table. We got up to shake hands with our German colleagues and say goodbye as we both made our way to the door. Their senior executive stopped us before we walked out. He was willing to up their offer by 10% and wanted to know if that was acceptable. I told them that it was. We signed a letter of intent and he told us they would draft a formal agreement and send it to our offices, which they did. We caught our plane to Amsterdam and were very happy about the deal. Merlyn was certain that I understood everything they said and until his untimely death, considered me the most seasoned negotiator whom he had ever met.

Not every negotiation went as well. Sometimes, they went downright lousy. The two of us were meeting an executive from a Japanese company with which we were hoping to do business. The executive in charge, along with his interpreter, flew to Chicago to meet with us. We met our Japanese contacts at the Hyatt Hotel in Oak Brook, advising them that we would meet them by the first floor elevators.

My first mistake occurred when they got off the elevator. One of the gentlemen was considerably older than the other. In my experience, it was always the executive who was the older fellow and the interpreter the younger one. Certainly seems logical. The proper etiquette was to speak to the executive, which I did, and the interpreter would then translate for him. Little did I know, however, that the executive was the younger man and the interpreter his senior. When we sat down to dinner, I thought I heard the interpreter, whose English was hardly perfect, say that the executive preferred fish-meat, by which I assumed he meant salmon. When the entree arrived, I could see that the man was unhappy. It turns out that he wanted a steak, which we proceeded to have brought for him.

We were also staying at the hotel and using its meeting room to conduct business. The plan was that after dinner, we would get down to the nitty gritty of the business discussions. This was a very common way of conducting business, and, after adjourning, it was the custom for everyone to take off his jacket and loosen his tie a bit. Our Japanese friends did neither, and though we would be at it until 4:00 that morning, we still had made no progress in our discussions. I began to see these men as kamikaze pilots waiting to smash into our aircraft carrier. There was no mazel that night.

Lucas had approached me in helping it acquire a company that sold wholesale auto parts to large concerns like J.C. Penney's and Sears. Since I had a client in the automotive after-market with a customer base that included these big retailers, I arranged a meeting between the parties. In 90 days, Lucas bought the company then asked if I would serve on the board of directors as secretary of the corporation as well as local counsel. Shortly thereafter it bought Hyperloop and I stayed on the board and served as local counsel.

All officers of a Lucas-controlled company were entitled to visit (between once a year and once every three years depending on your position and the size of holding) a Lucas facility anywhere in the world. This amounted to a fourteen-day all expense paid trip, complete with first class airfare and hotels. I took Paula to the Far East and we visited Hong Kong, Singapore, and Taiwan.

What happened to Hyperloop? Hyperloop was sold to Lucas successfully and we did well on the the deal though Ralph Gabric was careful to avoid the corner of State and Madison whenever he was in Gene Becker's company. Lucas eventually sold it to a company named Cincinnati Milacron which effectively ended our relationship with the entity. It was a great run for us and gave me a great deal of satisfaction to see Hyperloop grow as it did. The next enterprise that I would take on was like nothing I had ever tried before. Like everything else I did, I was to dive in head first.

Old Orchard Chevrolet

It was 1982 and I had been back to practicing law full time. I represented several very successful automobile dealers, none more successful than the one operated by my lifelong friend, George Shepard, who owned a Chevy dealership in Lake Bluff. Through George, I met a friend of his, Jim Long, who owned Long Chevrolet in Elmhurst and was one of the largest Chevy dealers in the world. The more I started meeting these dealers, the more impressed I became with the businesses they were running. A thought began to ruminate inside my head and it was

Various views of the the dealership

ten o'clock at night when I gave George a call. I told George that I wanted to become a Chevrolet dealer, and, frankly, he thought that I had been drinking or had flat gone crazy. I assured him that neither was true.

The problem as George saw it was that Chevy would be reluctant to grant a dealership to anyone who had no previous experience in the field. Though that would have given most men pause, it did not bother me one bit. I was ready for any challenge and always felt that business was business. With all due respect to the dealers that I'd met, my gut told me that if they could do well, so could I. George must have figured that I was serious and suggested I take a drive by Mancuso Chevrolet in Skokie which was the only Chevy dealership in the area that was for sale.

I took the close proximity of the dealership to my home as a good omen. It was almost walking distance. Everything else was positive. The size of the building and the many rows of cars were impressive, but what really caught my eye was the large, fenced vacant space that was part of the lot. While I knew little to nothing about autos, I felt I had some knowledge of real estate. The three and one half acres of prime real estate that composed the lot made my mouth water.

Rising early the next morning, I phoned George and related to him what I have just told you. According to my friend, the first person I must pass muster with was the Chevy's regional manager. Jim Long used to give parties at his home in Lake Geneva and I was a frequent guest at these shindigs. It was there, amidst a whole host of Chevy big shots that I had met the regional manager. Like Dan Donahue, this guy was a big and gregarious Irishman who seemed to have taken a liking to me, so I was raring to go. George arranged a breakfast for the three of us a few weeks later and to assuage any fears that Chevy might have about a new dealer, the plan was that George would be my partner. He suggested that I let him take the lead in the breakfast meeting and he told the regional manager that if they approved the sale of the dealership to us, he would treat the dealership as if it were his own. On and on the meeting went from one topic to another until it seemed as though we had touched on everything under the sun except my becoming a dealer. As we adjourned, the big guy got up, and with his blue Irish eyes fixated on me like a police officer interrogating a suspect asked me, "Sam, why in the hell do you want to be a dealer?" I looked at him, then I looked at George, and, with a straight face said, "Because I want to be as rich as all these damn dealers I represent." How did he take my answer? He liked it so much that he started to laugh uncontrollably and then put his big right paw on my shoulder and said, "Sam, that is the best damn reason I ever heard. If that is your goal, then we'll make it happen."

Lorraine and George Shepard

That got the ball rolling. After filling out many forms and attending dealer school in Detroit, I was officially approved. George Shepard would have a minority interest in the dealership and would help manage it. While we kept some of the employees, I wanted to bring in fresh talent. We hired a sales manager, a used car manager, and a finance, service, and parts manager. I wanted to run the business with the same type of entrepreneurial vigor that I had for every for other business in which I was involved. One of the keys to making money in any business is incentivizing key managers. Each manager would be paid a salary with a bonus based on the profitability of his individual unit. His bonus would be based on net profit, with my salary being excluded from the formula. Otherwise, I could have paid myself a hefty salary, thereby deflating the numbers. I wanted them to know up front that this was going to be a square deal.

With the team assembled, we got to work selling and servicing cars. How did the transition go? We sold more cars in the first three months of the Pfeffer regime than they had the whole previous year under the former owner. I would say it was a combination of hard work and mazel as you will soon see.

There were some concerns among the employees that there would be major changes. They centered on union contracts, the service department being union workers. I had the right to terminate the union contract and they would have to recertify. Sensing their anxiety about the future, I gathered the group together. I told them that I was not going to terminate their contract. If being members of a union was going to make them happy and content employees, then that was fine with me.

Instituting monthly meetings, I asked the employees to make a list of what improvements they would like to see that would enhance the workplace. They were not shy. Fans in the work area would make the summers more tolerable and I had them installed immediately. The following month they complained about the area that they used to clean up in and hang up their clothes. I had the place renovated to their satisfaction. The next month focused on the choices available in the vending machines which they claimed paled in comparison to what could be found at the nearby hospital. I instructed the vending machine company to stock the machines similar to the way things were stocked at the hospital.

By the fourth meeting, they stated that they were happy with all of the improvements and had no further requests. I then told them. "I have been very happy to grant all of the requests that you have asked for. But now it's my turn. The first thing is that I do not want you to charge a customer until the work is performed. Please do not take anything home that is not yours. The special paper towels that you dry your hands with are expensive. If you want these paper towels then I will arrange for you to be able to purchase them for the same price as we pay."

The guys took this all very seriously. We had established trust and they did not want to violate their end of things. One day, one of the fellows from the parts department came to me. He had noticed a box on top of one of the racks. Upon inspection, he found all kinds of cleaners, paper towels, and even some parts. Someone was clearly planning on taking home this box of goodies. I asked the man to keep an eye on the box and take notice of when it left the rack. After lunch he came to me and told me it was gone. I convened a meeting of the parts department and asked if there would be any objection if we went out and viewed the contents of the trunks of all those with access to the parts department. We did, and, lo and behold, the box was sitting in the trunk of the assistant parts manager who was leaving to go to a new job. If you thought that the parts manager or I were the most upset about the pilferage, you would be mistaken. One of the guys was so hot, so angry at the man, that we had to restrain him. He wanted a piece of the guy right there in the parking lot. After letting him go, we practically had to escort the thief to his car for his own protection.

The loyalty could be seen in other ways. The union to which the mechanics belonged was getting ready to strike. The Old Orchard union representative told the powers that be that his members did not want to strike Old Orchard Chevrolet. He told them that though we were a union shop, our three closest competitors were not. They felt that a strike at Old Orchard would have a negative impact on our business which would undoubtably have been true. The union was amenable to the request.

The bond also became personal. Part of being the boss is that your people will bring their problems to you. Being a lawyer didn't hurt either and I would hear about their personal, financial, and family struggles, seeking to help whenever I could. Though I was no marriage counselor whenever a fellow would complain about his wife, I would tell him to take his wife out to dinner and have him use my credit card for the meal. It was a small gesture, but they really appreciated it. The wife would call me and tell me how much it meant to her that I cared.

Our annual Christmas party was probably where the mutual trust and affection were solidified. We would hold it on the floor

One of our custom-built vans used in the Fourth of July parade in Skokie. Left to right: Saul Chez and Steve Fifer (Service Director) with Saul's children.

of the dealership by moving all of the cars out, and have the whole thing catered. I made sure to give everyone a turkey for the holidays, and, in turn they would collect a dollar from all 120 employees and buy me a lovely gift.

There are also headaches that come with running the show, but the goodwill that I had built up helped mitigate the problems. Two female employees had filed a harassment suit against the office manager. The suit was subsequently settled, but what was interesting was that they did not file the suit against Sam Pfeffer, only against the office manager. This had to run against the advice of the EEOC lawyers but they did not want to hurt me in any way.

One day as I was walking through the dealership, there was a young woman standing by the service department. She was in tears. I walked up to her and asked her what the problem was. She told me that she had bought a used car from one of our salesman but it did not have a radio. He promised her that he would put a radio in the car and that it would look like it came from the factory. When she came to pick up the car, it had a small radio that filled about half of the space of the compartment. The salesman was off that day so she was told to see the man who installed the radio. We went to see my employee who installed the radio and I asked the lady to go in the waiting room as it would take some time and we promised to drive her to the shopping center. I then asked my porter who installed the radio to come into the office. He was one of my most reliable porters, and, in addition to his regular work, he earned extra income by snowplowing, cutting the grass, and trimming the bushes. He said the salesman, whom in the interim we had instructed to come immediately to the dealership, had told him to take an old radio and install it in this woman's car. I asked the porter if he knew of the rule that no used or new car may be worked on without written authorization from the department's manager. He said that he knew of it, but that he was doing Bill, the salesman, a favor and did not think he had done anything wrong. In the meantime, Bill arrived and was sent into my office. I explained the situation to Bill and asked him for an explanation. Bill hemmed and hawed. I told the manager to take Bill with him because Bill was no longer employed. I turned to the porter and told him that he was through as well. About an hour later, I got a call from the porter's wife. She told me how much he loves his job, and how proud he was of it, assuring me that he would never make the same mistake again. I told her that it was true; that he would never make the same mistake again here. The next day he came in with the union agent claiming that he was fired without cause. The porter admitted what he had done and the union agent agreed that this was indeed cause for being fired.

 We often took inventory on a spontaneous basis so no one knew when it would happen. I always noticed that when we took inventory on Saturday, there was always a van missing. On Monday, it was always back. After this occurred several times, it dawned on me that one of the porters would take it for the weekend. I went to see the Chief of Police and asked if he would have one of his cars go by an address of this particular porter to see if the van were nearby. He did, and found our van four or five houses down from the porter's home. The police would be glad to arrest this young man if I so wanted. I declined, and, on Monday, when the porter was back at work, I called him into my office and told him that the Evanston Police may arrest him as a weekend van stealer. He finally acknowledged what he had done, explaining that he had taken it for the weekend. I fired him on the spot. Just like with the previous incident, I received a phone call, in this case from the porter's mother. She told me how much her son loved his job. He was a good kid and I treated him very well, but you just cannot put up with this kind of behavior. He had a lesson to learn and whether he learned it or not, I will never know.

Publicity and promotions are what car dealers are known for. Looking for anything that would bring us traffic, and, therefore, business, we initiated a program that proved to be a real success. We had one of our vans painted all white and had a figure painted on it that looked like one of those old-fashioned crossing guards whom we called the "Old Orchard Ranger." The Ranger would drive down the Edens Expressway from Chicago north to Highland Park. If there were any vehicles that had broken down, he would stop and lend assistance. If the car needed a tow, he would have it towed anywhere the driver wanted. This was always a free service. That was not our only gimmick. We would blow up some balloons and attach them to the car. The balloons read, "Help! Help! From the Ranger of Old Orchard Chevrolet." Detroit was so impressed that it included our idea in one of its monthly newsletters.

General Motors is famous for holding a variety of contests based on the number of cars sold. During my tenure, we won a fair number and got to travel all over the world, including an African safari. Contests were also in play for sales for each of the departments. I made sure that if the department won the contest,

Article about our emergency vehicle called "Rescue Ranger"

the manager would get the trip as I had heard that there were dealers who would take the trip themselves. I also inaugurated in-house contests, making sure that the figures needed to win the contest were attainable. Sometimes the prizes were cash or even a free dinner. You would be surprised by how much people love these kind of things and our low turnover was testament to that.

I began to look for ways to increase our sales beyond our traditional retail customer base. For years, the City of Chicago had bought only Fords for its police squad cars. Apparently, the mayor was close to a particular Ford dealer. When Harold Washington became mayor in 1983, he promised to hold an open bid for all cars purchased by the City. I went to speak to our General Manager and asked him if he knew anything about squad cars. Though he did not, he knew someone who had bid for state police cars in the past. I met the gentleman in question and was sufficiently impressed by his knowledge of squad cars, and I agreed him to pay him for the job. I'd compensate him for time he spent working on the bid and would provide a bonus if the bid was accepted.

Knowing someone at City Hall never hurts and though I did not know any high-level people there, I did know someone who had served as a "gopher." Being there for many years, he knew everyone including the women who worked in the purchasing department the massive paperwork passed through. I asked him if he would arrange for me to meet them. I realized that invoices could sit on someone's desk for weeks. I bought a two-pound box of candy for each of the six women who would be handling the paperwork. It was not a bribe of course, and the only thing I asked of them was that if we happened to have the mazel to win the bid, that they would move the paperwork through without delay so we could receive prompt payment. They agreed to process the payment quickly.

Guess what? We won the bid. In fact, our bid was so much lower than our competitors' that we were awarded an additional fifty cars. We were ecstatic and received congratulations from the president of Chevrolet as well as from numerous other top executives. But with the good comes the bad. The regional manager of GMAC (General Motors Acceptance Corporation, GM's financing arm) informed us that GMAC expected payment within 60 days after delivery. Beyond that time, they had the legal right to take over the dealership. I called my friend, the gopher, who arranged the meetings with the six ladies and I went again to City Hall and told the women that I had won the bid. They applauded and I gave them the second box of candy and they told me that the invoice would go through just as soon as they received it.

The women were good to their word and we had a check within 21 days of delivery. But there was a problem: once the checks were written, the funds had to be made available. Alderman Burke, head of finance for the City Council had to approve the funds to be deposited for the checks to clear. He was dragging his feet because he had figured that we were connected to Mayor Washington, so that even though everything was approved, he did not deposit the funds into the account. I called a lawyer friend whom I knew was friendly with Burke and asked him if he would call Burke to tell him about me, and that I did not know Washington, that I had no political connections, and I had bid independently. Within 24 hours the funds were deposited and I breathed a huge sigh of relief and my heart rate returned to normal.

Everyone thought I had major clout in City Hall. The Chevy dealers who were located within the city limits were furious and pressured the City Council to enact some ordinance that prevented any suburban dealers from future bids. They would eventually get their way.

We also sold automobile parts to the City including the fire department. With our contract came the stipulation that if it went over 60 days, interest would be added in order to ensure that we did not lose money. One July, my parts manager informed me that we had not yet paid by the City and that the invoice was 90 days past due. I was very unhappy that he had waited so long to tell me and subsequently found out that the fire department had ordered some cords for its air conditioning units. I instructed our people not to release the cords until we received all past due payments. One of the local television stations at the time was doing a story about why all of the ambulances of the fire department were not operational. The problem was ambulances could not be dispatched until they had the cords and we were in summertime. A man from the fire department was very upset about this situation and was calling our parts manager to complain. I had the switchboard redirect all of this man's calls to me. I spoke to him and he was just plain abusive, cursing and yelling at me. I simply hung up on him.

Thirty minutes later I received a call from a man who identified himself as the administrative aide to the Fire Chief. He wanted to know why I had refused to ship the cords. I informed him of the past due amounts and he promised to hand deliver to me the next day the entire sum. I told him I would release the cords and the fire department sent its truck to the dealership to pick up the parts that were needed and had them installed immediately. By evening all of the ambulances were operational. The administrative aid showed up with the check as he had promised. Every future payment from the fire department was within 30 days.

Perhaps the most exciting development during my years as a car dealer occurred when I appeared on ABCs "Nightline" with Ted Koppel. What was the reason for this? This was the period when the Big Three automakers first offered 1.9% interest rate to the public. The "Sun-Times" wanted to run a story on the new financing and instructed one of the press photographers and a reporter to do this at a dealership. If you remember, I had represented a lot of press photographers in my law practice and one of them came to snap some shots of Old Orchard Chevrolet. A feature writer came along as well and the article appeared on the front page at the same time that the "Nightline" photographers were in Chicago. One of the producers saw the "Sun-Times" article and called me and asked if he could shoot the dealership for a show that was airing that evening. They spent five or six hours with us and as part of the story, I was questioned by the crew about the new rates and these clips were interposed during the show. I was not in favor of this type of financing and told the

Chicago Sun-Times article about the new rates introduced by the auto industry (August 1986)

reporters that I thought it was setting a dangerous precedent. Once customers became used to these rates, it would be very tough to wean them off and raise them to traditional levels. Little did I know how prophetic those words would be for in 2010 you can buy a car at 0% on many models.

"Nightline" was a very popular show and the next day, I was swamped with calls. Not only friends and family, but my fellow car dealers wanted to know how I had managed to get on Ted Koppel's show. I had a standard answer: "What are friends for?" All these guys must have thought that we were long-time buddies. Though I never explicitly stated as such when I said, "what are friends for?" such an impression was no doubt created. In truth, I have never had the privilege of making Koppel's acquaintance.

The car business is an up-and-down game but for me it was mostly up. However, the domestic car market was beginning to lose sales to the import market. Old Orchard needed an infusion of several hundred thousand dollars for working capital. Remember George Shepard was my partner, owning 49% of the dealership. But he shared in the profits 50/50. During the years that Old Orchard was in operation, interest on mortgages began to drop. Twice during that period of time, I was able to refinance our mortgage for a much lower rate which resulted in our saving hundreds of thousands of dollars, savings which George shared equally. We needed working capital though, and I asked George to have his dealership, Shepard Chevrolet lend Old Orchard the necessary funds, but he declined. So, I was forced to seek these funds from personal friends and I signed a personal promissory note so they would not have to worry about repayment. These funds were eventually repaid once I sold the franchise, a story which I describe next.

I received a phone call from Chevrolet requesting a meeting. Not knowing what was up, I agreed. Chevrolet asked me if I would consider selling my franchise back. I was flabbergasted because unless there is real trouble that was an extremely rare occurrence. There was in fact, trouble, but it had nothing to do with me as you will soon see.

What did I tell the Chevy people? I informed them that everything was for sale, that is, with the exception of my wife, who owns our home. They laughed at my joke but they were dead serious about getting me to sell. I told them that I would think it over. On the surface, the whole thing didn't make any sense. But I figured if they wanted it so badly, there must be a reason. And I was to learn that reason when I received a phone call from a contact whom I had within the hallowed halls of General Motor's corporate headquarters.

My contact was an intensely loyal GM guy, but he was unhappy about what was behind the company's pitch to get me to sell. Eventually, he spilled the beans and it was to prove a most interesting tale which surely occurred in other businesses as well. There was a nearby dealer, an African-American fellow who claimed that Chevy was treating him unfairly. He claimed that these dealers were given secondary locations and he had threatened to expose their poor treatment of African-American car dealers. What really frightened GM was that he threatened to bring Jesse Jackson and his organization into the mix. As a public company, GM was terrified of any negative publicity, and certainly of any possible boycott. They were anxious to placate the man and asked him which dealership he thought was most attractive in his area. He mentioned ours and they told him they would see if they could get it for him. So, with this information in hand, I knew I had GM in a very favorable position. If we were playing poker then you could see that I was holding four aces. I did not want anyone to see my cards, not even my own lawyer or partner. I told no one of the phone conversation. After several months of negotiations, we agreed on a price and all I will tell you was that it is that it was a premium one. Part of the deal was for the lease on the property, and, as you shall soon see why, I did not want the new dealer's name on the lease. The fifteen-year lease had Chevrolet as the lessee. Now I just needed to collect rent from General Motors, which, of course, gave me little pause. It was among America's largest and most profitable industrial companies. No one at the time could have imagined it would have the kind of trouble that the car company has experienced in the last couple of years. A bankruptcy and government ownership were still more than decade away.

How did the new dealer do, coming into the dealership in the go-go economic times of the 90s? Well, this fellow had the dealership there for several years and ran into all sorts of problems despite, the $1.3 million that GM spent in renovating the building. Notwithstanding, he lasted for about five years and GM bought him out. Chevy brought in several other dealers. They did not fare much better. By 2006, they had put their last dealer in and had essentially given up on having a viable dealership at the location. The lot was vacant but they were still paying me rent and were scheduled to do so for three more years when the lease ran out. Once again, they came to me with a proposition. First they wanted me to sell them the dealership. Now they wanted to buy out of their lease early. Like the sale of the dealership, I was in a favorable position and I worked out a deal with General Motors in which it ended up paying Old Orchard 92% against its original offer of 50%. This resulted in our receiving a very substantial sum which, of course, I shared with my partner George. Now there was only one question left for me; what to do with the large lot? The dealer who was leasing the property at the end of the thirteenth year had an option to purchase the property. That dealer served us with notice of his intention to purchase. I was very upset because I felt that we would not get the top price. Fortunately for us, the dealer decided to terminate his lease having lost millions of dollars and was vacating the property. I had him sign a waiver of this provision in the lease which precluded any other person from having any other option to purchase the property. Although the letter was never tested in the courts, it deterred Chevrolet from selling its lease to a third party with that person having an option to buy. Chevrolet remained the lesee for three more years and eventually we reached a buyout agreement. Mazel again!

    The only thing left to do was to find a buyer for the property. Remember when I first laid my eyes on the lot, how enamored I was with this piece of prime real estate. There were various real estate brokers who had clients that may be interested in purchasing the property, all large box retailers who needed a location for their stores. At that time, I was also approached by the president of Rush Hospital whom I knew. He informed me that Rush would have to seek a partner to continue in the operation of the hospital and eventually chose nearby Evanston

Hospital. He asked me not to negotiate directly with any other potential partner. His feeling was that Evanston and Rush could strike an agreement provided the Old Orchard lot was part of the deal. The president and I negotiated and agreed on a price, shook hands, and I promised him that I would not contact Evanston Hospital. After many months, a formal contract was signed between Old Orchard and Rush Skokie. After many months, Evanston and Rush reached an agreement and the property was sold as part of their agreement. I was now out of the business.

Clio Awards

The movies have their Oscars, the theater has its Tonys, and television has the Emmys. In the world of advertising, there are the Clios. It all started out as a rather small affair, run out of a New York City brownstone by a man named Wally Ross who had been the owner of the newsletter, "Ross Reports on Television." Ross brought on an assistant named Bill Evans whom he ultimately sold the business to in the early 1970s. Evans expanded the entire operation which consisted of a gala evening celebration at the Waldorf Astoria where all of the prominent members of the worldwide advertising community would gather just as those in the motion picture industry would on Oscar night. This was a for-profit operation and the money would be made through the fees paid each time an ad agency submitted an entry. Evans increased the categories and media for which awards were given, thereby increasing the revenue.

Bill Evans did very well at this and with a staff of eleven, put on some great gala evenings year after year. But as the decade of the 1980s came to a close, trouble awaited Evans and the Clios. Evans was spending money like a drunken sailor and there were rumors that he had become a heavy drug user, rumors which turned out to be fact when the NYPD Narcotics Squad raided his apartment. By 1991, his staff had quit after he missed one too many payrolls and the show that year did not go real well. Evans did not show up at all, and the caterer ended up filling in as master of ceremonies. The evening collapsed and like a scene out of a movie, people stormed out, with some grabbing the unclaimed Clio awards. Clio is named for the Greek muse of history and after that night it looked like the Clios were, in fact, history.

As you are reading this, you are probably thinking, great Sam but what does this sordid tale have to do with you? Well, I'll tell you. I had a legal client named Jimmy Smyth who had founded a company in 1972 called Optimus. Jimmy was an interesting fellow. He was from a large working class Irish Catholic family in the Austin section of Chicago. His ambition was probably fueled by his hardscrabble youth, and believe me, he had plenty of it. He had real talent, too, and ran Optimus which was a video post-production company, meaning that it was a critical final element in the process of producing television commercials. His clients were some of the largest ad agencies and Jim had built the operation to thirty people or so. Smyth was something of a creative genius and Optimus was doing some cutting edge work.

There was only one problem with the operation. To do that cutting edge work, Jim had to have the best video equipment around. The problem with this equipment was two-fold: it was expensive to purchase and it became obsolete very fast, nearly every year. Jimmy was always scrambling financially and had acquired a good deal of debt from a variety of lenders. Holding them at bay was my job. By 1985, things had gotten serious.

The lenders requested a meeting at Optimas' office, a meeting that would be presided over by a committee of the creditor's lawyers, all guys from white shoe firms. I was ready for them and had discussed with Jim the somewhat unorthodox game plan for handling them which he agreed to follow. The meeting was not going well as the lawyers were going over the litany of complaints and trying to squeeze us out of a reasonable negotiating position. Finally, after these guys were done, I looked at the lead lawyer, and went over to him and dropped a set of keys on the conference table. I said to him, "you are right. My client does not deserve to be running this business. Here are the keys to the office. Good luck!" Just like the minister who was hounding me when I handed him the deed to our building, I knew the last thing these creditors wanted was to own a post-production video company. You can make such a dramatic play only when you have some idea of how it will be received. Jim and I then walked out of the conference room and we had just gotten back to his office for coffee when they asked us to come back into the conference room. The lawyer handed the keys back and we proceeded to hammer out a revision of the loan agreement.

Jim got some breathing room but caught the break of his career in 1986. It was terrific mazel when he was approached by the Creative Services subsidiary of Anheuser Busch in St. Louis which was looking to add a post-production capability to its in-house staff. "Would he be willing to sell?" they asked him. Would he ever. The sale was negotiated for multi millions and Jim had enough to pay off all of his creditors with enough left over to retire. A happy client, Jimmy bought a yacht and was content to sail the Caribbean, at least for a time.

Paula and I were off sailing with Jim and his wife Ellen in 1992 when he told me about the debacle with the CLIOS. He was very familiar with the scene, having won CLIOs himself and had heard that there was a major fallout from the disaster at the dinner in 1991. By the following year, Ruth Ratny, a woman from Chicago who ran a local newsletter on the video production

Paula and I with Jimmy and Ellen Smyth aboard their yacht in the Carribbean

science called "Screen," put in a bid along with several others from the bankruptcy court. She had a backer with deep pockets and with experience in a similar business whom I will leave unnamed, but then attempted to cut him out of the deal when she claimed that she had bought the trademark for Bill Evans for $10,000 and a promise to pay Bill enough money to meet his "needs." She attempted to reorganize the thing as the New Clio Awards. Well, the whole matter ended up in litigation and the key person to testify was one of Bill's employees who explained how the whole supposed deal transpired. The court ultimately ruled that the sale of the trademark was not a valid sale of the company and that she either had to come up with a bid that was market value or it would be put to an open bid.

In the interim, the court allowed Ruth Ratny to put on the show in 1992. The show was hardly a great success, attracting roughly one-third of the crowd and the entries of the previous shows. The future of the Clios was seriously in doubt. Ruth knew Jimmy Smyth and came to see if he would want to invest in the company since she had little cash and had lost her other backer. She wanted Jimmy's cash but seemed to give up little in return, so we decided that Jimmy should make a bid directly to the bankruptcy court, a fair bid that was ultimately accepted. I became a minority partner, owning roughly one-third of the Clios—not too bad for a kid from Spring Valley who knew next to nothing about advertising.

True, we got the Clios for a good price but that was largely because after the disaster in 1991 and the lackluster show of 1992, the asset that was the CLIOS was in serious jeopardy. The advertising community had soured on them and it was our job to help restore confidence in the value of the awards. Fortunately, Jim had a plan to accomplish this. Since the Clios were truly an international award, Jim decided that we should travel the world to meet face to face with the leading executives and figures in the advertising community. When I say we, there was another person whom I should mention: Michael Demitreadus. Michael had been with the Clios for many years and is one of the most knowledgeable people in the advertising awards area. We took out a map and with the help of a travel agent began plotting our course. Jim would handle the United States and Great Britain. The rest of the world was ours.

The obvious question you are probably asking yourself is, "Sam, you didn't know anything about the car business, but bought a dealership. Well, you had general business experience and a group of talented managers around you. But this is the advertising field. These guys have their own lingo and their own way of doing things. How can a novice in this area help restore confidence in the Clios?" No need to worry. I was way ahead of you. Jim and Mike gave me a crash course in advertising and I was a willing student. I learned the jargon and the codewords. Even came up with a half hour spiel that I could give to any advertising audience. I was like a politician about to hit the stump.

Jim made important structural changes to the Clios. The actual statutes are made by the same folks who make the Academy Awards. The company, RS Owens, is located here in Chicago and Jim came up with a new design for the award. He also cut down on the number of awards so we went from 14% of the submissions winning to 1-2%. The more who win the more it becomes devalued and Jim helped bring back the prestige to the brand. He also changed the venue over time, bringing it to cities other than New York and it was held at various locales, helping generate additional interest in the show.

By now you probably realized how much I love to travel. Mike and I ran up the frequent flyer miles. One of our key targets was Japan. We had taken two junkets there but had found only limited success. I then received a letter from the CEO of a major agency based in Tokyo. He was retiring from the business and was going to start an advertising school. Seeking advice, he sent out letters to all major companies involved in advertising throughout the wold. I received the letter that was sent to Clio and it was my job to respond. I replied with a three-page letter which apparently impressed him. His secretary called me and told me that he was planning on framing the letter and putting it behind his chair in his new office. She also told me that he would like to meet with me on my next trip to Japan. When that occurred several months later, I called his office and found out that the man was at the bedside of his father, who was critically ill at the time. He had arranged for me to go out to dinner with his administrative assistant and the assistant to the administrator, both of whom were fluent in English. It turned out to be a great evening and was the breakthrough we needed. The CEO then advised the other major agencies that he was going to submit ads to the Clios. It was obvious that if the leading agency was sending ads in, then all the others would follow, which they did. We met with great success in Malaysia, Singapore, Australia and Korea. We were a big hit in the Far East.

In Korea with one of the Clio Award representatives

Seoul was particularly receptive. I spoke on three separate occasions there. My first speech attracted about twenty agency executives. By my third speech I had a crowd of about sixty industry people. They not only had Clios submitted, but, through an interpreter, told me that they were committed to bringing their people to the gala awards show, which we began holding that year in San Francisco. At the show in San Francisco, we had one hundred and twenty Koreans.

Mike and I attended trade shows to gin up interest. In Bali, we caught a break. We had set up a booth where we showed the Clio winners for the last ten years. In attendance was a gentleman who was in charge of an advertising school in South Africa. We had been trying to get in to see Nina de Klerk, who was the head of the trade association and the sister-in-law of the country's Prime Minister, F. W. de Klerk. The South Africans were not participating in the Clios because of the 1991 disaster in New York.

When Paula and I arrived in Johannesburg, we learned that Nelson Mandella, who had shared the Nobel Peace Prize with President de Klerk, had convened a meeting of influential business leaders to explore the ways in which he might increase the number of blacks in the advertising industry. I also spoke before students and execs in Johannesburg and was warmly received. Since the meeting that was held with representatives of Mandella ended early Friday, I wanted to see if Ms. de Klerk could meet with me that afternoon. I was informed by her secretary that our meeting is for Monday morning and was scheduled for 30 minutes. We met Monday morning and our thirty minute meeting turned into a friendly 2½ hour gabfest. She promised a meeting with the head of the association and that this would be tantamount to getting us approved for the South Africans to resubmit for evaluation. This was a big win for us.

We had other successes in Africa as I had previously met the president of Namibia, Hage Geingob, who had received an honorary degree from Columbia College. Since I was on the board of Columbia College at the time he received the honorary degree, he had extended an invitation to any board member who wanted to visit Namibia. I took him up on his offer. We were given the royal treatment in Namibia, taken to one of the finest game reserves in the world. At the time, Namibia was having an advertising contest. As a representative of the Clios, I was asked to become involved in the contest. I discussed with Jim the idea of awarding a trip to the award show in New York that year. Jim agreed. This got me on television shows and in the leading newspaper. I went over big in Namibia. It was a beautiful country and a highlight of my travels throughout the world.

By 1995, the show had made it back. It was enormously satisfying rescuing it from the brink. Two years later, Jim was approached by BPI Communications, a subsidiary of VNU of Holland, which published "Adweek" and other trade publications, with an offer to sell. That company was expanding beyond publishing and saw considerable synergy between the two entities. We took the offer and the deal closed in November of 1997. That firm still operates the show which is now a four-day extravaganza held in South Beach. Jim went back to his yacht and Mike went back into the fray, becoming executive director of New York Festivals, which holds award shows in the communications field. Several years later, he brought Jim in as CEO. The yachting life gets boring after a while I suppose, but retirement for me meant devoting my energies to helping those who did not have my good mazel.

CHAPTER 5

Charities

St. Joseph's Parish and School

In the introduction, I identified my feelings about charity and helping others as a primary motivation for me to write this book. It is something I have been involved with since my youth. Of course, the more success I enjoyed, the more I could give and the more I could do. Sometimes opportunities to do good developed in the course of my legal and business career. As I was thinking about my involvement with St. Joseph's Parish and School and Mallinckrodt College, two Catholic institutions, I see how seamlessly it all transpired.

When I owned Old Orchard Chevrolet, we were advertising a fifteen-passenger van in the newspaper. We had originally ordered it for a Korean church, as one of our salespeople was a member of that church. After taking delivery of the truck, the church called us and told us that it had made the determination that it could not afford it. We were in a bind and needed to unload it in a hurry. If you remember from the last chapter, there were heavy interest payments to GMAC once the vehicle was delivered, so we needed to sell it and sell it fast. The price we were asking for in the paper was $1 over cost.

A few days later, a call came in from a church that was interested in the van. On the other line was Sister Stephanie Schmidt

Sister Stephanie and I at St. Joseph's School (since closed) in front of the beautiful mural made by the students

Fr. Sebastian Lewis

who was affiliated with St. Joseph's Parish. (Old St. Joseph, as it was known, was founded in 1836, concurrent with the City of Chicago. Along with Old St. Mary's and Old St. Patrick's, it is among the oldest parishes in Chicago. Originally, it was located near where Holy Name Cathedral is today. In 1871, with the Great Chicago Fire, it burned down and then was reorganized at State and Chicago Avenue before its present location was finished being built at 1107 North Orleans.)

I returned the call to Sister Stephanie and she told me that their school, St. Joseph's, needed a large van to take the children to various activities. Their vehicle had seen its better days and was no longer serviceable. So, what was preventing her from coming down to the showroom and buying the van? Well, their major obstacle was money. They had only six hundred dollars, but told me that if they could raise ten thousand dollars for the van, a charitable foundation would match the sum. However, there was only one problem in all of this. They had no way of raising the ten thousand dollars.

If you remember from my discussion of my law practice, I was a co-trustee of various charitable trusts with different major banks and that we would be making allotments on one of these trusts within the next two weeks, which signaled the end of the fiscal period. I suggested that Sister Stephanie and Father Sebastian Lewis, who was the pastor of the parish, come out to the dealership and we would see if there was a way of helping them. They came by and the van seemed to be exactly what they were looking for. I sat them down and told them that there was a possibility of getting them the ten thousand dollars. Of course, as the co-trustee, I had a major role in choosing the charities, but I wanted to ensure that there would be no conflict of interest in making the grant. Therefore, the letter that I had them write indicated the grant would be used to buy the van from Old Orchard Chevrolet. My co-trustee felt that there was no conflict of interest and that this particular grant met all of our requirements. Sister Stephanie wanted to know how the letter should read, so I told her that I would dictate a letter that would help meet the charitable gift. She sent the letter to the corporate co-trustee and he called me after receiving it, then told me that we can give them the ten thousand dollars. I had him call Sister Stephanie and inform her that the money would be available to St. Joseph's and ask her what the charitable foundation needed in writing to confirm that fact. All was accomplished as he sent St. Joseph's a letter which indicated that a check would be forthcoming and any other language that the other foundation required. They then showed that letter to the foundation had promised the matching grant and now they had the funds. She called me and was so excited that I sent the information to the insurance company, and, meanwhile, we had the van undercoated, Simonized, and ready for delivery.

We arranged to have the van delivered within a week, so I drove into the City along with one of my managers. As we neared St. Joseph's, we were greeted with a sight that I will remember all the rest of my days. Before me were three hundred black children singing hymns in my honor. Can you imagine being serenaded by three hundred kids? Where else could you get such treatment? It was quite a scene and I could barely contain myself. I think anyone would have felt some tears well up if he were greeted like that. And it wasn't over yet. They held a party at the school which a number of church dignitaries attended. Lo and behold, the Jewish kid from Spring Valley had become a hero.

Sister Stephanie was ecstatic about the van and saw the events which had unfolded in purely religious terms. To her, it was a matter of Divine Providence and she asked me what parish I belonged to; I told her that I was not Catholic, not even Protestant, but Jewish. She paused for a second and said, "Thank you, Lord!" What did she mean by that? She expressed to me that the purpose of her life had now been fulfilled. To her, this fulfillment very much related to her religious order. The religious order that she belonged to was Our Lady of Sion and it had an interesting history to it. It was founded in mid-19th-century Rome by two Jewish apostates from a prominent family of bankers. Both of them were to become priests. Though their original charter involved outreach to Jews, their mission changed over time to an educational one as well as one to promote understanding between Catholics and Jews. Though I have no way of knowing for sure, I suspect that the Holocaust and the Church's role in it, as controversial as that has been, must have influenced in some way the nature of Our Lady of Sion.

The man running the show at St. Joseph's was Father Sebastian Lewis. Though we were of different religions, we shared many things in common. Father Sebastian had attended St. Bede's Academy in Peru, Illinois, around one and a half miles from Spring Valley. As you probably noted in my many references to Spring Valley, a small town makes for the ultimate small world where people are acquainted with one another. In keeping with that idea, Father Lewis was well acquainted with the Buckman family. While a student at St. Bede's, he was a star athlete, and, after being ordained a Benedictine monk, returned to St. Bede's to teach for a decade, coming to St. Joseph's as assistant pastor, and, after nine years, took over as pastor. He would remain there for forty years before retiring in 2001.

Due to his Peru connection and Father Sebastian Lewis' warm personality, we instantly felt comfortable with one another. After the van had been delivered, I received a phone call from Father Sebastian one day. He suggested that we have lunch and meet at a restaurant named O'Brien's, and there was a reason for that. The O'Briens were prominent members of his congregation and were major donors. Anyone who ever said there is no such thing as a free lunch never ate at O'Brien's with Father Sebastian.

The lunch conversation revolved around what was called the school's "Outreach Program." This consisted of people who volunteered by helping the students with their homework after school had let out. The parents of most of the children worked all day and therefore this after-school program was imperative for the success and well being of the children. The volunteers and the children needed to be fed during the hours of the program and there was a special board of directors that was organized for the sole purpose of raising funds for this endeavor. Father Sebastian asked me if I would serve on this board. Naturally, I would be the only non-Catholic on the board, a status that I was getting pretty used to by now.

The main vehicle to fund the program came from an annual benefit dinner held at—you guessed it—O'Brien's. The O'Briens paid for the whole evening, complete with fine food and liquor, of course. Though St. Joseph's charged one hundred dollars a person, the seating was limited, so they raised the same amount of money every year. Though the O'Briens were very generous in underwriting the event, there needed to be another way to raise additional funds. After developing a friendship with the Father, I felt it was time to make a suggestion. There were two kindergarten classes with approximately twenty children in each class. Anyone in attendance at the dinner could "adopt" one of the kindergarten children for an additional $150. Of course, this was not a legal adoption but was more like a sponsorship. They would receive a picture of the cute kid at the dinner and get a Christmas card and report card, which served as a thank you.

Father Sebastian was somewhat reluctant to initiate my idea. As you may have gathered from their problems in acquiring the van, the parish was very poor. Finally, he spoke to the board and they unanimously approved the idea. The suggestion was made that I be the one to introduce this program at the next annual dinner. We were not sure how many people would become sponsors and sure enough only six stepped up that first year. But within five years, we had increased the number to forty. That amounted to $6,000, which doubled our annual funds raised at the dinner.

The school had many other needs besides this after-school program and I sought to do what I could to improve the school. During my time, I helped oversee a complete expansion of the school's library. We made sure to have both old-fashioned resources like World Book encyclopedias and new ones, like computers so that the kids would have the same opportunities as those of better-funded schools. Though I was very proud to play a part in all of this, it was a concerted effort by everyone on the board. We attracted so many new contributors that Father Sebastian was running out of wall space to hang all of the new plaques—a good problem for a school to have. A new universe was opened to these children and many lives were changed. Money helped but it was the initiative of the dedicated teachers which made it all happen. Then it was up to the students themselves to progress in their education and a fair number of them went on to college and most importantly, have gone on to lead productive lives.

I should say a word about the neighborhood. St. Joseph's is located adjacent to an area known as "Cabrini-Green." Originally the area was German and then Italian. Then public housing came in and what made this near north-side project so unusual was its location. Most public housing was built on the west or south sides, concentrated in predominately African-American neighborhoods. But Cabrini-Green, as it came to be known, was adjacent to Lincoln Square and not all that far from the high rises of the Gold Coast and the ritzy shops on Michigan Avenue. The contrast was a stark one as the series of public housing projects built there became cesspools of crime and drugs. Gangs were everywhere. Two police officers were gunned down by snipers. A girl was brutally raped and poisoned. Mayor Jane Byrne, flanked by a bevy of police officers, moved into one of the worst of the public housing projects there in what can be described only as a political publicity stunt. She lasted all of three weeks with the extensive police detail that kept watch over her leaving as well.

Into this steaming cauldron of violence and poverty, stepped Father Sebastian Lewis. Though the population was overwhelmingly non-Catholic, it was invited into the church and into the school. To give you some idea of the mettle of the man. I quote from the "Tribune's" obituary, "In 1985, when asked why he and the other ministers had come together to take back Cabrini-Green playgrounds, he told the Tribune, 'We are doing this to answer the resident's cry for help.' And help he did. He created scholarship programs for kids, all the while taking up the cause of the residents. If they were looking for a better life, they could not have had a better ally than the Father. He finally retired in 2001, and, with this event, my involvement with the school came to an end. It is something I am really proud of and something which gave me so much pleasure. What happened to my friend? He didn't retire to Florida, but, instead, went back to his old stomping grounds of St. Bede's in Peru, Illinois, appointed as prior of the monastery there. In 2003, St. Bede's Academy elected him to their athletic Hall of Fame. Obviously, Father Sebastian epitomized all of the qualities that the institution was trying to implant in its students. He set a powerful example. In 2006, he passed away. A great loss. A great man."

Mallinckrodt College

The dealership seemed to be a portal to meeting all kinds of interesting folks, and, as in the case of St. Joseph's, this next group turned out again to be Catholic. One day, as I was walking through the dealership to my office, I happened to notice that there were two nuns dressed in full habit purchasing a new Chevy from one of my salesman. This was not something you saw every day and I went over and introduced myself and welcomed them to the dealership. They told me that they were affiliated with Mallinckrodt College in Wilmette. At the time, it was a two-year college located not far away from my home. I told them that we would extend every possible courtesy and charge them the same price that we do our own employees when they purchase a car from us. Naturally, they were pleased.

The following day I received a call from Sister Patrice Noterman, who was the head of the school. Before purchasing the car from us, she had been driving a beat-up old truck with a snow plow attached to the front so she really appreciated the

Mallinckrodt College
Blessed Pauline von Mallinckrodt
(Courtesy of Sisters of Christian Charity, Western Province Archives)

opportunity to drive a new car. I told her to feel free to stop in whenever she was going past the dealership, and, if she called in advance, then I would arrange to meet her.

One day, the sister took me up on the invitation and we ended up having coffee together in my office. We discussed a whole host of matters including the financial condition of the college. She asked me if I was Catholic and just as when Sister Stephanie had asked, I told her that I was Jewish. Why did she want to know? Apparently she was interested in having a non-Catholic businessperson on the Board of Trustees and asked me if I would consider such an assignment. The board consisted of several nuns, a priest, and several lay Catholics. Sam Pfeffer on this board would be quite a novelty and I told the sister I would be very honored to serve.

Several days after my meeting with Sister Patrice, I was delivered a copy of the school's financial statement. I was shocked to learn that the school was heavily in debt. Buildings were in dire need of repair. The library was undergoing a major renovation at the cost of $75,000. Well, you are probably wondering what is coming next. This appeared to me to be an opportunity to help as if Providence were prevailing again. I was involved with another trust at the time (not the same one that gave the $10,000 to St. Joseph's), which, in this case, was giving away $75,000 and was in the process of making decisions about our recipients. I was aware of the fine work being done by the nuns who were the educators at Mallickrondt. The college was able to exist because of the low cost of paying the nuns (the order was given a small stipend which was used for the living and maintaince of the order). One of the trusts that you have heard about was nearing the end of its fiscal period and we were poised to make a distribution. I discussed the matter with the co-trustee and we agreed to disburse the $75,000.

Sister Patrice was naturally overjoyed at the turn of events and insisted that there should be a dedication held for the renovated library. A Sunday afternoon was chosen and Sister Patrice thought that it should all be done in the proper ecumenical spirit. In keeping with that, she suggested that the rabbi of my synagogue deliver the keynote speech. It was a beautiful event and has to be one of the few times that cloistered nuns dressed in their full habits had assembled to listen to a rabbi. Talk about ecumenicalism. That was some scene.

Most Catholic colleges are run by religious orders and Mallinckrodt was no exception. Other similar institutions in the United States had the educational institution legally separated from the religious order. This involved the order entering into a lease agreement with the college. I proposed doing this at Mallickrodt. Why did I want to do this? Did I have something against the order? Of course not, but with such a separation in place, the college would then become eligible to receive funds from the federal government. The nuns of the Mallinckrodt religious order were reluctant to enter into such a lease as they occupied the top two floors of a four story building. The nuns were concerned that they might one day become evicted from their home. After the dedication of the library, Sister Patrice asked me to speak with the nuns and impress upon them the need for the lease and that such an arrangement would not be harmful to them. I spoke to them and explained the situation. Judging by their response, it was clear that they had complete trust in me. They agreed to sign the lease, and, sure enough, we received some federal funds.

I tried to do whatever I could to help Mallinckrodt, but it became clear over a period of time that it was too late to revive the college. The debt load was too burdensome and the ongoing capital needs too hefty for such a small institution. I had a heart-to-heart with Sister Patrice about the situation, a difficult but necessary conversation. I laid out the financial picture and told her, in my opinion, the most prudent course of action would be to sell the school to a suitable partner. She agreed and we discussed that the most likely purchaser would be Loyola University.

We ended up holding some pretty extensive negotiations with Loyola University and eventually came to terms although I did not have any direct participation in the meetings that were held. One of the requirements on our part was that the nuns be permitted to stay in their residence. Loyola agreed and had the resources to make the kind of physical changes that were necessary. One of the first things it did was re-wire the entire building at a cost of one million dollars. This was in 1991 and Loyola operated its School of Education at the Wilmette campus for about ten years, finally selling it in 2001. It sold the campus to a developer who was going to convert the large and beautiful building to condominiums, eighty units in total. Remember that I had given the nuns my word that they would always have a home on the grounds that had been their home for so many years. Since the development necessitated them being displaced, the developer agreed to build a small building behind it which would comfortably house the nuns. They were quite pleased with their brand new home.

The nuns wanted to do something to thank me for my concern for their well being and so for my seventy-fifth birthday,

The inauguration of then Sister M. Patrice Noterman as President of Mallinchrodt College. From left to right: Sister M. Andre Blanchard, provincial superior of the Western Province; Sister M Patrice Noterman; and Sister Marcella Ripper. Sister Marcella had been Dean and later, President of the College.
(Courtesy of Sisters of Christian Charity, Western Province Archives)

they presented me with a most meaningful gift. At a special coffee, they gave me a photograph, lock of hair, and a metal engraving of the order's founder, Pauline Von Mallinckrodt (1817-1881), who started the order in her native Germany. This woman was not only the founder of their order, but she continues to inspire all of the nuns to the present day. Her famous words spoken back in 1849 were "Let the spirit of youthful joyousness be characterstic of us." Good words to live by.

    What became of my friend, Sister Patrice? While remaining president of the college and after receiving her doctorate, Sister Patrice decided to leave the Sisters of Christian Charity, and she became known as Dr. Patrice. She maintained her presidency of the college until the school was sold. Her life took an interesting turn after she had been invited to a college graduation party given by a young lady who had been a student of hers when she was the principal of a Catholic girl's grade school. The young lady's mother had passed away many years earlier and Sister Patrice rekindled a friendship with the family. Eventually, she married the father of this girl, who had a very successful career in law enforcement, including serving as the head of the FBI office in Chicago. Together, they are a happy couple with Dr. Patrice continuing her life of good works with various Catholic organizations.

Catholic Orphans of Acapulco

Acapulco, Mexico is one of the most beautiful sites in North America. True, with all of its tourist developments and resorts it has lost something of its pristine qualities, but beautiful it still is. Once the vacation destination of Hollywood's rich and famous, the seaside city on Mexico's west coast now is home to many college students looking for sun and fun during Spring Break. La Quebrada is the place where cliff divers jump 145 feet down to the water, one of its great attractions.

One group which frequented Acapulco comprised several businessmen who owned retail flower shops in the Chicago area. I was acquainted with them because I represented several of them in my legal practice. They were friendly competitors, so much so that they even vacationed together. They would all rent a home and have a great time in the Acapulco sun. These folks were all Catholic and quite religious to boot. They would attend the large church in the city but had decided that the following year they would like to try a smaller one which they reasoned might be more intimate.

The following year two of their employees in the flower shop business vacationed for a few weeks before the main group arrived. The two fellows found an orphanage which housed a small church. They were hugely impressed with the entire operation, the church, the orphanage, and, most importantly, the priest. In this case, the padre's name was Father Angel Martinez. When the main group came for its vacation, it heard about the orphanage from Leonard and Chuck and were most anxious to see it. They attended services on Sunday and realized that they found their new place of worship.

There are plenty of lapsed Catholics around but you tend to forget just how commited so many people are to the Church and its teachings. During their vacation, several members of the group met a young couple who had been married, though only civilly. They became quite friendly with this couple and told them that if they got married in the Church, then the group would pay for everything, including a fancy party which would include any guests that the couple cared to invite. The couple must have been touched by their generosity and were amenable to the offer. After the ceremony, the party got underway and apparently it was quite a celebration. As I remember, there was a line from a Western movie which went, "When these folks fiesta, they really know how to fiesta." And these folks knew how to fiesta. It was in the midst of this fiesta, in the wee hours of a frosty Chicago morning in the winter of 1976, that I received a phone call from Bud Alfirevic, one of the leaders of the group. Bud was a friend and a client who wanted to know if there was a way that we could form a charitable organization for the purpose of helping the orphanage and bringing eighteen of the children to the Chicago area for a visit. Like I said it was the wee hours of the morning, which except for my friend and client Joe K., was not normally a time when I answered legal questions. I told Bud that the hour was either too early or too late, depending on your perspective, and he was too inebriated, and, frankly I was too tired to discuss the matter. I told him to call me later that morning.

Bud called me at the office, and apologized for waking me up earlier. With great enthusiasm, he clued me in about the wedding and then informed me that they had promised the Padre that they would bring the youngsters to Chicago. We enlisted the help of a certain Catholic priest, a friend of Bud's, and we would hold fundraisers under the auspices of the Society for the Propagation of the Faith, a nineteenth century association

*With Padre Angel at the annual fundraising banquet
held here in Chicago*

begun in France designed to help the same kind of work that Father Angel Martinez was engaged in his Acapulco orphanage.

Padre Angel, as he is known, is an amazing man. He is only two years younger than I and is a real bundle of energy. He has been a priest for nearly sixty years and found his calling helping Mexico's unfortunate: the poor, the sick, the widowed, and, of course, the orphans, of which the country in general and Acapulco in particular are not in shorty supply. Charity begins at home and so it began with Padre Angel fifty years ago when he personally took in four youngsters. Since then, he has built facilities that not only house, feed, and educate the children, but he is providing extensive vocational training so that these young boys (he has also built a home for girls) will be able to provide for themselves. One of his latest projects is an ostrich farm which will not only provide much needed funds for the institution, but will teach the boys a practical skill.

Father Angel's Children's Home for Boys and Girls

The name of the orphanage is Father Angel's Children Homes for Boys and Girls. The vast majority of the monies donated come from the group that we formed, giving him the funding for all these new buildings like the new library, dorms, and school. After forming the charity, we began to hold annual dinner dances to raise funds for the orphanage. The event is going on its thirty-sixth year and the banquet hall owner where the dinner is held, Ted Kaminsky, supplies a large portion of the food and liquor as his personal donation. Any additional expenses, he charges us at cost. At our first dance in 1976, we charged fifty dollars a person and have raised the price only about twenty dollars in the intervening years. This included food, beverages and party favors. At the height of the event's popularity, we had two bands: a conventional American one and a Marachi one. In keeping with the Mexican theme, we had a tequila bar, which was greatly enjoyed by everyone including Father Martinez and me. Often by the end of the end of evening I was giving out blessings, though I was not ordained. In recent years, we have transitioned to a disc jockey. Each year a different florist would be in charge of the decorations. Though the florists were among the founders of the orginal group numbering forty or fifty, fewer than five of us remain. All of these services for the event are donated. One of the developments is that the Padre and I have become quite close and he has now become a monsignor. Our two backgrounds could not have been more different, but, like Father Sebastian and Sister Stephanie, we shared a common concern for humanity. I considered Padre Angel and I to be "comrades in arms."

It seems only appropriate that we have done something for the people of Mexico here in Chicago. The largest population of Mexicans in the United States resides in the Los Angeles area but number two is Chicago and the greater metro area has over one million Mexicans. One year we had the pleasure of having the Mexican Consul General and his wife in attendance. They remarked to me how amazed they both were that so much good has been accomplished on behalf of the orphans of Acapulco. And to think it all started out with a group of florists on vacation. Who says that each one of us simple folk cannot make a real difference in the world?

Before we leave this section which has dealt with three different Catholic organizations that I have been involved with, I must relate a story. Remember when I told you how our law firm was an exercise in ecumenicalism, with Pfeffer as the Jew, Becker as the Protestant, and Gabric as the Catholic? Well, Ralph had gotten lung cancer and underwent surgery in New York City at Memorial Sloan-Kettering Cancer Center. Ralph developed a severe infection after recuperating at home, with his fever running at 105. He was ordered back to the hospital in New York during Memorial Day weekend. I encouraged his wife, Joan, to take the kids to the local parade telling her that I would accompany Ralph to New York.

Ralph was in such bad shape that at the airport he did not recognize Paula. But thank God, the surgery was a success and after the surgery, he looked like a new person. On Sunday, I took Ralph to Catholic services and watched as the priest would anoint parishioners with holy water. Ralph, with his great sense of humor told the priest, "Don't annoint Sam with holy water. He sells us the holy water."

Thank God Ralph lived for many years after the surgery, but as he would attend the event for the Catholic Orphans of Acapulco, he loved to repeat the story of the holy water to Father Angel. The Father would bless people over the course of the evening (he would always give the women a rose) and when he would get to me he would say, "Sam, I am not going to to annoint you with holy water because you sell the church holy water." All in good fun, pushing our brand of ecumenicalism to its limits.

Columbia College

As you probably have figured out by now, I frequently get involved with organizations and institutions because of people I meet. Let me explain why that is. You meet a certain individual, get to know him a bit and become impressed with the individual and the manner in which he conducts himself. Such was the case with Columbia College. The president of the college in 1980 was Mike Alexandroff, who was very friendly with Seymour Gale, a senior partner in an accounting firm. Seymour was my consultant on all major accounting problems. Seymour was heavily involved with a variety of liberal and socialist causes and shared his political passions with Mike Alexandroff. They were part of an intellectual left wing clique that had among its most famous members Studs Terkel. Though I was very much a committed liberal, they were further on the left wing spectrum than I. Once you got to know these guys, it was impossible not to have great respect for their intellect and ideals even if you did not buy into their entire agenda. Seymour Gale, who was aware of my representing some very wealthy individuals, arranged a breakfast meeting with Mike and the three of us sat down and discussed Columbia College for two hours. Mike told me what he was trying to accomplish with the college and I listened intently. Foremost on his agenda was a heartfelt commitment to helping minority students receive an education. These students lacked the funds and the academic background that most colleges require. You may have picked up already that I have a soft spot for the underdog so Mike's vision appealed to me and piqued my curiousity.

Columbia College has a long and rich history. It traces its roots back to 1890 when it began as a women's college which offered preparation in speech and teaching. Named the Columbia School of Oratory, its founding and name were influenced no doubt by the Columbia Exposition, held in Chicago in that year. From the Columbia School of Oratory, it was renamed the the Columbia College of Expression in 1907. By 1928, the school was bankrupt though it survived as the "Ward of the Pestalozzi-Froevel Teachers College," a private teachers' college until 1939 when it was able to regain its independence as the Columbia College of Drama and Radio, and, finally in 1944, it became known by its current name, Columbia College.

The focus of the school since 1944 has been on communications, initally radio and later television, film, and video. Its founders, Ida Moory Riley and Mary Blood, were graduates of what is now known as Emerson College of Boston, a school with many similiarities to Columbia College. In that year of 1944, Norman Alexandroff, a Jewish immigrant who had come to the United States in 1902 as a fifteen-year old with no formal education, was a model autodidact, became president. Norman served the college for sixteen years until his death in 1960. His son Mike took over the following year and would serve as president of the college for thirty one years.

Mike worked to gain accreditation from the North Central Assocation and transformed the school into a modern, liberal arts college, albeit it with an emphasis on communications. The school expanded its physical facilities and had significant capital needs. I listened to Mike that day over breakfast and promised him that I would do anything and everything in my power to enhance the vision of Columbia College that he outlined to me.

I became a member of the Board of Trustees, and, eventually was awarded the status of "Lifetime Trustee." This, bestowed upon me by my fellow trustees, is a great honor.

Shortly after I became a member of the board, an opportunity developed to build an auditorium in the main Wabash Avenue building. For a communications oriented school, having a first class auditorium, is essential. The Woolworth Foundation had promised the school a matching grant of $250,000. If you were paying attention to the first two charities that I spoke about, you many remember that as the co-trustee of a sizeable trust, I was able to make a grant to the school. Well, I spoke to one of my law clients, Elizabeth F., about Columbia, and she was very enthusaiastic about making a $250,000 contribution to Columbia to help fund the auditorium. The theater at Columbia College is a beautiful room used for film screenings, lectures, and special events. We had a very nice dedication and Elizaebeth F., now long deceased, accomplished a great deal with this gift

The school was negotiating to buy a building on the southwest corner of 11th and Wabash. For many years this building had served as a warehouse for an auto parts company that was located in the South Loop. Well, the price tag on the building was $4,000,000, no small chunk of change, even by today's standards. Columbia had already incurred significant debt by acquiring other buildings that formed its South Loop campus and was hesitant to take on additional loans. While I was sympathetic to the College's position, I felt that this acquistion was necessary. It was to be used as the film and video arts building. This was a major growth area for the school and my feeling was that the growth would only continue.

The vote was taken and a majority of the board voted against acquiring the building. The chairman of the finance committee permitted me to recall the motion about the matter of the building purchase. In front of the board I recalled a matter that had occurred during my helm as the president of our synagogue. Well, my own syngagogue had a split, which, as you might surmise it does in many such splits, it had something to do with the rabbi. He left to start his own synagogue and took around 40% of our members with him. There was a certain lack of sincerity on the part of the rabbi and I decided to stay rather than leave. Our congregation decided that the best course of action would be to name as president someone who was not involved in the split, in this case it was my friend and prominent insurance fire adjuster, Ted Spak. He agreed to accept the presidency on the condition that I serve as his Executive Vice President because Ted did a great deal of traveling so a lot of the adminstrative burden fell on my sholuders.

Our synagogue had a serious problem on its hands, though not of a ritual or theological nature. It was a purely financial one. We were in the process of building a new synagogue when the division occurred. Talman Federal Savings and Loan had given us a construction mortgage of $1,500,000. The president of the bank was concerned that our ability to repay the loan would be severely hampered by the loss of 40% of our membership. There were rumors floating around that the loan would be canceled. By this time, I had become president of the synagogue, succeeding Ted. The bank wanted to cancel the loan. Although I had no proper authority to do so at the time, I met with the president of Talman and asked him if the loan would remain in effect if ten of our members would each sign a personal guarantee for $75,000. Shortly thereafter, I received a call from the president of Talman who told me that the decision was made to maintain the loan and would not require the personal guarantees.

Before I get too carried away with my discussion of one of the most thankless jobs that one could ever have, namely being a lay leader of a synagogue, let's get back to Columbia College. The building was an auto warehouse, and in this case, it was the warehouse of Warshawsky Auto Parts. Due to the special facade of the building, it was considered a historic landmark. At the time, Columbia had 40 members on its board. I said that if all of the members would each sign personally for $100,000, then the bank would give us the loan. Well, the motion was re-called and this time, the vote went in favor of buying the building, provided we could get the mortgage. Prior to receiving the mortgage, Columbia sent a letter of intent to Warshawsky's attorneys offering to purchase the building.

Remember that sometimes you need mazel. It came to us in the form of a gift to the college of $3,000,000 shortly after we made the decision to buy the building. The building became a big success and I have been able to obtain funds for the college to acquire additional facilites. After Mike Alexandroff retired in 1992, John Duff, a very capable educator and administrator, held the post for eight years before our current president, Warrick Carter, took over in 2000.

The Spertus Institute, orginally known as the College of Jewish Studies, and an institution that I was very familiar with, was moving to new quarters. Its old building was put up for sale when Spertus built its new building on the lot it owned directly to the north. Columbia was interested in buying Spertus's old building, and I made an introduction from Spertus's president to Columbia's. Columbia subsequently bought the building and is currently in the process of renovating.

As you may have gathered, Columbia College is a unique institution. It fosters in its students a sense of creativity in the classroom and prepares them for careers in a variety of different fields. Most of these involve the arts and media. I have always been a big fan of political cartoons and decided that one thing I would like to do would be to sponsor a contest for the students at Columbia in that field. I thought that this would not only bring recognition to hard working students but encourage them to seriously pursue this field. What has resulted from my vision is the Paula F. Pfeffer Political Cartoon Contest. In addition to the award there is prize money given away and I have taken the necessary steps to ensure that this will continue. We have a light luncheon at the school and the entire contest and event have been well received by faculty and students alike.

In June of 2011, I hope to be celebrating my 85th birthday. As you begin thinking about such milestones, you contemplate your life and think about what you have accomplished. Among my proudest achievements is my tenure of service to Columbia: that in some small way I was able to advance the cause of education. Most importantly helping students, particularly minorities, better themselves, gives me great *nachas* (satisfaction and pride). I always wanted to see young minority men carry pens instead of guns. I felt that only through receiving a decent education could this outcome prevail.

Shore Comunity Services

Columbia College was a well known institution in Chicago and produced many prominent alumni, some of whom are well known artists, photographers, actors, and others involved in every aspect of movie, television, and radio production. Collectively, they have had significant impact on the arts, the media, and the cultural life of our country. This is obviously very important, but there is a group of people who are not so well known. They are even well educated, though they are exceptional in their own way. I speak of those with mental and physical disabilties. If the graduates of Columbia College are often involved with professions that are considered interesting and cutting edge by employment standards, those clients of Shore Community Service do work that is repetitive, manual, and mundane. However, to them it is a lifeline.

Shore Community Services has been around for fifty years. It started out running educational programs for mentally retarded children and expanding its offerings to include vocational and life training to adults who are developmentally disabled. It currently operates centers in Park Ridge and Evanston, and several buildings in Skokie where they employ clients who work in light assembly for a variety of companies, in addition to a packaging plant in Morton Grove. The clients are more than just people who

Debora Braun, Associate Executive Director of Shore; Gerald Gulley, Executive Director; Mary Matz, Development Officer

punch a timeclock. The centers feed them and provide practical assistance in dealing with the types of challenges that these wonderful people face every day of their lives. Every aspect of the facilites was designed with the handicapped in mind, and, if you visit Shore, you will see some in wheelchairs and others using walkers. The staff has more than just empathy to supply. It is simply an exceptional group of people. It is true there are greedy and selfish people in this world, and I have met and dealt with my fair share over the years. But the folks who run and staff Shore are the kind of people who can restore whatever faith you may have lost in the human race. Like every other organization or business, leadership starts from the top. Jerry Gulley, Executive Director of Shore, is the rare type of person, with total devotion to his calling. To me, he is very much like Padre Angel, though he is in charge of a secular institution. There is a very real difference between a job and a calling, something which will become clear when you visit Jerry in his office. One of the

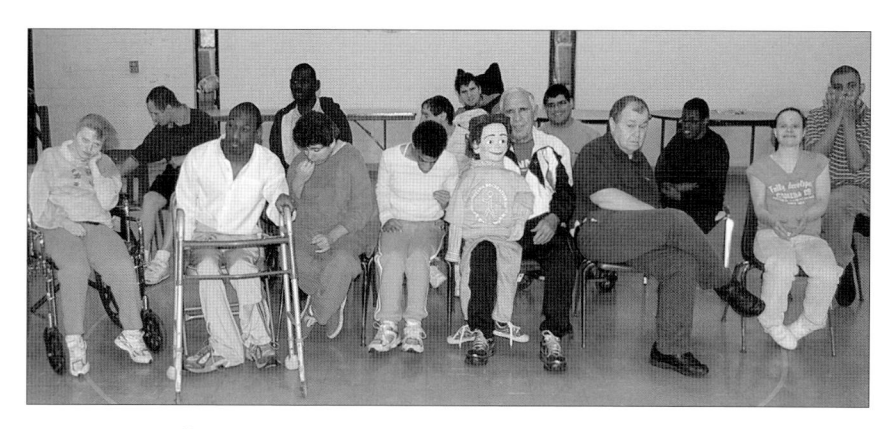

Mikey and I entertaining some of Shore's clients

first things you will notice about Jerry is that, like the clients of Shore who are developmentally disabled, he must deal with a handicap too. Having lost his eyesight during his college years, he refuses to let any physical impediment get in his way. The man is a genuine inspiration.

As I am writing these words, I am tremendously concerned about the future of Shore, which depends heavily on state and federal aid. I don't have to tell you how difficult that can be even in the best of times, to say nothing of the type of budget crises that we face today. The State of Illinois is four months in arrears in its payments and without additional funding, the threat of closure is never far off. It is a frightening prospect for all those who depend on Shore.

Much of my involvement revolves around helping Shore raise funds. As I mentioned earlier, I was able to interest one of my law clients, Joesph K., in Shore and he has been very generous in remodeling and rebulding the center in Morton Grove, adding another one third of space to the existing location. It was renamed in his honor. Shore Community Services frequently takes on the additional role of guardianship as the parents and siblings of clients may pass away and there is no one left to look out for them. They even have programs for seniors who are fifty-five and older. It is all quite a challenge to keep going.

I have been blessed in my life, no doubt about that. I call it mazel, but part of the responsiblity that comes with good mazel and abundant blessings is the responsiblity to help others. Whether their afflictions are economic, developmental, or physical, you must do what you can to help others. Everyone can do something, whether it is just to volunteer time or help in some other way. I consider myself a good friend to Shore and to show its appreciation for that friendship, they honored me with its "Man of the Year" award several years ago.

It was a great honor indeed, but, more important than honors is to find a new generation of Sam Pfeffers who can help organizations like Shore Community Services. I realize that this is no easy task and the best that I can do is try to set a proper example. I am sure that is what my grandparents and the rest of my departed relatives would want me to do. It is in such a spirit, that I have undertaken something very special. As this book comes out, I hope to be celebrating my eighty-fifth birthday. It is one of those milestone birthdays to be sure and one in which people usually throw a party. I have had plenty of parties thrown for me and felt that I did not need another one. Instead, Paula and I are taking the money that we would have spent on such a party, and are donating these funds to Shore in the names of our friends who would have been invited to my birthday party. It is quite a year for us this 2011, as in addition to my 85th in June, Paula will be celebrating her 80th in January, and on July 1st, we will have shared sixty wonderful years together. Our being able to make this gift to Shore in honor of our family and friends is most important to us.

CHAPTER 6

Family and Friends

I MAY HAVE BEEN BORN on June 16, 1926, but the most important date in my life was twenty-five years later on July 1, 1951. That was the day that Paula and I became husband and wife. It was a day that would change my life forever. Of course, we were not simply getting married, but saw this as a means of building a family. Together, we have been blessed with three children and eight grandchildren.

I speak a lot about mazel. The greatest mazel I have had was not in school, not in service, nor in law or even business. The real mazel was when Paula agreed to marry me. Why do I say this? I have always believed that it is important to be honest about yourself. I am not the easiest going of people whom you will find on this planet. When it comes to personality types, then Sam Pfeffer is most definitely the classic Type A personality. Why Type A? Well, you may have picked up in the previous chapters that I tend to be an aggressive, short-tempered, tightly-wound workaholic. That is not always a recipe for domestic tranquility. So, Paula deserves tremendous credit for putting up with me all these years and I am so incredibly indebted to her for making such a wonderful home for all of us.

Of course, whatever my faults, we have been a very good match. In many respects, Paula and I had personal histories that were quite similar. Paula's mother died when she was four

Paula's mother who passed away when Paula was only two years old

years old, a victim of influenza. She went to live with her father's sister, Anna Dickwolf. She raised Paula along with her daughter Miriam. Paula had a brother named Edward. He was raised by several of his maternal aunts. Though they did not live together, Paula and Ed were very close. Over the years I would become

Paula's brother, Edward as a P-47 fighter pilot during World War II

very fond of Ed, a real gentleman who had served during the war as a P-47 pilot and was in the original escort group for General Doolittle's famous raid over Tokyo.

How did I have the good fortune of meeting Paula? It was through Jerry Lichtenstein, the younger brother of a friend of mine, Irv Lichtenstein, that I met Paula. I was attending DePaul Law School at the time and had my own bachelor apartment on the North Side, near Kenmore and Argyle. I happened to bump into Jerry and told him that I was having a little party at my place the following Saturday night. Jerry brought Paula as his date. I remember when she walked through the door. She was very pretty, with a smile that radiated sweetness and innocence. There was something about her that captivated me, and though we spoke only briefly, it was clear that this Northwestern freshman was very intelligent. I thought to myself, "Not only beautiful but smart to boot."

We knew some people in common and our paths crossed in the next year or so. On one of those occasions, I asked Paula for her telephone number. She told me that she attended Northwestern, and though I was not quite ready to start dating her, I was interested in inquiring about some of her girlfriends at school.

On the Fourth of July weekend, I was out with my best friends, Gladys and Herman Sturman. The three of us decided to go to Riverview Amusement Park. For those reading this book from New York, Riverview was our version of Coney Island. I was trying to get a date for the occasion and was having no mazel. I called Paula to see if she had any friends who were spending the summer session on campus. I struck out again as she informed me that she didn't. During this time, Gladys whispered in my ear that I should ask Paula if she would like to join the three of us at Riverview, and to my delight, she agreed.

We picked Paula up and spent the better part of the afternoon and early evening at the Park. Paula and Gladys seemed to hit it off and after a couple of hours it appeared that they were old friends, which they would become soon enough. What to do next? Well, I have to be honest. I was dating a nurse at the time and the only reason that I was not with her on Independence Day was because she was on duty. She was also at the hospital most Friday nights so I started going out with Paula on that night and would see my nurse friend the following night. Well, I guess Paula must have tired of this arrangement and asked why we couldn't go out on Saturday night. Fortunately for me, the nurse was going home to Iowa to visit her folks that weekend, so I said why not.

This was going to be more than just a regular date. It was going to be a celebration of sorts for the law school summer semester was coming to a close. Harold Rappaport, one of my law school buddies, and I decided to visit one of our favorite eateries earlier that day which was a joint near Ogden and Harlem. Its speciality was foot-long hot dogs that went for a quarter. We were returning and driving down Ogden when a three-quarter ton truck crossed the median and hit our vehicle. It was a bad scene as I was seriously injured, and, fortunately, Harold was only slightly hurt. I was taken to Mount Sinai Hospital with severe enough injuries to my face and back that they did not even bring me to the x-ray room. Instead, they brought a portable x-ray machine to my hospital room. The x-ray technician happened to be a Jewish gal from Canada who is today still going strong at the age of 87. We became friends and I introduced her to her husband, Sam Miller, who since passed away, and they were married six weeks after they met. Together they had three children and numerous grandchildren and great-grandchildren.

The big date with Paula was scheduled for Saturday night, but as you might guess, I was in no shape to attend. In fact, I sat in a dark room, totally immobilized. There was a reason for the lack of light for the doctors in charge did not want me to move my neck and light forces you to do that. I asked someone to call Paula to deliver the bad news to her. While some guys may have used the story of a car accident as an excuse to stand a girl up, my story was completely genuine as the phone was brought to my ear and I proceeded to tell Paula all about the accident. I apologized for having to miss our first Saturday night date, but told her that we were on for the first Saturday night upon my release from the hospital.

To show you the kind of woman Paula is, she insisted on coming to the hospital and visiting with me. That was nice but

Sarah and Sam (Shabsai) Miller

presented a bit of a logistical challenge. Again, for you non-Chicagoans, the city is a grid and Paula lived on the far Northeast side, at Ashland and Pratt. Ashland is 1600 West and Pratt is 6600 North. Mount Sinai Hospital, while not clear on the other side of town, was still pretty far away as it was 2800 West and 1400 South. To get their via public transportation could take up to an hour and a half. Well, I started to think that this is quite a lady and sure enough she came to visit me. Since it was late when she left, her father was coming to pick her up. If you remember, the room was purposely dark when Mr. Freedman, whom I had never met, arrived. With him entering the dark room and me worried what he might be thinking, I blurted out, "Don't worry about anything, Sir. I can't move."

The visit impressed me sure enough, but it was clear to me that this was the beginning of a more serious relationship. I stopped seeing the nurse as things moved along nicely with Paula. Before we were married, Paula lived in a four-room, one-bedroom apartment with her Aunt Anna, Anna's daughter Miriam, her Aunt Rae, Rae's husband Jack, and their son, Merwyn, all of whom are now deceased. It was quite a group and with space at a premium, Paula slept in a folding bed in the dining room. But true to her character, she never complained. I should say that the reason that she moved in with her aunt after her mother passed does not reflect on the devotion of her father for her and her brother. To the contrary, David Freedman was very devoted, but he was a traveling salesman and was on the road all week. He was in no position to care for his young children but was with them every weekend. Like my own mother, he would remarry when Paula was a teenager, in her case when she was fifteen. The lucky bride was named Paula Hollander and the two stayed married for over thirty-five years.

Finally, it was time to ask Paula to marry me. There was only one problem. I needed an engagement ring. Everyone seems to have a friend or relative in the business and fortunately for me Gladys Sturman worked for a small jewelry manufacturer and distributor who also rented space to other jewelry wholesalers. Hy Spreckman was the owner of the business and his office had individual designers who sold retail jewelry. I told Gladys what I wanted in a ring and she introduced me to a designer, Don Lawrence, whom she thought would do a nice job for me and who'd be reasonable in his prices. Don was not only a talented designer, but a great guy, and he became a lifelong friend and tennis partner. Back then though his masterpiece of a ring was going to cost me $300. Guess what? I didn't have it.

I have been blessed to have great friends in my life. Fellows you can count on to help you out when you're in a bind. Harvey Goldstein was a friend and classmate from law school. We used to study and drive around together. He had a nickname that I

Harvey "Go-Go" Goldstein

will never forget. Since he was always the first in class to raise his hand, he acquired the nickname "Go Go Goldstein!" and it would be chanted in class like a football cheer. Harvey heard about my predicament and since he came from a comfortable background, he was in a position to help me. He lent me the $300 and I paid him back $25 a week. I remember telling my daughters this story. They could not believe their father did not have $300 but that was the truth.

Our wedding was held at the Hotel Belmont and it was a fairly simple event, a luncheon that all together cost $300. Can you imagine that the whole wedding for sixty people cost a total of $300? Five dollars per person, a sum which boggles the mind. Today, some couples would spend the $300 on flowers alone, and I am talking about the flowers that are on each and every table and not the flowers for the entire affair. Our wedding was officiated by our rabbi from Spring Valley, Rabbi Aisenstark, who was also a cousin of Saul Garten, a close friend who treated me like a close relative, and to this day I am very close to his widow and children. Saul was originally from Poland, and his entire family was wiped out in the Holocaust. He escaped by going East during the war and served in the Polish Army under the Soviets. After the war, he came to the United States via South America.

The wedding was going along smoothy until Paula circled me seven times as is traditional. What is not so traditional is what happened next, as suddenly her wedding veil caught on fire. Fortunately, we were able to extinguish it quickly. After the wedding, Paula and I went to visit our friends, Kenneth and Pearl Hirsch, who lived near the hotel. They could not attend because Ken's mom had recently died and Jewish law prohibits mourners from attending joyous events. We ended up having hot dogs for dinner at their house. The night kept on its exciting pace as we stayed at a hotel in Highland Park which was just ten miles from Chicago. The Moraine Hotel was a favorite spot for newlyweds. When we got into the car to leave, Paula commented that no one at the hotel even knew we were newlyweds. I told Paula she was correct, but, in truth, the front desk clerk had inquired if we were interested in the honeymoon suite, but I had to decline the offer because of my limited finances.

We took our honeymoon trip to Canada. Paula had gotten used to my sense of humor during our courtship but the question remained if she could put up with it during our marriage. I was also very big on being street smart whereas Paula tended to think the best of everything and everyone. When passing a cemetery, I asked her to venture a guess as to how many people she thought were dead in the cemetery. She thought for a while and, after doing some calculations in her head, gave me a number. I told her that all of the people in the cemetery were dead. The next day we passed another cemetery, this one even smaller than the first, and I put the same question to her. Again, she gave me a number. She was just very earnest and sincere, but I realized that I would have to be street smart for the both of us. Fortunately, I had no problem.

As we were entering Canada, Paula wanted to stop at a souvenir shop. I told her not to take the prices listed on the items as the final price, that what you ultimately bought it for was open to negotiation with the proprietor. Walking into the shop, our eyes were drawn to a table filled with little cigarette boxes. When you opened the little drawer of the box to get a cigarette, a small pelican which was attached to the box would pick up the cigarette. It was a cute item and Paula became very enthusiastic about the prospect of buying one. She did not seem ready to negotiate, which was contrary to the advice that I had dispensed to her in the car only ten minutes earlier. Well, the owner must have figured he had a live one and had piqued her interest when he told her that these were made by the local Indians especially for him. He told us that these Indians spent many a cold winter night carving the cigarette boxes just so tourists like us could enjoy them. Well, of course we bought one and later that day I took out the cigarette box and showed Paula that the only carving that the Indians made was to remove the words on the bottom of the box that read "Made in Japan." When we arrived at the scenic and very romantic Niagara Falls, we saw shelf after shelf of those cigarette boxes.

Canada proved an excellent choice and we visited many places in Ontario including the capital city of Ottawa. We traveled as far east as Quebec City. Of course, ever the practical type that I am, I considered the trip to be a real success since we arrived safely back in Chicago with $75 of the original $350 with which we had started out.

Our first apartment was at 4021 North Kedvale in Chicago, a third floor one-bedroom walkup. Since many of our friends had babies, we decided that it was imperative for us to have some additional company until we could afford a child. In our case it came in the form of a very frisky pooch we named Bumbo. We had grown a bit tired of listening to the endless talk of brilliant and precocious toddlers whose every sound and step seemed proof positive that the child would someday be a future Nobel Laureate. The truth is that a one-year old dog seemed far more advanced than a one-year old baby, and Bumbo was certainly that. If nothing else, he could be toilet trained a whole lot faster or so I thought. On Sundays I would take Bumbo out for a walk. He was a just small puppy at the time and I did not realize that small male pups do not lift their legs when they confront a fire hydrant, a skill which they develop as they mature. I spent many a frustrating morning demonstrating to Bumbo the proper technique. While we lived in this apartment, Paula's parents and my folks would visit us every Sunday evening. One Sunday, we told them that we would not be able to see them the following week as we had a wedding to attend. It's difficult to understand how the four of them could be so upset that we were ruining their Sunday but that was in fact the case. From this apartment we moved to an apartment on Devon and Lakewood. Bumbo moved with us but the apartment was an old-fashioned one. The living room being the first large room as you entered the apartment, and the bedrooms ran the length of the long hall. We noticed after we had moved in that there was a yellow stain developing by the legs of some of the furniture. We thought Bumbo may be the culprit. We put up a big gate to close off the living room, but to no avail. We decided to stay awake one night since Bumbo always slept under our bed. At about 3 A.M., we heard Bumbo quietly leaving and we followed him. He jumped over the gate, went to one of the legs of the furniture, and did his business before returning to his resting place under our bed. We decided that we could not train Bumbo and with all of his energy, it was clear that Bumbo was not cut out for apartment life so we gave him to a friend who had a home in the suburbs. Unfortunately, Bumbo's friskiness got the better of him when he met his demise chasing a ball out onto the street. When the girls came along, they decided that they would like to have a cat which, for obvious reasons, eliminated the problems that we had with Bumbo.

Paula and I always loved to entertain and we started out early in our marriage. These were mostly small parties, but when one of my friends from law school became engaged to one of the women who worked in the law school office, I suggested that our apartment, which contained relatively little furniture and no children, would have ample space to hold a large group. I was not worried about the noise level that this would cause since I was told that the neighbor directly below us was an older woman who was practically deaf. Together with my friend, Bill Bauer, we organized the shindig. An invitation was placed on the activity board at school notifying everyone that the first bottle of beer was free, but when the bathtub, which was filled with ice and bottles of beer, was empty, the next round would cost everyone one dollar. One of the DePaul priests, who just happened to be the dean of students, heard about the party and since it was related to school, he thought the prudent course of action would be to act as a chaperone. I don't know the exact number who came in and out of our apartment that night, but I can guess that it must have been around two hundred people, if you can believe it. Well, remember I told you about the woman in the 2nd floor apartment below us who could not hear well? Well, her vision was fine and throughout the night she got to watch her chandelier swing to and fro from the hordes that stopped in. She was certainly spooked and must have thought it was either an earthquake or that the place was haunted. She called her daughter to complain, and, never finding out the cause of the swaying chandelier, moved out of the building the following week. While we were certainly sorry to have unwittingly caused this lady such aggravation, we became very close with our new neighbors, Arnold and Fannie Gilmore. Though he has been gone for some time, we are still in touch with Fannie. Arnie was a car salesman and worked in a Chevrolet dealership with a man named George Shepard. George was the only salesman I knew who never gambled. He was a very prudent individual, and with his savings, bought his first piece of real estate which was a small apartment building in Skokie. George not only became a lifelong friend and client, but was a central figure in my becoming a Chevrolet dealer.

Ken and Dorothy Anderson were our next door neighbors and with whom we shared a common porch. Ken was a dentist and they had three fine children, all of whom entered the medical profession. Their oldest, Claudia, became a surgical nurse before going back to school to become a dentist, eventually taking over her father's practice. Eric became a doctor, and Susan a retina specialist at the Wheaton Eye Clinic in Wheaton, Illinois. Ken became our dentist, serving in that capacity for many years before Claudia took over. Though like many of our friends, Ken passed away, we are still very close with Dorothy who has been extremely kind in serving as our designated driver when we all want to go out together at night, since my macular degeneration does not allow me to do that.

Well, back to the story. Though we had a wonderful time living on Kedvale, after the birth of our oldest daughter, Beth, we moved to a much larger place at 6415 North Lakewood, where our other two daughters, Cara and Diana were born. Since everything is relative, our new quarters seemed perfectly palatial in comparison to the previous place. We lived in a two-story

Ken and Dorothy Anderson and family

building consisting of a large living room, dining room, kitchen, three bedrooms, and two bathrooms.

Miss Birdie, who lived with us, was a black woman and a devout Jehovah's Witness. She did a wonderful job helping us raise the children. The children were very attached to her and Diana always called her Grandma Birdie until we moved to our home in Wilmette. There, Nina, the daughter of one of our neighbors, explained to Diana the rudiments of these things, thereby disavowing her previously held belief that this lady whom she loved was actually her grandmother. She came crying to me when she heard this from Nina, now a cardiac specialist at Children's Memorial Hospital. I told her that while Nina was technically correct that Miss Birdie was not her actual grandmother, Miss Birdie loved her every bit as much as any grandmother loves a grandchild, so she should go on calling her Grandma Birdie. That solved that.

The pattern at the time was to move to a home in the suburbs, and so in 1963 we went north to our current home at 119 Hollywood Court in Wilmette. Of course, Paula was not only a tremendously devoted wife and mother, but I knew that she would never be fully satisfied with the life of a suburban housewife. I felt it was important for her to have a life that was independent of her husband and family and encouraged her to pursue her education.

When we got married, Paula was in her sophomore year at Northwestern and began working full-time in an insurance agency while going to school at night. Once she became pregnant, Paula was a full-time mother. After Miss Birdie began helping us, Paula resumed her studies on a part-time basis, ultimately receiving her baccalaureate from Northwestern University. After graduation, Paula went on for a master's degree in history at Northeastern Illinois University. One night I found Paula crying in the kitchen. Why was she in tears? The head of the history department had told the class of graduate students that he could not understand why people were getting graduate degrees in history when there were few jobs, if any, teaching history. I then asked Paula what her purpose was in getting a graduate degree. Was it for her own intellectual desire or merely to get a job? I had been under the impression that it was to further her own academic goals. That ended the tears and she continued her education, eventually obtaining a master's degree. During the commencement exercises, all three of our girls ran to the front of the balcony where we were sitting and yelled, "That's our mom!" What a moment!

While at Northeastern, Paula had a professor who would exert significant scholarly influence over the course of her career. June Sochen is a fine academician who has published numerous books and articles in American History, particularly in the history of feminism and African-American history. They became close lifelong friends, and, after receiving her master's degree, Paula became a history professor at Mundelein College. This college, like Mallinckrodt, was a Catholic women's college that would eventually be absorbed into Loyola University.

Paula was enjoying her teaching but set her sights on getting her doctorate. At the time, Northwestern University allowed anyone with the proper academic credentials, who was a full time teacher, to enroll in its Ph.D. program and take the first year course load over a two-year period. While the burden lessened, the cost did not. All of the other Ph.D. requirements remained the same. The acting dean at the time was opposed to this policy since he felt that the candidate would be less likely to complete her doctorate since she carried a heavy teaching burden. Well, Paula was certainly committed and it was at Northwestern that she studied under George Fredrickson who served as her thesis advisor and intellectual mentor. Fredrickson, who would leave Northwestern for Stanford, passed away only two years ago and did groundbreaking work on the history of race. His book "White Supremacy: A Comparative Study in American and South African History" compared the history of race relations in the United States with that of South Africa. Paula had written her master's thesis on A. Philip Randolph, the labor and civil rights leader and organizer who fascinated her. Dr. Fredrickson encouraged Paula to continue with Randolph. Her dissertation was well received and she was awarded her doctorate. There are no words to describe the pride that the entire family felt when Paula received that most prestigious degree. Remember the dean who did not think that anyone teaching full-time possessed sufficient commitment to see through to the doctorate? Well, the man not only apologized to her, but handed Paula her diploma. Talk about justice.

A. Philip Randolph is a most important figure in both labor and black history. Paula was able to show that he laid the groundwork for Dr. Martin Luther King's famous march on Washington and was often overlooked by observers of the Civil Rights

Paula receiving her Ph.D. from Northwestern University

Movement. Fortunately for Paula, she was able to meet Randolph who was an elderly gentleman living in New York at the time. Despite his advanced age, he was very helpful to Paula and she had access to his private papers and the library of the AFL-CIO, important because Randolph founded the Brotherhood of Sleeping Car Porters, the first black led union.

Paula's dissertation was adopted into a book that was published by Louisiana State University. Titled "A. Philip Randolph, Pioneer of the Civil Rights Movement," it was a tremendous achievement and was shortlisted for a Pulitzer Prize. Again, words are not sufficient to describe the pride that I felt in my wife

THE HISTORY FACULTY

AND

THE VICE PRESIDENT FOR ACADEMIC AFFAIRS

INVITE YOU TO JOIN US

TO CELEBRATE THE PUBLICATION OF

A. PHILIP RANDOLPH,

PIONEER OF THE CIVIL RIGHTS MOVEMENT

BY

PAULA M. PFEFFER

REFRESHMENTS AND BOOK SIGNING

IN PIPER HALL

IMMEDIATELY AFTER THE DEAN'S MEETING

THURSDAY, MAY 24, 1990

4:15 p.m.

Celebrating with Paula at her book signing. Left: Don Lawrence, our friend; right: with me

when I first laid eyes on the book. The only disappointed person was my own mother, who reckoned that with her daughter-in-law being a doctor, Paula could write all her prescriptions. When I tried to explain to my mother the nuances of the Ph.D. and the M.D. degrees, she was a bit incredulous, responding with the famous, "How can you be a doctor and not a doctor? You're either a doctor or you're not a doctor."

With Mundelein College's merger with Loyola, Paula continued as a tenured professor there until 2006. She loved teaching and writing and would be doing both still today were it not for the Parkinson's disease which makes many things extremely challenging. With the same determination she showed in getting her doctorate, she applies every day of her life. She inspires me. Not only has she written and spoken about the evolving role of women, she has lived it. A sign hangs in her office at home which reads, "Well behaved women rarely make history." Though she is certainly kind and gracious, she has, in her own way, made history. But as proud as I am of her many academic and scholarly achievements, I must say I am most proud of the example she has set for our three daughters. It has helped them become accomplished people in their own rights.

Our Children and Grandchildren

As I wax nostalgically about the days when our daughters were young, I am brought back to the reality that they have grown up and gone on to have families of their own. Beth attended New Trier High School and while that famous school has sent thousands of its graduates to nearly every academic institution for higher learning in the country, she was the first from New Trier to attend Douglass College in New Brunswick, New Jersey. Founded as the New Jersey College for Women, it was part of the New Jersey State University system and was highly regarded. It attracted some of the top female students in New Jersey and was particularly strong in its language offerings, which were of great interest to Beth.

Our oldest daughter also excelled in science and took many courses though not in pre-med. She received a degree in dietetics, and, in order to become a licensed dietician, was obligated to spend a year working in a hospital setting. Beth chose Cook County Hospital in Chicago. She did well there and was offered a permanent position as a dietitian. Together with a doctor and nurse, she joined a team and even wrote a manual on the dietitian's role in hyperalimentation, which was to provide food to the main artery of the heart.

Coming from the suburbs, Cook County Hospital was quite a change. It takes in many gunshot patients and the initials G.S.W. were not anything she had ever seen in her studies. She learned soon enough what it meant. One day our daughter came to us and said that she was quitting her job and wanted to go back to school to take all of the pre-med school required courses, which I had suggested during her undergraduate studies. However, she was deterred from doing so then due to her pronounced fear of blood. Apparently, her job experience had cured any such phobia since if the doctors and nurses were not available, she would have to make the necessary incision to insert the feeding tube.

Although she was offered the opportunity to live at home and take her coursework in the Chicago area, she chose to move back to New Jersey and took her pre-med courses at Rutgers. She was accepted at Loyola Medical School. Beth chose psychiatry and is currently practicing in the area. Though she is now divorced, her marriage led to three wonderful children: the oldest, Sara, 20, is attending the University of Arizona; and Zachary, 16, together with his sister Dianarose, 15, are currently students at their Mom's alma mater, New Trier High School.

After graduating from the University of Wisconsin, our middle daughter, Cara, got her master's in education at the University of Illinois and is involved in one of the most challenging

Our daughters, from top to bottom: Beth, Cara, and Diana

professions anywhere. She teaches autistic children and those with severe physical and mental disabilities. Cara met her husband Norman while she taught at a convalescent center that Norman's family, the Galpers, owned. Norman's father was so impressed with Cara that he insisted that his son meet her when he returns home from Philadelphia, where he was attending graduate school. Meet they did and subsequently married. While having children she took some time off from working but volunteered from time to time to work in special needs classes at the school where her children attended. When she returned to work, she became a full time instructor with special needs children, many of them with autism. As I mentioned earlier, this is a most challenging profession and given my own commitment to Shore Community Services, I take particular pride in the work that my daughter is doing. Of course, this work is in addition to her job as mother to her own three children. Briana is 21 and is a junior at the University of Southern California, achieving straight As and has been invited as one of seventeen students to take her second semester as a junior at the University of Westminster in London. Ari, 18, just finished his first semester at Reed College in Portland, Oregon and has ambitions to become a university professor. Adam, 16, is the youngest and is a junior in high school.

Though they are divorced, we have remained close to Cara's ex-husband, Norman Galper, and his parents, Sol and Charlene Galper, who have provided significant support for our grandchildren's education. Norman is an incredible father to our grandchildren and we appreciate the honor and respect he gives us. These days divorce is quite common, but notwithstanding, Norman has been a good father to our grandchildren.

Diana is a practicing lawyer specializing in environmental law. Like Cara, she attended the University of Wisconsin, and remained in Madison after her graduation while her fiance, Carlos Martin, completed his senior year. Diana got a job at the university working with one of the chemistry professors. Her initial job included ordering supplies and cleaning the equipment. The professor who headed the department began showing her how some of the biogenetic experiments are conducted. When the professor left the university for a private company, his first assistant who was a PhD, and Diana, who had only a bachelor's, joined him. At her new job, Diana conducted experiments and discovered a new method of manufacturing genes. This technology was sold by the company to other biogenetic firms which used these genes it in its own experiments. Her procedure was patented and she observed that the patent lawyer knew little about biogenetics. When her fiance was graduated they moved to Los Angeles and Diana took a job at UCLA doing work similar to what she had done in Madison. She decided to go to law school and for two summers worked in a law office which specialized in patent and trademark law. She discovered that environmental law was more interesting. While in her last year, one of her fellow students needed a partner for moot court and they ended up in the final competition. Although they lost, one of the judges, an environmental lawyer, was highly impressed with Diana; he told her that his firm was adding two lawyers and that he was on the hiring committee. Of the 600 applicants, she was one of the two selected. This firm merged and she now is a member of a mega-firm. She has refused partner tract because of wanting to spend time with her children. She is very conscientious and often comes to work very early in the morning so she can attend school events for her kids.

Diana and Carlos have two daughters: Nicole, 16, a junior at Culver City High School, has set her sights to become the first woman president of the United States. Carolynn, 13, attends private school. We enjoy the relationship with our grandchildren who call us frequently, keeping us informed of the goings on in their lives. It makes us proud and happy.

Wilmette is more than just the place where our family came of age. We chose Wilmette primarily for its proximity and easy access to Chicago. Using rail transportation, I could be downtown in twenty minutes. Other benefits include the varied recreational offerings such as fine tennis courts, skating rinks, and superb lakefront facilities. In 1976, the year of the Bicentennial, I was appointed the vice chairman of Wilmette's Bicentennial Commission. It was a two-year commitment and was

Our grandchildren
Photo 1: Sarah and Dianarose
Photo 2: Cara, Adam, Brianna, and Ari
Photo 3: Zachary
Photo 4: Standing: Carlos, Nicole, Sarah, Zachary, and Beth.
Seated: Carolynn, Diana, Me, Paula, and Dianarose

an opportunity to give something back to the community. The Commission sponsored a whole host of educational and cultural events throughout the year, allowing our residents the chance to increase their knowledge and appreciation for this country as well as celebrate its birthday. But the highlight surely has to be the construction a beautiful fountain in front of our town hall which is a lasting tribute to what Abraham Lincoln once referred to as the "last great hope on this earth."

Family is an essential part of life. You have probably noticed that throughout this book, whether in speaking about my childhood, schooling, service, or professional life, I have placed a premium on friendship. I have met so many people from so many different walks of life that I could write a book just about my friends. Yes, when it comes to friendship, I have had great mazel. I hope that my friends feel the same way about me.

Many of the friends who have enriched my life over the years are no longer with us. I think of them often. One such person was Frank Macri. I met Frank through a politician friend of my Uncle Sam and Frank cut quite a figure. He was a very handsome fellow, who looked great in a fine Italian suit. His profession was well chosen, as he sold high-end men's clothing. Blessed with the perfect personality for the job, Frank was among the most modest and sincere folks whom you could ever hope to meet.

One day Frank called and told me that he had four tickets to the big Northwestern football game. I thought that was great, and since we lived so close to the stadium, I suggested that he and his wife come by and we would all go to the game together. He told me that he would like to give me all four tickets to the game. Why, I asked him. He told me that he could not go to the game because it was his Sabbath. Frank looked as Italian as Dean Martin, and growing up in Spring Valley, all the Italians I knew were Roman Catholic. Not Frank Macri, though. He was a devoted Seventh Day Adventist. It just goes to show that things are not always as they appear. So here was this guy named

My handsome friend, Frank Macri

Macri giving a Jewish guy named Pfeffer tickets to a football game because he can't go on a Saturday.

Friendship means experiencing the joys and the sorrows that are life itself. Frank, with his ready smile and upbeat demeanor, experienced his share of life's low moments. His first wife Josephine, died far too young. They had a daughter named Linda and Linda had one child, Gregory, who contracted cancer at an early age. Frank spent a great deal of time with the boy, keeping his spirits up and they often attended church together. Gregory's cancer was thought to be in remission and the boy grew into a young man who lived life fully, got married and had two beautiful children before the dreaded cancer returned to his body. Gregory, who was by then in his early thirties, eventually succumbed to the disease.

As they say, "life goes on" and it was to Frank's great credit that he was able to keep going despite the onslaught of these events. A number of years after Josephine's death, Frank remarried a lovely woman, who like himself, was deeply committed to the church. Marie's parents were missionaries in India and Pakistan for over 40 years and she was born in Pakistan, not returning permanently to American soil until she was 18 years old. Marie and Frank were married for twenty years until Frank's death. It was a happy life together, a life which centered around church, family and friends. And as I sit here thinking about Frank Macri's, I can only say I was proud to be his friend.

My Three Doctors

If you remember from the beginning of the book, I had given serious thought to becoming a medical doctor. Well, mazel dictated that things would not go that way. But, as a family, we were fortunate to have several excellent medical professionals looking out for us. Many of you are familiar with the television show that ran in the 60s and 70s: Marcus Welby, M.D., which featured Robert Young in the the title role. That kind of doctor, the caring, do everything family physician, is nearly extinct today but we had such a man in Dr. Leonard Goldberg. House calls were the order of the day and he made plenty of them. In all of the brouhaha today about the high cost of medicine, Dr. Goldberg's fee for coming to your house and examining you was an exorbitant three dollars. Naturally, over the course of a number of years, he had the chutzpah to raise his fee to five dollars.

In the days before specialization, he delivered all three of our daughters. When they went away to college, not only they, but their friends as well, would call him for medical advice which he dispensed free of charge. Eventually, Dr. Goldberg retired

Dr. Leonard Goldberg

but I was fortunate to have Jerry Buckman, my cousin who has been like a brother to me, as our family doctor. Given the way I feel about Jerry, and his great medical skills, this could not have worked out any better. It gave Paula and me a wonderful sense of security.

Our daughter Cara contracted chicken pox and encephalitis at the age of six. It became very serious. Dr. Goldberg contacted the medical authorities involved in infectious diseases. An ambulance was at the ready, and though Cara didn't need it, Leonard and Jerry stayed by her bed the entire night until she was out of danger. What devotion!

Jerry, in addition to being a great guy, is a wonderful doctor, and after serving us and many other patients, eventually retired. We were again in need of a doctor and I contacted Dr. Leonard Berlin, a family friend, who was Chief of Radiology at Rush

*Dr. Jerry
Buchman*

*Dr. Lawrence
Layfer*

Hospital of Skokie to get a referral. Leonard knew our family well and was familiar with all of the doctors at his hospital. He recommended Dr. Lawrence Layfer to be our family physician.

Again, we were blessed with great mazel with another outstanding doctor. He is not only a highly skilled practitioner, but a very learned biblical scholar as well. Quite a combination! Of course, you would prefer not to have to spend too much time at your doctor's office but these things are frequently out of your control.

Our family was hit with our greatest health challenge when Paula was diagnosed with Parkinson's disease. Dr. Layfer recommended Dr. Christopher Goetz who is in charge of the Parkinson Disease and Movement Disorders program at Rush Chicago. He is widely considered one of the experts in treating this terrible disease and brings not only great expertise but great compassion to his practice.

Sometimes when you start seeing a specialist, your family doctor takes a back seat. In our case, Dr. Layfer stays very involved, having Paula see him every three months. He stays on top of her condition and offers us hope. If we forget to set up the appointment, he will personally call the house to schedule it. He seems old-fashioned that way.

I have titled this book, *Born to Survive*. Nobody expected me to make it from being born three months premature and my days sleeping in a shoe box. But I suppose I had a certain will to survive, and thank God, I have had wonderful mazel. My health has been, by and large, very good. I have seen friends and family suffer many illnesses over the years, and, sadly, some have died much too young. I still remember the basketball star who was in St. Margaret's Hospital with me, and I remind myself just how fleeting youth and good health can be. So, I am grateful to God for all of the blessings I have been given.

Fifteen years ago during a routine visit to my ophthalmologist for some new glasses, I received some bad news. They call it macular degeneration and I had it in both eyes. I don't want to bore you with all of the details but objects that are right in front of one start to become blurry. One still keeps a lot of peripheral vision and it is common enough among older folks like me.

I saw various specialists in this area. Once, while in California, Paula and I were called into the office of a major eye doctor at the UCLA Medical Center. He told Paula with very little feeling in his voice, "Dr. Pfeffer, your husband is going blind." The worst three months of my life followed this grim pronouncement as I lived in constant fear that one day I would not be able to see anything.

Thankfully, this day never came. I went to see Dr. Alice Lyon, a leading specialist in macular degeneration at Northwestern Hospital. She has been treating me for the past fourteen years, doing everything medically possible to maintain as much of my vision as she can. I am legally blind in my right eye and have developed glaucoma and cataracts in both eyes which is not a winning trifecta. So it was time to see another specialist, and Dr. Lyon recommended Dr. Angelo Tanna. Between the two ophthalmologists, they have allowed me to see as much and as well as I do. That I can still see the smiling faces of my grandchildren, makes me very happy and I am very grateful to both doctors.

During the past year or so, our country has been engaged in a major debate over health care. Surely, there are changes that can be made but we tend to forget just how dedicated many of the medical professionals truly are. As a family, we have been blessed in the extreme to have some of these folks working to help us live our lives to the fullest. Our entire family owes them much. You may have heard of the operatic trio known as the Three Tenors. I talk about this trio of three doctors who have made beautiful medical music for our family.

CHAPTER 7

Fulfilling My Remaining Goals

RETIREMENT CAME IN 1995. I suppose it was inevitable, but for someone who had spent his whole life working, it was quite a change of pace. From my boyhood in Spring Valley, I learned the value of hard work. It was a great lesson and I tried to work as hard as I could work ever since that boyhood. Now that part of my life was essentially over and it was time to find other ways to channel my talents, my energy, and my spirit. But like many retirees, a question lingered: how do I accomplish that? As you will see, I was to find my own unique path.

MIKEY AND ME

I was 69 years old and in good health, thank God. In thinking about things that I could do now that I had more time to do them, there was one area which leapt to the forefront. You may remember from the beginning of this book that I loved taking the children to the ball game. You may also recall that I helped found the Little League in Spring Valley. One can reasonably infer that

I love kids. One would be right. The first thing I wanted to do in my retirement was to make a difference in the lives of children. One way to make a difference is to bring laughter and joy to the face of a child, particularly to children who have suffered major illnesses in their young lives. I decided that I wanted to entertain children. But how to do it? I didn't want to be a clown and I can't sing, so I thought I was somewhat limited in helping kids. I decided I would learn how to become a ventriloquist. I mean, what youngster doesn't enjoy watching a ventriloquist in action?

Well, how do you become a ventriloquist? Fortunately, I had a friend whose uncle was a part-time ventriloquist. I contacted him and he told me that the only person he knew who was engaged in ventriloquism instruction was a fellow out in Woodstock, Illinois. So, I called this fellow and we talked about ventriloquism. His rates seemed fair, and, soon enough, I was taking the fifty mile trek to rural Woodstock twice a week for lessons. Some of you may have heard of Edgar Bergen and Charlie McCarthy. I suppose ventriloquism attracts a different sort of person and the instructor was not your run of the mill type of guy. He lived with his mother, and, while he never married, there were six other family members to keep him company. Of course, they came in different sizes, were male and female, and had individual tastes in clothing. He referred to them as his children, and why not? He had made them all himself, constructing them from head to toe. When we would go down to his basement, the room in which he instructed his pupils, he would speak to the various dummies, and, of course, they would answer him.

I had been taking lessons for about six months when I asked my instructor if I may rent one of the dummies in order to practice my ventriloquist skills. Apparently, he was a very protective parent because he responded as if I should know better, "I never let my children go anywhere with strangers." He did, however, agree to make me a dummy if I gave him an idea of what kind of a dummy I wanted. For those of you who think every dummy looks alike, you are sadly mistaken. The key ingredient in building a dummy is to capture the facial expression that you want to use for your ventriloquist act. He proceeded to make me a perfect dummy.

After one year of lessons, my instructor gave me the go-ahead to begin performing my own shows, and, unlike law school where you needed to pass the bar, there was no comparable accreditation or licensing agency in performing this kind of act. My instructor did, however, recommend that I concentrate on children between the ages of four and eleven. My first audiences were the children and grandchildren of my friends and it was simply amazing to see how differently each child reacted to the dummy. Some were afraid; some didn't like him (the dummy—not me, I hope); and some wanted to hold him on their lap. Many of the younger kids thought he was real and would get quite angry with me whenever I scolded him. From this audience, I transitioned into performing at kids' birthday parties and for the children at hospitals, which proved to be among the most rewarding of all of my ventriloquist experiences.

The question, when I started, was what to call my dummy. So, I asked him, and he told me that his name was Mikey, but that's not all he told me. Like a good Jewish dummy, he had a Hebrew name, too, which was Moishe. So, when I performed for a general audience, Mikey did the performing, and when I performed for Jewish kids, he was Moishe. Fortunately for the act's sake, he was not afflicted with an identity crisis.

I held a performance at Shore Community Services where I sit on the board of directors. This show was for disabled children. As part of the performance, I would have Mikey go up to a child, and if the child was a girl, he would tell her how pretty she looked, and, if a boy, how handsome. There was one little girl who sat with an attendant directly in front of us. When we came up to this little girl who suffered from a certain autistic disorder, she pushed Mikey away. We then started our routine for the entire group, but between parts of the act, Mikey would wave to this little girl and tell her, "I like you," and on the performance went.

Several times, we would go over to the little girl and she no longer moved Mikey away from her. The performance was a success and everyone filed out of the room. Everyone, except that little girl. She wouldn't budge, and as her helper tried to get her to leave, she shook her head "No." I then realized that she considered Mikey a friend and brought him close to her. She put her arms around Mikey and gave him as big a hug as such a frail little girl could. Everyone who had remained in the room smiled, Mikey included. Only then, did the little girl assent to leave the room.

As I mentioned earlier, entertaining children at hospitals is very special. In one of the hospitals, I encountered a mother who was walking with her 4-year old daughter and the daughter's portable IV. The girl was Hispanic so I put Mikey next to her on the floor and said, "La senorita es muy bonita." The little girl got all excited, and with a smile on her face, said to her mom, "Look! He speaks Spanish!" Perhaps Mikey had a little bit of Miguel in him.

One of the most interesting performances took place at Children's Memorial Hospital in Chicago. The hospital is equipped with close-circuit television in each room. This way, everyone could see the show, even those who couldn't attend the performance in person, which we held in the studio located in the hospital. The parents of those patients who were ambulatory filled a good 12 seats alone. We first went around to the children and had Mikey shake hands with each of them. Mikey, being the affectionate type that he was, then paid his respects to all of the moms by giving them a kiss on the cheek. Now, at the front of the room, Mikey exclaimed "You boys and girls sure are lucky to have such beautiful mommies." We then commenced with our show followed by a question and answer session. The way we did it was that the children would call out the answers to Mikey's questions, including those children in their own hospital rooms who could use their phone to answer, and then Mikey would tell them if they were right or wrong. Those with the correct answer (eventually all of the children) would then receive a small gift.

Since Mikey was, at times, Moishe, I felt it important that he earn his keep by entertaining Jewish children, particularly those with disabilities or other challenges. One Sunday, we found ourselves performing before just such an audience. Each of these special needs children had a person, in this case a college student to assist them. There was one little girl whom I shall never forget. She was the only one who had not one aide but two people helping her. Her eyes would tear up constantly, her facial expression was frozen. It became evident to me that of all of the children, she should be the one for me to concentrate on the most. We went through our usual routine, but every once in awhile, I would abandon the chair that Moishe and I sat on and approach her. Putting Mikey close to her, he would raise his little hand and wave saying, "Hi! You're cute!" We would then go back to our routine. After finishing, Moishe went up to the little girl and gave her a kiss on the cheek, waved to her, and said, "I love you." Her reaction was to smile back at Mikey. Everyone in the room looked on in silent disbelief. Why the astonishment? It was the first time anyone had ever seen her smile.

Despite all of the joy and satisfaction that being a ventriloquist has given me, I eventually had to give it up. Why? My hands became so arthritic, that, sadly, I could no longer hold Mikey. After I finish writing this book, I hope to work with a new teacher and have him craft a dummy which would be easier for me to hold. I am anxious to again bring some happiness to children with handicaps and other afflictions as well as entertain at joyous occasions. I miss seeing those young smiles and bringing such joy to others gladdens my own heart.

The Trips to Israel

Like most Jews of my generation, I was an enthusiastic Zionist and consider among the most amazing events that transpired in my lifetime the founding of the Jewish State in 1948. I was

Israel Leadership Award, 1980

active in Israel Bonds and was even honored with its "Israel Leadership Award" in 1980. I had been to Israel three to four times prior to retirement but now that I was retired, Paula and I had a wonderful visit.

FULFILLING MY REMAINING GOALS

Several months after returning from Israel, the phone rang in my Wilmette home. The caller identified himself as being from B'nai B'rith, the Jewish service organization, and informed me that I had won an all expense paid, seven day trip to Israel. You will not be surprised to find that I was a little skeptical when I first heard this news. I told the caller to send me a letter verifying the matter and sure enough received just such an official letter a few days later. Apparently, my mazel was beyond good. B'nai B'rith was scheduled to have its international conference in Israel and decided to hold a drawing in which it would randomly choose one of its 60,000 members for a free trip. Of the tens of thousands who could have been chosen, the person picked was Sam Pfeffer.

The trip was for two, but since Paula and I had both been to Israel, and she was busy teaching, I decided to take along someone who had never been to Israel and who would be unlikely to go on his own. Hershel Rapoport was someone I knew through the synagogue. Every Saturday, he would lead the congregation through the prayers at the beginning of the morning services. Long since retired, I figured Hershel would jump at an opportunity to travel. I was not wrong.

I knew that Hershel's family were lovers of the Land of Israel. His father had wanted to move to Israel, but, as is not unusual, his mother felt that since their children were in the United States, she could not leave. Hershel's late brother, Rabbi Shlomo Rapoport was a prominent rabbi and educator who headed the Ida Crown Jewish Academy. He had promised their parents that upon their passing, he would bring their bodies to Israel, and so Hershel contacted one of his cousins who lived there and they were able to visit the graves of his parents on several occasions during our trip.

Our seven days in Israel were busy ones and I arranged on our one free day for Hershel to take a tour. The most interesting event was a special dinner in which Prime Minister Benjamin Netanyahu was to be the featured speaker. While the convention events were going on inside the hotel that day, Hershel and I wandered into an outside garden where the dinner would take place. There was a dais and a reserved table surrounding the dais. I reasoned that the prime minister would be square in the center of the dais so I told Hershel that we would be sitting in the table directly facing him. Hershel pointed out to me that the sign said "reserved" but I told him that I had arranged it all in advance, which, of course, I had not.

The time came for the big dinner to begin. We were there early and sat at the reserved table as I had told Hershel we would. As everyone filed in, no one asked us to move. The prime minister finally walked in together with his contingent of bodyguards. Hershel was thrilled as not only did he get the opportunity to have his picture taken with the Prime Minister of the state of Israel, but he got the chance to shake Bibi's hand.

Though Hershel has had his ups and downs in life including a recent family tragedy, he tells me he counts our trip together as one of the most exciting events of his long life. In looking back at those seven days, I cannot tell you how happy I am that I chose Hershel to accompany me.

With Paula still actively teaching at Loyola, I was looking for a new volunteer project. I met someone who was volunteering at a military base in Israel for two weeks fueling vehicles and doing other such work. While this is a wonderful program, it did not particularly appeal to me. I inquired at the Jewish Federation offices in Chicago about other such opportunities and learned that there were two-week and four-week programs whereby one could go to Israel and teach English. That appealed to me. Chicago has a sister city in Israel called Kiryat Gat. All I needed to do was pay all of my expenses with the exception of lodging which was provided for me. Everything was going fine until the offices here found out that I was over seventy-five years old. They required a letter from my physician who attested to my being in sufficient health to take on such an assignment. I gave the letter to the woman in charge of the program and was accepted as a participant.

Kiryat Gat is located about thirty-five miles south of Tel Aviv, twenty-seven miles north of Beersheba, and forty-two miles from Jerusalem. Of course, the country is so small that nothing is very far from anything else and Kiryat Gat is only 15 miles from the Gaza Strip, well within striking distances of its rockets, though it was not a concern when I traveled there. Though the city has a long biblical past, the modern Kiryat Gat emerged as a development town in the mid-50s and eventually grew into a city by the time I arrived there. However, it was small enough at the time that it did not have a movie theater.

In the area around Kiryat Gat, they grow beautiful roses and it was my impression that these flower growers, who already had some knowledge of English, would be my students. Two days before I left, they told me that I would also be teaching elderly Israeli retirees who spoke little or no English. So, off I went and was met at the airport and taken to my apartment in Kiryat Gat. The refrigerators and shelves were stocked with food, so what more could one want?

Of course, I was not in Israel on vacation, but was there to teach. Despite all of the different and varied experiences that I had in my life, this would be my first experience in the classroom. It looked to be baptism by fire if you will pardon the expression. Although Paula had given me a few tips since she had spent over thirty years as a professor, I was still a bit nervous and knew not what to expect my first day. Well, that first day turned out to be a first class disaster. The fifteen or so men and women in each class spoke and understood almost no English and I speak very little conversational Hebrew. I was in big trouble. I contacted the Jewish United Fund (JUF) office at Kiryat Gat to tell them about my situation and talked them into providing me with a translator. Fortunately there was a young woman who was doing her *Sherut Leumi* (alternative national service) in the town. This beautiful and bright girl, whose English was quite good, helped me communicate with my students.

I was pretty much on my own as to how to teach my charges and decided that, like teaching children, I would begin with something that everyone had, namely a body. Starting with the top of one's head to the bottom of the feet, I would say a word in English. My interpreter would then write the word in both English and Hebrew. This worked so well that I moved to teach them a song, which, in this case, was the old-time classic, "Row, Row, Row Your Boat Gently Down The Stream." Pretty soon, they had learned the song so well and sung it with such enthusiasm, or as they say in Hebrew, *hitlahavut*, that the other classrooms in the building that we used asked us to close the door. Apparently, this made its way back to the JUF offices in Kiryat Gat and Chicago.

In the evening, I was scheduled to teach the rose growers who were working during the day in the fields. I was asked if I was willing to take on an additional class during the day, in this case, Ethiopian immigrants, a group known as Falashas who interested me a great deal. They were living in a large building which was surrounded by a large steel fence. Though it sounds restricting, they were free to come and go as they wished. Most of them preferred to stay within the confines of their homes.

The Ethiopians are an extraordinary group and perhaps my interest in exotic Jews, if I can use that word, began at this time. Though they are black, they look much different than West Africans in that their features are very delicate. Again I had an interpreter to help me. I started teaching about a dozen or so boys and girls between the ages of nine and seventeen. But rather than focus on the human body, I decided to teach them about their families, their mother, father, brothers and sisters.

I did make one mistake, but it was not a pedagogical one. I began giving them candy, allowing them to come up during class and take a piece of candy as a kind of reward for coming to class. Of course, I could not foresee where this was headed. During the class they began taking the candy and then would leave. Word spread that you could go to this class, get candy, and then leave. At the next class, there were twenty students in attendance but no candy. Instead, I brought out some inedible pencils and told them they would not get their pencil until the end of class. Though they were not happy, they stayed to the end and the classes began to get larger each day until we had a total of about forty children. By the end of the lesson, I had told them about my own family and had each one write a letter to each of my eight grandchildren. In this letter they would describe their life in Ethiopia and the transition to their new existence in the Holy Land. On my last day with them, they gave me presents such as drawings that they had done in my honor and told me how much they loved my class and me. I can barely contain my emotions when I think of those kids and what they had been through.

I also taught Ethiopian adults and when I finished teaching the kids at 4 o'clock in the afternoon, I took a bus to meet and teach the rose growers. Though most of my students were engaged in that vocation, I also had a Russian fellow who worked for Intel, the giant computer chip maker headquartered in Silicon Valley. Intel had built a huge plant near Kiryat Gat and that gentleman, who had been a professor back in Russia, was in charge of quality control at the plant. He was to make certain that dust did not end up on the chips. This fellow was my transportation back to KIryat Gat as he lived together with his wife and daughter in a predominantly Russian neighborhood in the city. We would often stop at a little restaurant for supper. On my last day, he took me on a tour through the state-of-the-art Intel facility, as sophisticated technologically as anything we have here.

Of all the groups whom I taught, the rose growers proved the most difficult to teach. In true Israeli style, they felt they knew it all, and did not think I could be of much help. Since they could read English, I had brought some different articles culled from magazines and would ask the class to read the piece to themselves and then we would discuss the content of the article in a group format. Interestingly enough, the opinions of my students were divergent enough as to actually cause arguing among many who were friends. And Israelis do know how to argue. Eventually, I won them over, and by the end of our time together, they had a dinner in my honor.

Some of my students in Kiryat Gat, Israel

Sam with some of the Ethiopean students

One of the many benefits to my teaching was that I would be invited to the home of my students for Sabbath meals. In addition to the excellent cuisine served there, I got to see three generations interact. It occurred to me that I had never seen such happy and content people before, this despite their limited economic circumstances. Returning to Wilmette, I received a call from the JUF office. Apparently, I was a big hit and realized that there was a lot to be accomplished in retirement. The satisfaction of giving was never so pronounced as my experience of teaching in Israel. There was something else happened during my time in Israel, and it would lead me to one spectacular adventure.

Taking a Torah to Northeast India

I was enjoying my retirement when one day I was throwing out some old magazines. "Hadassah Magazine" was one of the several that were slated for the recycle bin when I came across an issue, October 1999 to be exact, that piqued my interest.

MENASHE'S CHILDREN COME HOME

by Wendy Elliman, Hadassah Magazine, October 1, 1999.

Reprinted with permission of Wendy Elliman

"Some Israelis are more willing to give land to the Palestinians than to give a warm bed to brothers who left a long time ago, says Esther Thangsom, 24, who came to Israel 18 months ago. "Others go out of their way to welcome us back.

But is doesn't matter whether people make the way home easy or hard, because God helps us, she says in her calm and gentle manner. "We're a patient people. We've waited almost 3,000 years; we can wait almost 3,000 years; we can wait a few years longer."

Thangsom is part of a new immigrant community in Israel that now numbers 340. They are known as Bnei Menashe or Shinlung, names acquired at different stages of their long journey. The first signifies their belief that they're descended from the Israelite tribe. According to their tradition they lived as part of the Hebrew nation till the days of the First Temple, when they fled east from the Assyrian conquerors of 744 B.C.E. and, 400 years later, farther east still from the armies of Alexander the Great, through Tibet and into China. Believing they were the only Jews left, they lived quietly under the Chinese until the Middle Ages.

Late in the thirteenth century they were threatened once again-by conversion to Christianity. They fled south to Indochina, where they acquired their second name. For two generations they found refuge in a remote valley of caves; Shinlung means cave dwellers. The Chinese eventually found them, seized their holy parchment (which they believe was the Torah) and drove them into today's Thailand and Burma. From here many migrated into the north Indian provinces of Mizoram and Manipur, where it is estimated 1.25 million to 4 million live today. There are 10,000 actively Jewish Bnei Menashe in 13 towns. Of this number 3,500 have formally converted to Orthodox Judaism.

"We never felt we belonged in India," asserts Ruth Thangsom, 25, Esther's sister. The family comes from Manipur and their features, like those of other Bnei Menashe are Mongolian. "We felt lost. We don't look like Indians, we don't think like them or identify with them. We were sojourners. We always knew we belonged to the land and people of Israel. In college, when I was studying for my B.A. in English literature, I used to think: What I want more than anything is to be in Israel, where I can live according to the Torah and the mitzvot."

"I grew up with a longing to be Jewish and to come to Israel," says Esther, a psychologist who is studying social work. "I used to tell my friends at boarding school in New Delhi: "I'm not Indian. It's a geographical and political mistake that I'm here. One day, I"ll live in Israel."

"I've wanted to come to Israel ever since my midteens when I [found out about] Israel," says Shmuel Joram, 38, a draftsman who grew up in Mizoram. Like so many Bnei Menashe he speaks quietly and respectfully, but with determination and conviction. Today Joram, the Thangsom sisters and their brother Yitzhak, 30, an economist, all live in Jerusalem. They have formally converted to

Judaism and are citizens. If they don't yet feel Israeli, they have a strong sense of having found their place. "In my heart, I resented undergoing conversion when I feel so utterly Jewish," says Yitzhak with controlled dignity. "But as our path back to our roots was through Christianity, I accept it was necessary."

After the loss of their precious parchment, they nursed a tradition that one day a white man would come to return their holy books. When a Reverend Pettigrew arrived in India from Britain in 1813, ablaze with Baptist fervor and copies of the Christian Bible, the Bnei Menashe believed the prophecy had been fulfilled. Large parts of the book, from Adam and Eve to the Exodus from Egypt, echoed their oral tradition. Within a decade, the whole community was Christian.

"Our grandfather was orphaned young and raised by missionaries," says Yitzhak. That's how our family became Christian. Our father reversed it. He was a deeply religious man who sought the truth. I remember him giving me a siddur and telling me: Judaism is the true faith." The way back was shown by a community member who came to be regarded as a modern day prophet.

"His name was Challa Malla," explains Joram. "In the 1950's, he had a vision that the Bnei Menashe were Israelites. His vision ignited the community. They stopped working and began preparing to return to Israel, expecting daily the appearance of the Messiah. A delegation was sent to the Israeli consulate in Calcutta."

This first attempt to return collapsed quickly in the face of opposition from local Indian authorities and Jewish leaders. But a connection had been forged and the Bnei Menashe stayed in touch with Jewish communities in Calcutta and Bombay 600 miles away. Members like the elder Thangsom embraced their Judaism.

"When you find the truth it hits your heart," Joram says. "I remember my father weeping because he had found the true faith."

In the 1970's a group of educated middle-class BM made a formal decision to return to Judaism. They built synagogues, took on Sabbath observance and brit mila. It was shortly after this that Rabbi Eliyahu Avichail first heard of them; one of the many letters they wrote asking for help in coming to Israel was passed along to him. "I was interested, of course," Avichail says. After several attempts he obtained permission to go into Manipur and Mizoram, an area closed because of a border conflict. He also met community representatives in Calcutta and managed to bring two of them to study in Israeli yeshivot, so they could return to India as Jewish teachers.

"The more I got to know the community, the more certain I became that their tradition was true and they were indeed descended from the tribe of Menashe," says Avichail. "Their customs are very close to prerabbinical Judaism. They have songs thousands of years old, with words from the Bible. One is: 'Let us go to Zion!' even though they didn't even know what Zion was. They gave their children names unknown in the surrounding Indian community, such as Apram, Yakov, Sinai and Shilo. Among their customs are white garment that resembles blue and white tzitziot. The eating of blood is prohibited. They have laws of family purity and follow a lunar calendar. Corpses are seen as impure.

"All this is too close to be coincidence-and too far to have been recently brought to them. These are ancient customs, corrupted over time."

In their scrolls there were strange stories about Adam and Eve, the Flood, Avichail points out. "The Tower of Babel, for example, was built to wage war on God, Who turned the stones to poison, whereupon the builders forgot their language and were dispersed."

Avichail began his long struggle on their behalf. "In 1988 we made a symbolic beginning, converting 24 in Calcutta," he says. "But then as now Israel's interior ministry reaction was: Do you want to submerge Israel with these people? But I persisted, and ended up pleading the case before the Supreme Court. It found in our favor and in 1989 I brought over the first group and settled them in Kfar Etzion."

Avichail's aim is to bring the 10,000 or so Bnei Menashe who are today practicing, if not yet converted, Jews. With every incoming group, however, he faces a major struggle. "In 1993 I brought [some] with the help of the Christian Embassy in Jerusalem, which paid for the plane, "he says. "Days before they were due, a scare story was leaked to the Hebrew press that 'untouchables' were about to flood the country. This delayed their aliya by seven months and they'd already sold their homes and businesses. I turned to the Lubavitcher Reba, who was by then very sick. 'Should I be doing this?' I asked him. 'Yes!' he said. 'Bring them to Israel!'"

"Israel's Chief Rabbinate has been good to us, says Yitzhak. "They insist on a full Orthodox conversion [bet din and mikve] but I think they go easier on us than other converts by not making us wait months before being called to the bet din. They recognize our genuine faith. The absorption ministry has also been helpful and is giving [us] temporary resident status so we can live in absorption centers while we study Hebrew and Judaism.

"But the interior ministry is very different. They delayed granting us citizenship for almost a year after the bet din converted us. Their tactics included streams of questions about our conversion, like: How did you step into the mikve? They insisted each of us produce a full genealogical tree. It was only when we threatened to go to the Supreme Court that they gave us our citizenship papers."

Today the Bnei Menashe are scattered throughout the country: they have settled in and are doing well. Some are in higher education, others run small businesses, many live on settlements—Kiryat Arba, Ofra, Beit-El, Eilon Moreh, and Gush Katif. Most are politically right wing, all are ready to serve in the army, and all, without exception, are religiously observant.

"We didn't know all these people in India, but we feel very close," says Ruth. "There's always somewhere to go on Shabbat and festivals and we share one another's weddings and bar mitzvahs. There are already sabra Bnei Menashe in the community."

The Thangsoms and Joram are still living and studying in the Nahalat Zvi yeshiva, where they prepared for conversion. "It's home to us," Joram says. "The rosh yeshiva [yeshiva head] totally accepts us 'raw' from India. He carries the spark of holiness within him. I'm planning to stay on for another year. Then I'll think about my career and how to earn money and settle down."

Ruth, too wants to continue her Jewish studies. "Without learning you miss out on what it takes to be a Jew," she says. "Every Jew needs to find his own path, but you can't find it without knowledge." After full-time study, she'd like to teach.

"You have to be educated in your faith," says Esther. "We'd be missing the point of being in Israel if we didn't like to teach.

"For the remaining Bnei Menashe in India who are interested in living a Jewish life, moving to Israel would be more than enough for the moment. Many enjoy comfortable middle class lives, but their hearts are in their ancestral land. They also faced danger 18 months ago, when their communities in Manipur were attacked by neighbors from the Naga tribe. Two synagogues were burned and several people were killed.

But this isn't why the Bnei Menashe want to come. "They want to live in Israel for the same reasons that we do," says Joram, "the same reasons that any Jew wants to live in his own land. Because it's ours. Because it's home."

Map of northeast India

I was heavily affected by the article. It was more than just being fascinated by an exotic sounding people. I wanted to do something to help these people. After all, their greatest desire was to live as Jews and in the State of Israel. All they wanted was something that many of us take for granted. I contacted the writer of the article and the photographer. It was more than the just the words that tugged at my heart. It was the pictures, the photos of the B'nai Menashe that got to me. I found out more about the group and the author told me that what the group wanted besides being able to come to Israel was to obtain a Torah scroll. I also contacted Esther Thangsom, one of the people quoted in the piece, who was living in Israel.

As you may remember from the article, Esther came from a prosperous family which was in contrast to the vast majority of the B'nai Menashe. Since I was planning on going to Israel to teach, Esther had told me she would try to get some of the community members together so I could meet them. She also put me in touch with her brother, Issac, who was back in India and was heavily involved in real estate and rented office space to the Indian government. Though he did not come to Israel because of these business interests, he would prove to be a help as his father and uncle were members of the Indian government.

When I arrived in Israel to teach I contacted Esther. She was unable to gather the community together, but, instead, took me to see Rabbi Avichail, who, as the article mentions, discovered the group and was responsible for the first wave of those coming to Israel. Rabbi Avichail is quite a man, oozing with a type of religious sincerity that is so rare in today's modern world. He was a student of Rabbi Tzvi Yehudi Kook, a yeshiva head and leader of religious Zionism, who was himself the son of Rabbi Abraham Issac Kook, the former Chief Rabbi and preeminent religious philosopher and personality. As the group's leader and mentor, Rabbi Avichail mentioned to me the need the community in northeast India had for a Torah scroll and asked me if I would bring a Torah to them. I told him that while I was planning

With Rabbi Avichail at his Jerusalem apartment

a trip to India, I had no intention of trekking to northeast India but if I changed my plans and visited the region, I would indeed bring them a Torah.

Back in Chicago, I told Paula all about my trip and my meetings with Esther and Rabbi Avichail. We discussed our upcoming trip to India which included stops in Delhi, Kashmir, and the Taj Mahal, all locations in western India and nowhere near Mizoram, Manipur, and Nagaland where the B'nai Menashe could be found. It was not to be my first trip to India as I had previously traveled and toured there for a month several years earlier and had simply loved the place. Since Paula was not able to go at the time due to her teaching schedule, I had promised to take her in the summer when she would be on vacation.

Paula must have detected that my curiosity over the region was peaking, and, being an academic, she suggested that I go to the library and read up on the area. After poring over assorted travel books and other sources of information, there seemed to be one conclusion: don't go to northeast India. Why not? The region featured on and off internecine fighting, violence that centered on political and national differences among a variety of different groups and tribes. And to make matters worse, it was situated near Burma in an area rife with poppy growing drug activity which meant drug lords and violence. So, of course, the more negative things I heard, the more I wanted to go.

I applied for a visa to India which I received. But, when I asked if this would allow me to visit the three provinces where the B'nai Menashe lived, I was told that it would not. To enter Mizoram and Manipur, I required a special permit from what amounted to India's State Department. In order to obtain the special permit, their form required the recommendation from someone in a high political office in those two provincial states. So I received the documents but now I just had to find someone of significance in those states who would be willing to vouch for Sam Pfeffer.

If you remember my trip to Norway, I had met high level government officials, but when it came to India, I did not have any such contacts. What to do? I decided to speak to a friend of mine, Sabra Minkus, who was president of our synagogue. Sabra's family owned a company that purchased raw materials from various countries around the world, thinking that maybe she may have a contact in India. She had done business with the former Bhutanese ambassador to India who happened to be acquainted with the commissioners of the two states where we were looking to obtain entry. The ambassador was willing to contact them, and, sure enough, they vouched for us by returning the signed documents to the Indian Consulate in Chicago. The documents were then sent to the Indian State Department and two weeks later the docs were sent to the Indian Consulate in Chicago. (who are equivalent to our senators) and they returned them back to us. Within two weeks we had our permits and were ready to travel to an area known as "the Wild West of India." Now that we had our permits, we still had time to decide whether we really wanted to go. I remembered my words to

Bruce Sheridan, chair of the Film and Video Department, Columbia College. Producer and director of This Song is Old.

Rabbi Avichail and together with Sabra and Paula discussed whether we should take the trip.

Serving on the board of Columbia, I had a meeting on a committee that I served on whose function was to discuss all new requests for facilities prior to its being brought before the full board. In this case the film department was looking for extra space and after the meeting had adjourned, we all sat around drinking coffee. Someone asked me, "Sam, what are you doing in your retirement?" So I proceeded to tell about my upcoming trip to India and bringing the Torah to B'nei Menashe.

Bruce Sheridan, chair of the Film Department was in attendance and after hearing the tale, suggested that we had all the elements for a pretty good film, one which he considered to be a humanitarian documentary. Such a documentary would give the students at Columbia College hands-on experience in a real world film and provide the college with positive publicity. I sat down with Bruce and we laid out the roles that everyone would play in the making of such a movie and eventually came to terms so now our mission to India took on even greater importance.

It all sounded good except for one minor detail. We had no Sefer Torah. I thought that was going to be the least of our troubles as I figured we would be able to find a Sefer Torah from the arks of one of the Chicago area synagogues. There were surely some that were little used and it seemed to me that our cause was sufficiently compelling that one of those synagogues would donate one. I figured wrong.

We needed to buy a Torah. First we had to raise the necessary funds. Three of my friends contributed equally along with us. Paula and I donated money in honor of our children and grandchildren. Sabra Minkus, who had become as enchanted with the idea of bringing the Torah to northeast India as I was and would join us for the trip, had donated funds in memory of her husband, Morton. Gladys Sturman donated in memory of her husband Herman and our friends Morris and Clarice Simon in memory of the six million who perished in the Holocaust.

The next step was to call in an expert. I went to speak to Avi Fox, who owns a large Judaica shop and is very knowledgeable in these matters. The first thing I learned about the enterprise was that as in the car business, there is a great variety of price when it comes to Torahs. A newly written Sefer Torah could cost between forty and fifty thousand dollars. A "pre-owned" Sefer Torah could go for anywhere between five and twenty-five thousand dollars, depending on its condition. My mazel was good in this case as Avi had informed that he had just received such a Torah scroll from Israel recently. We agreed on a price and our rabbi and a scribe went over the scroll and made corrections as necessary. So we finally had our Torah and were good to go.

Still, one final detail needed to be worked out. How do we get the Torah to India? The logical thing to do would be to check it as baggage on our flight but as our rabbi correctly pointed out,

Beth Hillel Academy students and teachers touch a Torah carried by Sam Pfeffer around the Beth Hillel Synagogue in Wilmette earlier this month. Pfeffer flew to India Sunday to deliver the Torah to the Bnei Menashe, who believe they are a lost tribe of Israel.

TORAH: Handwritten Torah bought for $12,000

CONTINUED FROM PAGE 1

Pfeffer.

"I hope Israel will open its doors to these people as they did to Jews from the former Soviet Union," Fox said.

The road to converting the Bnei Menashe, however, is likely to be longer than Fox hopes. When Pfeffer arrives in the Indian states later this week, religious ceremonies will be held for the locals, who will see a Torah for the first time.

Eventually, Pfeffer hopes Israel's religious court will come to the region to perform bona fide conversions that would confer the legal right to immigrate to Israel, like all recognized Jews. Efforts to convert the Bnei Menashe began in earnest about 18 months ago, when Amishav, an Israeli organization committed to reaching out to "lost Jews" seeking to return to Israel, established a Hebrew school in Aizawl, the capital of Mizoram.

Over the last decade, Amishav brought about 800 members of the Bnei Menashe to Israel and helped them convert to Orthodox Judaism. They now live predominantly in the communities of Kiryat Arba, Gush Katif and Beit El. Last year, Israeli Interior Minister Avraham Poraz decided to bar additional members of the tribe from immigrating to Israel, said Michael Freund, director of Amishav.

"Sadly, I can only conclude that Mr. Poraz's policy is one of racism, which discriminates against the Bnei Menashe because of the color of their skin," said Freund, referring to their dark skin and Asian features.

The Bnei Menashe claim a connection to Judaism from the time of King Solomon, though these ties are disputed. At that time, the tribes of Israel split into two kingdoms.

In 723 B.C. the Assyrians conquered the kingdom of Israel and took 10 tribes into exile, and they roamed across the world. Some say they escaped to China.

The Indian tribe believes that Christian missionaries in the 19th Century forced them to abandon their Jewish identity and convert to Christianity.

In 1951, three years after the state of Israel was established, a local chief told the tribe that God had told him his people should return to their religion and original homeland. That began the movement for the Bnei Menashe to go to Israel.

The tribe has tried to maintain rituals that resemble those in Judaism, including their use of the lunar calendar.

They also chant songs about crossing the Red Sea and returning to Zion.

But because theologians and politicians disagree on their connection to Judaism, the tribe is ineligible to immigrate to Israel under the country's Law of Return.

Neither politics nor religious arguments discouraged Pfeffer, a member of the Beth Hillel congregation in Wilmette. Added a member of the Beth Hillel Congregation in Wilmette. While he was teaching English in Israel last year, Pfeffer met a woman from the Bnei Menashe who was among the 800 allowed into Israel. Pfeffer became determined to help the estimated 6,000 others left behind.

When Pfeffer returned to the United States, he headed for the Indian consulate in Chicago to try to get a visa to visit Manipur and Mizoram. But officials told him the states were off-limits to foreigners. Pfeffer then used his connections through Jewish firms doing business in India and eventually received the permits.

His next obstacle was to find a Torah, and that's when he found Rosenblum's.

"There are many things involved in getting a Torah," Pfeffer said. "I had no idea that the Torahs go for so much money. Mr. Fox had just received a Torah from Israel so I told him I wanted to speak to my rabbi to make sure it met all the religious requirements."

Once his rabbi gave the green light, friends and Pfeffer pitched in the $12,000 for the Torah. Then he made plans with two members of the Beth Hillel Congregation to make the trip.

"I am so excited, and the elders in the village are excited," Pfeffer said.

"They say they could have 1,000 to 2,000 people for the reading of the Torah because they never had a scroll to read from before."

The Chicago Tribune article about the Torah and B'nai Menashe

Sabra Minkus with Torah scroll

this would not have been appropriate as the Torah needs to be treated with great respect as it is a holy object. So it occurred to me that I needed to buy a seat for the Torah. We happened to be flying Lufthansa so a week before our trip I drove to the O'Hare airport with Torah in hand to speak with one of the managers of Lufthansa. The woman I met with was in fact the top person at O'Hare, and I explained to her why we were traveling to India. She had never seen a scroll before but understood that it was an intricate part of the Jewish religion. Apparently she was very impressed with our mission because she asked me to wait a minute while she checked the manifest for the flight. She then told me that there was extra space in first class and that the Torah could fly for free. Ever the negotiator, I tried to see if I could fly first class and the Torah could fly business class. Our lady from Lufthansa pointed out that there was a difference between a person and a Torah; a Torah does not eat. I could have told her that the Torah is, in fact, compared to water since it sustains us spiritually, but she was technically right that the Torah does not eat and so left it at that. I thanked her for the wonderful courtesy that she and Luftansa had showed the Torah. As I drove back to Wilmette that day I could not help but think given the history of the airline in question, there was a fair amount of historical irony in our Torah flying first class without charge.

Before we left, Rabbi Kensky, our synagogue's rabbi, expressed a desire that the children in our Hebrew School should do something to help the B'nai Menashe children of Izawal and see the Torah before it began its journey. We arranged a special one hour program for the children. Each youngster contributed twenty-five cents that would go to the kids in Izawal and the adults that attended contributed substantially greater sums. We took the Torah around so the kids could kiss it. It was not a ceremony that lacked fanfare. Someone had notified the Chicago Tribune and they sent a reporter and photographer. Not only did this turn out to be a front page story but it was picked up by other newspapers in the Tribune family. And it was not just local publicity we garnered as our travel agent sent a copy to the local agent in India and when we got there, we were treated as celebrities.

Bruce Sheridan had arranged for a cinema photographer, a sound man and helper to take our pictures upon our arrival in India. We were unaware that that we were being photographed but once we met the cinema photographer, whose name was Harsh Varma, we discovered that he was also a location director and a representative of the BBC (British Broadcasting Company) in India. Varma is a well known media personality in the country, having done several stories about northeast India for Indian television. Those in India's more populated cities have rarely traveled there and knew about as much about the area as I did.

Despite what I heard about the region, nothing quite prepared me for the scene that greeted us when we landed in Izawal by way of Ceijhwati. The airport was surrounded by machine gun toting army troops. They came aboard the plane and inspected

With B'nai Menashe children at synagogue located 20 miles from Imphal. Paula is in the top row.

all of our baggage as well as inspecting all of us through a pretty rigorous search. We were finally allowed off the plane when Paula proceeded to take a photo of the airplane. Two army officers spotted this and were not too happy about it. They ushered Paula into an office inside the terminal. After being questioned, she was released minus the film. It was true what they said about northeast India. It was certainly not flying into Delhi.

When we arrived in Izwal it was election day and no buses or taxis were running. Fortunately I had arranged for someone to meet us at the airport and drive us into town without realizing that it was what amounted to a legal holiday. Good mazel!

Izawal had an educational facility that taught children Hebrew and the rudiments of the Jewish religion. But it was a very practical education as they needed to be self-sufficient in their ritual practices. They made kosher wine and matzoh for Passover. At the school, we showed everyone the Torah and gave them the money that had been collected on their behalf by our synagogue in Wilmette. They held a service and entertained us with their

*At a small B'nai Menashe synagogue outside of Imphal.
(Note the clapboard roof.)*

special dances done in full local costume. I mention this because they are famous for their embroidered bright colored clothing. They gave us beautiful shawls as gifts.

The next day we flew to the capital of Manipur, a town named Imphala. As we exited from the airport with the still wrapped Torah we were met by hundreds and hundreds of B'nai Menashe waving Israeli and Indian flags, singing *Hatikva* (national anthem of the state of Israel) and dancing with all their hearts. Some were even moved to tears and the three of us shed tears as well. All the excitement had caused so much commotion that we were disturbing the traffic pattern and the police ordered us to disperse. Our B'nai Menashe friends loaded on to buses and we hopped into some private car as all the while they were still singing and shouting in Hebrew.

We found ourselves in what amounted to the Impahl convention center. It was the largest building in town. As we made our way to the center, the distinct sound of long trumpets welcoming us could be heard. If I had known any better, I could have sworn it was straight out of Kipling's *The Man Who Would be King* and we were the newfound royals.

The first thing I noticed when we entered the auditorium was the piety of the crowd present. Men and women sat separately. The second thing I observed or rather felt, was the heat. It must have been one hundred twenty-five degrees and though I was sweating through my shirt, the crowd seemed little affected. There was no air conditioning and the ceiling fans offered little relief. How to communicate with our friends? Well, the leaders of the community had learned enough to greet us in our native tongue and we had Isaac Thangsom to serve as our interpreter and his English, reflecting his classical education, was superb.

We then turned over the Torah to them and told them that that this Torah we brought them was their Torah as the Torah was then marched several blocks to their synagogue, with a prayer shawl acting as a canopy for the scroll. There was a large procession following behind, singing Hebrew songs. We had Friday night dinner and the next morning for Sabbath services, the Torah was read from. There was an overflow crowd and you can imagine the emotion, the crying and the shouting, that took place in the synagogue that day. Finally, the B'nai Menashe were united with their fellow Jews the world over. They were reading from the same portion of the Torah that every other Jew, every large synagogue and small prayer house from Brisbane to Buenos Aires, from Boston to Bombay. We had accomplished our mission.

Still, we wanted to take the Torah around to the B'nai Menashe who were scattered in little villages throughout the countryside. One of the villages we visited was named Chandiapur. Because we needed to wait for some camera parts to arrive, we were four hours late. The people did not care. They waited patiently in the boiling sun.

You must be wondering about the wild, wild, west part of northeast India. In the United States, you rarely see soldiers

*Top: With oldest living B'nai Menashe woman. Rumored to be over 100 years old, she asked if she could have her picture taken with me. She referred to me as "her hero."
Bottom: With B'nai Menashe leader.*

unless they are traveling or you are on a military base. Well, the army was everywhere on our trip, in some cities you would see soldiers on foot or riding in armored vehicles. Sandbags surrounded government installations and tanks trolled around government buildings and financial institutions as if an attack

With Hillel Halkin and Sabra Minkus

was imminent. At one point we began to notice that there were two men in plainclothes that would follow us around wherever we went. It was clear that they were from one of the security services. As it turned out they were Indian secret service but their reason for keeping an eye us related to one Harsh Varma. His father was a senior member of the Indian parliament and he had requested the detail. It was nice to know that in the wild wild west, someone was watching over you.

Upon our return to the United States, Bruce Sheridan thought that our film would not be complete if we did not tell the story of the B'nai Menashe who had arrived in Israel in the mid 1990s and had staked out a life for themselves in the Jewish state. Bruce arranged for a film crew to work with us in Israel and we were most fortunate to have as our chief cinematographer a top notch person who had just got garnered major awards for his work on the documentary, *Area K*. It was an important film because it highlighted Jewish settlers helping Muslim fishermen and the relationship that ensued between the two groups. That is until the Muslims were pressured by the events of the bloody intifada to discontinue their cooperation.

Our work on the film put us in touch with many fascinating people. None were more fascinating than the well known Israeli journalist Hillel Halkin. From a distinguished rabbinic and scholarly family, he is a superb writer who among his numerous books wrote about the B'nai Menashe in his *Across the Sabbath River*, bringing much notoriety to the group. As well as producing a fascinating book, Hillel Halkin stayed involved with the subject of his work. He had originally traveled to China with Rabbi Avichal and apparently like yours truly, became fascinated with these Mongolian looking souls. I spent a significant amount of time with Hillel, learned a great deal from him, and he figures prominently in the film.

Another person we met who plays a large role in the life of B'nai Menashe is Michael Freund. Like Hillel Halkin, he is a native New Yorker who made *aliyah*. He was working in the government when he met Rabbi Avichail and worked with him for several years in the organization that he founded named Amishav before founding his own group called Shavei Israel. Though Rabbi Avichail remains the spiritual mentor and hero of the B'nai Menashe, Freund's group has done a great deal to help them, both in terms of bringing them from India and acculturating them into Israeli society.

The Sephardic chief rabbinate sent several rabbis to investigate the claims of the group that they are, in fact, descendants of a lost tribe of Israel. Traveling there in 2004, by March of 2005 the rabbis announced that they determined that the group are indeed descendants of a lost tribe. Of course, that finding does not remove the need for a formal conversion. The original group that Rabbi Avichail brought over in the 1990s came over on a tourist visa and were converted in Israel. But ten years later the more practical approach was to have the rabbinate convert them in Manipur so they could be brought over as Jews under the law of return, which allows any Jew the right to live as an Israeli citizen.

The costs to bring 6,000 Jews from India would normally be absorbed by the Jewish Agency, the organization which takes a leading role in significant immigration matters. Helping out were the International Fellowship of Christians and Jews with an offer to pick up the entire tab which includes the chartering of planes until all the B'nai Menashe arrive in Israel. Unfortunately for the sincere souls that comprise the B'nai Menashe, they became caught in the politics of the two countries. The Indian government did not want them to leave in one fell swoop and were only going to allow groups of 50 or 60 of the 250 or so permitted to leave at one time. There had been an Indian law enacted many years earlier that forbids proselytizing, a law put into place by the Indian government to protect the Hindu majority from Christian proselytizing. But in our case it was the Christians clergy who were worried they are losing from their flock some of their own numbers, people like Esther and her siblings. (Christian missionaries had made significant numbers of converts throughout northeast India including a fair number of B'nai Menashe, some of whom have since converted or are in the process of converting to Judaism.) Of course, the B'nai Menashe argue that this is not the case since the group was originally Jewish and the rabbis are just allowing them to become knowledgeable in the religion of their ancestors.

The other part of the equation is on the political realm. In so much as relations between India and Israel are strong and there is ever growing military and economic cooperation between the two countries, the Indian government placed pressure on their Israeli counterparts to cease the conversions. The key government body in Israel on matters of immigration is the Interior Ministry and the fate of the B'nai Menashe seems tied not only to the party in control of the Prime Minister's office but in the coalition government, the person who is appointed to be Interior Minister. In general, the left-wing parties have opposed the B'nai Menashe because it is believed that they will be unfriendly to a leftist viewpoint and as citizens, they are unlikely to vote for one of the left-wing parties. Therefore, the office has been a frequent stumbling block in the group's coming to Israel. This is truly a sad situation and it is important to place pressure on both the rabbinate and the government to see this matter through.

As we were making the film, we were most anxious to see how the immigrants were adjusting to a society so very different from their own. Unfortunately due to the color of their skin and their unique past, the B'nai Menashe were hardly in high demand so they had to go where they were welcomed and very few communities were interested in having them settle. One which did was Kiryat Arba, adjacent to Hebron. Hebron is the final resting place of the Biblical Patriarchs and Matriarchs and therefore very holy to Jews. No place is more closely associated with Jewish genealogy than this place and for a group claiming a connection with the one of the Jewish tribes, this is more than just a touch ironic. It seems to be just another chapter in the amazing story of the descendants of the tribe of Menashe. But as with anything in the Holy Land, there is plenty of security to be found in Kiryat Arba. The Jews are vastly outnumbered, were massacred in large numbers in Hebron by Arabs during the riots of 1929 and the threat for a repeat of that carnage is never very far from the surface of life in the region. Only an army presence and barbed wire protect the B'nai Menashe and the other Jews from serious bodily harm. The B'nai Menashe have gone from the wild wild west of northeast India to something only a little less volatile. Do they mind? When you speak to them, they seem happy and content to live as Jews in a Jewish country. They have returned home, even if it only took 2,700 years.

It was in Kiryat Arba that we met Issac's mother and two sisters. There they recited some of the lines of an old village song which is similar to Miriam's song, which is found in the book of Exodus when the Jewish people leave the land of Egypt. It is from this very toucing song that Bruce Sheridan titled our film, *This Song is Old*. In Kiryat Arba we met some of the younger generation who seem to be adjusting rather well. We met Israel Defense Forces (IDF) soldiers and, for all intents and purposes, they seemed perfectly Israeli.

Wilmette man, filmmaker help Jews from Asia integrate into Israel

BY RUMMANA HUSSAIN
Staff Reporter

Retired Wilmette lawyer Sam Pfeffer fulfilled the dreams of a group of Indians believed to be members of one of the lost tribes of Israel when he presented them with a Torah during a visit to Asia last year.

"The scroll was the one item they lacked to make them part of the Jewish community," Pfeffer reminisced this week, describing the B'nei Menashe's reaction to the holy book. "They just went wild."

Israel's chief Rabbi Shlomo Amar has recognized the group as legitimate Jewish descendants and orchestrated plans to bring them back "home," ending their 2,700-year exodus from the Middle East. Pfeffer, a Columbia College board member, is intent on capturing part of the journey.

He and Columbia College film and video department Chairman Bruce Sheridan will travel to Israel on Sunday to interview Amar's aides for a documentary on the plight of the 6,000 to 7,000 Jews from the far northeast Indian states of Manipur and Mizoram.

"These people have been obscure and unknown to the world. Their dream has always been to return [to Israel]," Sheridan said.

Without a Torah

Pfeffer, 79, first learned about B'nei Menashe in 2003 when he spotted an article in a Hadassah Magazine issue he was about to throw out. He then contacted the article's authors, flew to Israel to study the matter and purchased a $12,000 hand-written Torah from a Chicago area bookstore for the Indian Jews. Without a Torah, it would have been impossible for the group to join the 800 B'nei Menashe's members already in Israel.

Although the congregations in the mostly Hindu country have been practicing Judaism for years, they have to be formally converted to Orthodox Judaism by rabbinical judges before they are given the "right to return" to Israel. Many of the men have to be circumcised, and the group must take Hebrew classes so they won't be "sticker shocked" when they come to Israel in a few years, Pfeffer said.

Sheridan said Pfeffer, a member of the Beth Hillel congregation in Wilmette, should receive credit for initiating the process to bring the Indian Jews back to their homeland.

"It's one thing to be in a position to do these type of things. It's another thing to actually do them," Sheridan said.

Sam Pfeffer (left) and Bruce Sheridan look over a map of Israel before leaving on a trip to plan a documentary. —KEITH HALE/SUN TIMES

The Chicago Sun Times article profiled our trip and film.

I returned once more to Israel to work on the film and this time Bruce Sheridan joined me. We now had a film and with Bruce and Columbia's students working hard, by 2009 it was ready for viewing. Yours truly serves as the narrator and I was pleased to find out from various friends that I am a pretty good narrator. But the story is so good that it could have survived even a poor narrator. It gives me great pleasure to see how well the film turned out and is still being shown at Jewish film festivals.

One of the most prominent of the Jewish film festivals is the one held annually in Atlanta, Georgia. It is scheduled to be shown, along with plenty of other interesting titles, in February of 2011. We are extremely excited about this showing and I reprint the blurb here:

THIS SONG IS OLD
Documentary
Director: Bruce Sheridan
Usa 2009 Digibeta 29 Min English

Seeking to uncover the truth about a remote mountain village in India that practices Judaism, **THIS SONG IS OLD** penetrates the question: what does it mean to be Jewish? The Bnei Menashe claim to be descendants of a lost tribe, Jews enslaved by the Assyrians, who escaped to China, eventually settling in east India. When retired Chicago attorney Sam Pfeffer hears their remarkable story, he decides to personally deliver a Torah to the village. His intercontinental odyssey becomes a larger campaign to officially recognize the Jewishness of these disciples who chant Hebrew inside mud walled synagogues, but are ineligible to emigrate to Israel. The road to *aliyah* is fraught with complications, as theologians and Israeli courts argue whether to confer legal status on the Bnei Menashe. **THIS SONG IS OLD** is a fascinating examination of forensics, political intrigue, and the religious fight to bring the Bnei Menashe "home" to Israel.

But if you thought that the trip and the film would be the end for me and the B'nai Menashe you would be mistaken. Together with Sabra and several other friends, we formed a charitable foundation named *Chazak* which means strength in Hebrew to help the B'nai Menashe and other Jewish communities that require assistance. It bears mentioning on why we chose that name. Just as we heard on that Sabbath in northeast India, all Jews read from a portion of the Pentateuch. Though it is one

Torah scroll, the Pentateuch consists of the book of Genesis, Exodus, Leviticus, Numbers, and Deuteronomy. Whenever we finish on of the Five Books of Moses, the entire congregation proclaims, "*Chazak, chazak, v'nitchazek.*" which means "Be strong, be strong, and may we be strengthened."

One of the proudest developments in the community has been the ordination of a B'nai Menashe community member to become a rabbi. Shlomo Gangte is not only ordained as a rabbi but also is a qualified mohel (religious circumciser) and a shochet (ritual slaughterer). The initial thought was that he would travel back to India and provide religious instruction and services there but family circumstances have kept him in Israel. This is a boost for the community there and to help tend to the needs of the B'nai Menashe who are spread out there, we have purchased a used car to assist him in this most worthy position. We are hoping to do a great deal more.

Many people are interested in the work we are doing and I hope many more will become involved. Sabra has taken this on with great energy and vigor. But I want to leave, you, the reader, with one message about this very interesting chapter in my life. Remember what I told you previously; that it does not take much to make a difference in this world. You can contribute your time and your talents, you can write a check, but, above all else, you need to give of yourself. I hope that as I am concluding this book, that you remember that message and give it some thought. It is more simple and far easier than you would think. Look what transpired from an old magazine article. And believe me, there is nothing so special about Sam Pfeffer. You can do it too.

A Torah Crown in Wilmette

Bringing a Torah to northeast India was surely an exciting experience. To travel half way around the world with a Torah scroll was nothing I could have ever imagined. But a good deed is a good deed whether half way around way the world or in your own backyard. This next story took place right here in Wilmette.

Rabbi Paul (Moshe) Raitman is a long time friend but you may be surprised to learn that what brought us together was not Torah but tennis. We were in fact partners for 15 years on the court. Rabbi Raitman comes from Australia and from a tennis playing family there. He is a perfect example of how deceiving appearances can be; with his beard and religious garb no one would ever think he would know how to hold a tennis racquet much less play the game well. He is a spectacular player and any stereotypes that people may have of religious or Chassidic Jews are crushed as they see Rabbi Raitman crush a tennis ball with a serve that would make his countryman, John Newcombe, proud. Not only can he serve and volley but he covered the court like Rod Laver. I have really enjoyed playing with him. Not only is he a great doubles partner but simply one of the best amateur tennis players that I have ever seen.

For many years, Rabbi Raitman functioned as the cantor of the local Chabad center of Wilmette. Three years ago, he decided to form his own congregation, The North Shore Jewish Center-Congregation Or Simcha. Believe it or not, our mutual interest was tennis and we discussed little of religion over the years. As with many Lubavitchers, Rabbi Raitman was very careful not to foist his beliefs on an individual who may not share them all and, of course, I behaved likewise. It was on this basis of mutual respect that our friendship grew. When Rabbi Raitman told me he was opening up his new synagogue, I told him that I would give him financial assistance.

When speaking of the B'nai Menashe, we spoke of the ancient city of Hebron, the piece of real estate first purchased by Abraham. The father of the Jewish people was known for his hospitality, keeping his tent open in all four directions, allowing strangers that were traveling from every direction the opportunity to stop. Rabbi and Mrs. Raitman follow this lead and their home is open to all on Friday night. There are a wide variety of people that can

www.pioneerlocal.com   September 2, 2010

Congregation Welcomes Handmade Torah Crown
By Kathy Routliffe

Rabbi Moishe Raitman (left) holds the Torah as Sam Pfeffer places a handcrafted crown, made in Israel, during a dedication of the gift Sunday at the Wilmette Community Recreation Center social hall, at 3000 Glenview Road.

Members of the North Shore Jewish Center-Congregation Or Simcha celebrated the crowning of their Torah on Sunday, at a special evening tribute held at the Wilmette Community Recreation Center social hall, 3000 Glenview Road. The event was made possible by a donation from congregation member and Wilmette resident Sam Pfeffer, Rabbi Moishe Raitman said last week. Raitman said Sunday's dedication of the silver Torah crown, handcrafted in Israel, was made in honor of the 60th wedding anniversary of Pfeffer and his wife, Pearl.

"At the beginning of the summer he approached us and said he wanted to do something for us. We had a few options, but we thought the best one was the glorification (of the Torah)," Raitman said.

Sunday's celebration began with a viewing of "This Song is Old," a documentary about Pfeffer's earlier decision to obtain a Torah for the Bnei Menashe community of north-east India. The community is a group of people claiming descent from a lost tribe of Israel, who followed Jewish laws and traditions, but who did not have a Torah.

"This was a wonderful combination of his donating the Torah crown and his mission to the community in India," Raitman said. "It represents a bridge, and the bridge is the person himself, being instrumental in reviving a community that is trying to survive over there, and the continuation of our community here."

Pioneer Local article about
Torah crowning ceremony

*With Rabbi and Mrs. Raitman, Paula and Beth
at Torah crowning ceremony*

be found at the Raitmans for Sabbath meals. Of course, yeshiva students are particularly enthusiastic eaters and you can find a fair representation of them at the Raitman's table on Shabbat. The job of preparing those meals falls on Esther Raitman. She does a tremendous job, and the meals that we have spent at the Raitmans have been particularly enjoyable and festive. While Paula and I were over for one Friday night meal, we once asked the Rebbetzin how she does it. She told us that she would get a migraine headache on Friday afternoons but she was so duty bound and committed to making the Sabbath meals a special experience for her guests that she was able to fight through what must have been very painful. Apparently, doing something for the sake of Heaven allows one to persevere a good deal. It is the spirit of such hospitality that my grandmother and Aunt Mary, who would prepare meals for the many Jewish guests who came through Spring Valley a century ago, would appreciate.

As I mentioned when discussing Shore Community Services in Chapter five, this is a special year for Paula and myself. She is turning eighty, I am reaching the age of eighty-five and we are celebrating our sixtieth wedding anniversary. While the synagogue had a Sefer Torah, they did not have any ornaments that are commonly placed on the Torah, silver objects that serve to beautify that most holy object of our people. We decided that we would make a contribution of a Torah crown in time for Rosh Hashanah services. We even had a ceremony and reception covered by our local paper. I hope it will be used often, exposing the many Jews of Wilmette to the beauty of the Torah.

Long Lost Relatives

The B'nai Menashe, for all their fascinating past were akin to being long lost relatives of the Jewish people who are being reunited into the body of their family. It is a wonderful thing to see family brought back together and sometimes it actually happens in your own life, or at least it happened in mine. It was this past June of 2010 while I was in the middle of working on this book, that I received a phone call from Liverpool, England. The man on the other end of the line was named Gregory Abrams and I had a feeling that this was something out of the ordinary, though I never could have imagined to what extent. Gregory was friendly and courteous and told me it would take some time to listen to the story of what he had to say. He further went on to tell me that he would understand if I did not want to pursue the conversation, but he, his wife, and their family were convinced that his wife and I were biological first cousins, that I was the son of Paul Pfeffer, her uncle. Well, you may remember from the first chapter that my father divorced my mother when I was still a baby and I had no memory of him. He had completely abandoned my mother and me, which I grew to dislike because my mother worked so very hard to support us. But I told Gregory,

"Listen, you didn't call collect and you didn't ask for money, so speak as long as you would like."

Apparently, Gregory's wife, Rochelle (Shelly), had heard rumors over the years that Paul Pfeffer, who happened to be a favorite uncle of hers, had once married and fathered a child. She heard most of this from her half-brother who had survived the Holocaust, but had since passed away. Her father, Nathan, who had been a rabbi in Poland, had lost his first wife, son, daughter, and father in the inferno of the Holocaust. Shelly never knew what to make of these rumors but when she and her husband were planning a trip to America to attend a wedding in Los Angeles, her son suggested that they try and find out if there were any Pfeffers in Chicago. She figured she would try to see if these rumors had some truth behind them.

It was not the first time she had tried to find her long-lost cousin. She attempted through the years to locate this person, but had assumed that her cousin lived in Texas. By the time we met, she and her husband had five kids, two of whom are married and one was planning to be married. They had planned on spending two days in Chicago and their son began to check the Internet. Eventually, he called his mother to take a look at a photo that he had found of me and when she did she began to cry and said, "Oh my God, there is Uncle Paul." Apparently, the resemblance with Paul was a striking one and she felt sure that she had found her long lost cousin. Gregory asked me if we would have breakfast with them at their hotel when they were in Chicago in August. Instead, I invited them to our house, which was easier for Paula. The day came and I picked them up at their hotel and drove them back to our home in Wilmette.

I would call it all a happy reunion, but, in truth, it was no reunion at all for we had never met. I was extremely pleased with the wonderful family that I had and was not necessarily on the prowl for additional members. But the Abrams' were extremely fine people and so I heard the story of my biological father's family. My grandfather, Jacob Pfeffer, was in the

My paternal grandfather who perished in the Warsaw Ghetto.

My first cousin who was killed in Auschwitz

lumber business in Poland and was quite successful. He traveled back and forth from his home in Poland to America, where of course, his son, Paul, had settled. Tragically, my grandfather was stranded in Europe when the war broke out in 1939 and he perished in the flames of the Warsaw ghetto. His other son, Shelly's father and Paul's brother, was named Nathan. Nathan was a rabbi in Poland with a family of his own. He and his son survived the horrors of a concentration camp; his wife and other members of the family all perished. He and his son remained alive by being chosen to work at the camp, and, after the war, he made his way to Italy where he met and married an Italian Jewess, who was Shelly's mother.

My only hostility toward my father was that he did not try to help my mother at all. My view of him is far different from Shelly's, who adored him. She proceeded to tell me that Paul remarried in 1952, and his brother, Rabbi Nathan Pfeffer had come to New York to perform the ceremony. They showed me pictures, and, after not knowing what ever happened to my father, I learned that he lived in the East and had a successful retail business. Apparently, he was a religious and charitable man as Shelly had seen him often over the years.

It turned out to be a wonderful meeting. Of course, they are thrilled to have found long lost family and have invited us to come to England to attend their son's wedding. Because of Shelly, we spent five days in England. This gave us the opportunity to meet the entire family who were most gracious and considerate to both of us. It added to my theory that without mazel, miracles don't happen. I am pleased that by finding me, I was able to fulfill Shelly's lifelong desire to find her long-lost biological first cousin.

I have taken you on quite a trip with *Born to Survive*. But as I sit at my desk in Wilmette, looking out at snow covered trees, my mind cannot help but wander back to another time and another place. That place is Spring Valley and though I am nearly eighty-five now, and I remember the stories told of me when I was newly born. I was the baby who weighed two pounds, the frail little infant who somehow was just born to survive. The word I use a lot in this book is *mazel*. It is surely one of my favorite words because I believe that it applies so accurately to so many of the events that I have lived through. But I must say that the greatest *mazel* in my life was the love and support of my entire family and everyone in Spring Valley. They were with me from those earliest days when I was so weak through my formative years when I grew strong in body, mind, and spirit. Without them, I would not be here.

No matter how many times I say it, it will never be enough, but I must conclude by saying how incredbily grateful I am to have Paula in my life for sixty years and for the children and grandchildren that God has seen fit to bless us with. Paula has given me her constant love and support and continues every day to regenerate that very love and support. Though I may have been born to survive and blessed with mazel, I could not have done it alone. A well known book about the life of the shtetl and I refer not to the Spring Valley shtetl but to the Eastern European one, was titled, "Life is With People." And that is surely true. My great thanks to all of the friends and relatives who are still with us for making my life so much more meaningful. To those who have sadly departed this earth, I will never forget you. You will always be in my mind and the place that you have in my heart is attested to by the many photos that you will see in the section ahead.

I now address myself to some very important readers, namely my current children and grandchildren, and my future descendants. I ask only one thing of you; that when you look look into the eyes of another human being, especially someone who is poor, ill or otherwise afflicted with a handicap, that you see him or her first and foremost as one of God's creatures. Think the best of them and do not judge them on the basis of race, creed or religion. Do all that is within your power to help them. That would be the greatest thing you can do for me. It constitutes the fulfillment of a very special destiny. The destiny of a small-town kid who was *Born to Survive*.

A Tribute to My Uncle, Maurice Buckman

The Good Lord, He did come out today
to pick another flower for His special bouquet

A man, whose generosity for his fellow man was that flower
for whom God knew He was calling upon this hour

A man whose unseen love was to give instead of take
left behind beautiful memories no one would ever shade

Memories of an outstretched hand and a giving heart
to help the poor and knew just where to start

The food on my table often did come from him
not as a gift of pity, but of love within

He was a true friend as one would say "I told you so"
because his soft pat on the back he'd say "I think I knew"

His words of wisdom were of simple choice
but his reassurance came in that gentle voice

He'd always say "Somebody loves you; somebody cares
and the Man will take care of you: The Man Upstairs"

He was as gentle a man as one would want to meet
always honest to those who needed help—never to cheat

He dug deep most of the time to really give
and I honor Maurice—one of the greatest to live

Now, God, Maurice Buckman is knocking upon your door
show him the streets of gold and a lot more

He was with You—him and his most loving touch
but tell him for us, oh Lord, he'll be missed so much.

This man, Maurice Buckman, wasn't only a tribute to his family, but to everyone who knew him. He was known for his dignity, his respect, and his love that was handed down to him. A lot of hard sweat and labor went into making him the man that he was.

He never intended to be a centerpiece to be looked up at or down upon. He felt he was no better or no less than his fellow man because his self dignity was the respect he had gained, the love for and from his fellow man.

Many things can be said about Maurice Buckman. His family can hold their heads high in praise of him. And what can I say? I'm one of the many who'll remember him and all I've got to say is this: Thanks, Maurice.

—Leroy Cassford

Photo Album

*Aunt Mary and Uncle Maurice Buckman;
Jerry and Rita Buckman and family;
George and Elaine Buckman and family;
Paul Dubrow and my cousin
Lilian Buckman Johnson*

Jerry Buckman's family:
Cary and family at daughter Miriam's wedding to Gilad Goldstein;
Lee Buckman and family with Ari Mendelson, Rachel's nephew;
Meryl, Brendan, Perry, Morgan, and Mari Buckman

*George Buckman's family:
Daughter, Marcie Goldstein and family;
Son, Terry Buckman and family;
Son, Arnold Buckman and family*

Sam's brother, Leonard Kligman and family;
Sam and Paula with Lenny and Sandy, Irv and Shirley Kligman;
Lenny and Irv Kligman

Charley and Charlene Steinberg;
Dan and Sandy Steinberg;
Sid Steinberg;
Al and Char Frank with Char's children

Ali, Adam, and Briana with Norman Galper;
My mother with Beth;
Sol and Sharlene Galper;
Robert and Lila Hodes

*Edward Freedman's family: Daughter Jo Marie Shamash,
Mother-in-law Mrs. Cussimano and wife Marilyn Fredericks;
Standing: Carol Cohen, Cara Galper, Paula, Beth Robbin
Seated: Aunts Annette Polland, Nell Cohen, Sidonia Bernstein;
Paula's cousins: Miriam Pearlman; Steve and Roberta Leons*

*Joyce and Larry Powell;
Rae and Peter Polland;
Rae with Ben Berger*

*William Evans, Paula's aunt Etta Hobson, and cousin Miriam;
Paula's Aunt Anna with cousin Miriam and daughter Beth*

The Abrams family;
Once a Month Club

Childhood friends: Chuck Sebastian; Sammy Abraham; the Eskins

*The Greenbergs;
The Willens;
The Lifshitzs;
The Benders*

Ted Spak Family;
Daughter, son-in-law and grandchild of Robert Spak;
Mr. and Mrs. Robert Spak

The Gene Becker family;
The Gabric Family;
Judy and Barry Siegal

Toni Causby;
Katarzyna (Kasia) Strozak;
Sam with Sarah (Seka) Siver

Dr. Sam and Ellen Nickel;
The Popletts;
Jane and Harry Peterson

Pearl and Ken Hirsch;
Reva and Irv Bernstein;
Rita and Bernie Hymen with grandchild

Nathan and Rosita Schloss;
Tom and Heather Borst and family

The Markowitz family;
Sam with Don Salamon;
Rabbi Allan Kensky and his wife, Dr. Adina Kiel

*The Gilmores;
Charles Wolk and Delphine Koensberg and the Rosens*

Drs. Erich and Trudy Gibbs;
Louise and Allen Hoover;
Dr. Julio and Gracia Battistoni

*Gene and Elaine Shepp;
Zev and Alice Weiss;
Carol and Al Feiger*

Arnold and Phylis Cowen;
Francine (Putchie) and Mike Wagner;
The Yablons;
Sheldon and Terri Rothstein

Earl and Sharon Abramson and family

*Fred and Idele Applebaum;
Phyllis and Lenny Berlin;
Haskell and Molly Schiff*

Arnold and Phylis Cowen;
Francine (Putchie) and Mike Wagner;
The Yablons;
Sheldon and Terri Rothstein

Earl and Sharon Abramson and family

Fred and Idele Applebaum;
Phyllis and Lenny Berlin;
Haskell and Molly Schiff

The invitation to my 50th birthday "bicentennial" celebration

Sam and Paula